Kaplan Publishing are constantly finding new ways to make a difference to your studies and our exciting online resources really do offer something different to students looking for exam success.

This book comes with free MyKaplan online resources so that you can study anytime, anywhere. **This free online resource is not sold separately and is included in the price of the book.**

Having purchased this book, you have access to the following online study materials:

CONTENT	AAT	
	Text	Kit
Electronic version of the book	✓	✓
Progress tests with instant answers	✓	
Mock assessments online	✓	✓
Material updates	✓	✓

KT-524-308

How to access your online resources

Kaplan Financial students will already have a MyKaplan account and these extra resources will be available to you online. You do not need to register again, as this process was completed when you enrolled. If you are having problems accessing online materials, please ask your course administrator.

If you are not studying with Kaplan and did not purchase your book via a Kaplan website, to unlock your extra online resources please go to www.mykaplan.co.uk/addabook (even if you have set up an account and registered books previously). You will then need to enter the ISBN number (on the title page and back cover) and the unique pass key number contained in the scratch panel below to gain access. You will also be required to enter additional information during this process to set up or confirm your account details.

If you purchased through Kaplan Flexible Learning or via the Kaplan Publishing website you will automatically receive an e-mail invitation to MyKaplan. Please register your details using this email to gain access to your content. If you do not receive the e-mail or book content, please contact Kaplan Publishing.

Your Code and Information

This code can only be used once for the registration of one book online. This registration and your online content will expire when the final sittings for the examinations covered by this book have taken place. Please allow one hour from the time you submit your book details for us to process your request.

Please scratch the film to access your MyKaplan code.

Please be aware that this code is case-sensitive and you will need to include the dashes within the passcode, but not when entering the ISBN. For further technical support, please visit www.MyKaplan.co.uk

KAPLAN

PUBLISHING

MANAGEMENT ACCOUNTING: BUDGETING

STUDY TEXT

Qualifications and Credit Framework

AQ2016

The Study Text supports study for the following AAT qualifications:

AAT Professional Diploma in Accounting – Level 4

AAT Level 4 Diploma in Business Skills

AAT Professional Diploma in Accounting at SCQF – Level 8

British Library Cataloguing-in-Publication Data

A catalogue record for this book is available from the British Library.

Published by
Kaplan Publishing UK
Unit 2, The Business Centre
Molly Millars Lane
Wokingham
Berkshire
RG41 2QZ

ISBN: 978-1-78415-998-6

CONTENTS

STUDY TEXT

INTRODUCTION

HOW TO USE THESE MATERIALS

These Kaplan Publishing learning materials have been carefully designed to make your learning experience as easy as possible and to give you the best chance of success in your AAT assessments.

They contain a number of features to help you in the study process.

The sections on the Unit Guide, the Assessment and Study Skills should be read before you commence your studies.

They are designed to familiarise you with the nature and content of the assessment and to give you tips on how best to approach your studies.

STUDY TEXT

This study text has been specially prepared for the revised AAT qualification introduced in September 2016.

It is written in a practical and interactive style:

- key terms and concepts are clearly defined

- all topics are illustrated with practical examples with clearly worked solutions based on sample tasks provided by the AAT in the new examining style

- frequent activities throughout the chapters ensure that what you have learnt is regularly reinforced

- 'pitfalls' and 'examination tips' help you avoid commonly made mistakes and help you focus on what is required to perform well in your examination

- 'Test your understanding' activities are included within each chapter to apply your learning and develop your understanding.

ICONS

The study chapters include the following icons throughout.

They are designed to assist you in your studies by identifying key definitions and the points at which you can test yourself on the knowledge gained.

 Definition

These sections explain important areas of knowledge which must be understood and reproduced in an assessment .

 Example

The illustrative examples can be used to help develop an understanding of topics before attempting the activity exercises.

 Test your understanding

These are exercises which give the opportunity to assess your understanding of all the assessment areas.

Quality and accuracy are of the utmost importance to us so if you spot an error in any of our products, please send an email to mykaplanreporting@kaplan.com with full details.

Our Quality Co-ordinator will work with our technical team to verify the error and take action to ensure it is corrected in future editions.

UNIT GUIDE

Introduction

This unit is about the use of budgeting for planning, coordinating and authorising the activities of an organisation, and for controlling costs. The unit provides skills and knowledge to improve the performance of an organisation by setting targets, constructing achievable plans and monitoring results.

Students will develop a range of skills within the context of planning and control. These include management accounting, statistical analysis, written communication and variance analysis. The application of standard costing, and its links to budgeting, is also included, although the topic is covered in detail in the Management Accounting: Decision and Control unit.

Students will also develop their business awareness. In particular, they will gain elementary understanding of production planning (efficiency, adjusting for changing inventory levels, material control, staff planning, plant scheduling) and aspects of marketing (competition, promotion, product life cycle and so on). In this context, performance measures are used to set targets and monitor performance. These are not high-level financial indicators, such as return on net assets as learned in other units, but detailed measures relevant to specific budgets. As an example, average hourly labour rate would be relevant to the control of a direct labour cost budget.

Budgeting could be described as the art of the possible. Budgets are constructed from forecasts and plans. Forecasts relate to external factors, over which management may have very little influence. Plans relate to the organisation's activities and must be managed.

Management Accounting: Budgeting is a **mandatory** unit. Its content links with Management Accounting: Decision and Control but the application here is specifically to budgeting.

Learning outcomes

On completion of this unit the learner will be able to:

- prepare forecasts of income and expenditure

- prepare budgets

- demonstrate how budgeting can improve organisational performance

- report budgetary information to management in a clear and appropriate format.

Scope of content

To perform this unit you will need to know and understand the following:

Chapter

1   Prepare forecasts of income and expenditure

1.1   Identify internal and external sources of information used to forecast income and expenditure

2

Students need to be able to:

- select the appropriate sources of data to use for forecasting

- describe their sources of data when issuing forecast.

Budget data is drawn from a wide variety of sources within the organisation and externally. Students must be able to suggest an appropriate, reliable source for each piece of information required in budget construction. They will not be expected to have a detailed knowledge of, for instance, government statistical publications, but must be able to demonstrate that they know which external source, or which member of the organisation, to go to for data required for forecasting.

In a multiple-choice task, candidates are required to suggest an appropriate, reliable source for each piece of information required in budget construction. Candidates are not expected to have a detailed knowledge of, for instance, government statistical publications, but must be able to demonstrate that they know which external source, or which member of the organisation, to go to for data required for forecasting.

1.2   **Use statistical techniques to forecast income and expenditure**   3

Students need to be able to:

- Apply the following techniques:

    – sampling

    – indices

    – time series, trends and seasonal variation.

These techniques have been learned in previous units. Extended application of each technique is not required at this level but students must be able to demonstrate their use as tools for forecasting. Assessment focuses on the use of published wage and price indices; sampling techniques used in market research and the application of time series to sales forecasting. Only simple calculations are required.

Chapter

1.3 **Discuss the purpose of revenue and cost forecasts and their link to budgets**

2,3,5,6

Students need to be able to:

- differentiate between forecasts and plans

- describe how each forecast contributes to the budgeting process

- describe the methods of dealing with the uncertainty inherent in forecasting (planning models, regular reforecasting, rebudgeting, rolling budgets and budget flexing).

Some aspects of business performance are within the control of the organisation and can be planned. Others are subject more or less to external factors that must be forecast. For example, budgeted sales revenue may be calculated from forecasts of market demand and market share.

Cost budgets may be influenced by forecasts of world markets and national inflation. These forecasts are used to develop the planning assumptions on which budgets are based. These assumptions must be clearly stated so that variances from budget can be analysed and understood. Students must be able to distinguish between forecasts and plans, and describe how each forecast fits into the planning process. They must also be able to recommend techniques for dealing with the uncertainty inherent in forecasting. These techniques include planning models, regular re-forecasting, re-budgeting and flexible budgets.

Candidates are required to distinguish between forecasts and plans, and describe how each forecast fits into the planning process. They must also recommend techniques for dealing with the uncertainty inherent in forecasting. These techniques include planning models, regular re-forecasting, re-budgeting and flexible budgets.

Chapter

1.4 **Identify the impact of internal and external factors on income and expenditure forecasts**   2,3

Students need to be able to:

- advise on the reliability of forecasts

- describe the stages and features of the product lifecycle and their impact on income forecasts

- describe market trends and competitive pressures

- explain the expected impact of promotional activity

- identify and describe external events affecting the reliability of cost forecasts.

2 **Prepare budgets**

2.1 **Identify budgetary responsibilities and accountabilities**   1,2,4,5,6

Students need to be able to:

- describe the role of the budget committee

- describe the duties and responsibilities of the budget accountant

- describe the budgetary accountabilities of senior managers in typical organisations (Chief executive and heads of marketing, sales, production, purchasing, finance and human resources)

- select the appropriate managers to provide information required to prepare budgets

- classify and allocate direct costs to appropriate responsibility centres

- identify appropriate responsibility centres and recovery methods for all types of indirect cost.

Chapter

Students must understand that the structure of a budget needs to be appropriate to the organisat For instance, if there is a production departmen marketing department and an administration department, the organisation's budget will need include a production budget, a marketing budge an administration budget.

Appropriate profit centres, cost centres and investment centres will need to be created and the budget must be structured accordingly. The budget responsibility of managers must be consistent with their authority. Students are assessed on their ability to assign accountabilities to appropriate senior managers at various stages of the budgetary control cycle.

**2.2   Identify and calculate the effect of   5
production and sales constraints**

Students need to be able to:

- identify budget limiting factors, for example, a production bottleneck, possible market share or access to finance, shortage of material, labour, plant capacity, factory space

- calculate the production limit.

Budgets have to be based on what is practically possible. Every business has a budget factor (limiting factor), which could, for instance, be a production bottleneck, possible market share or access to finance.

Candidates are required to identify budget limiting factors (constraints in capacity and limitations on costs and sales) and to prepare or revise a budget to fit within such a constraint.

KAPLAN PUBLISHING

		Chapter

2.3 **Prepare planning schedules for physical production resources** 5

Students need to be able to prepare the following planning schedules:

- production plan (volumes of inventory, production and sales)

- material usage and purchases

- staffing, labour hours and overtime

- plant utilisation.

Candidates are required to prepare the underlying 'physical' plans upon which budgets are calculated. This involves calculating the production plan and the resource plans for materials, labour and production facilities and making appropriate adjustments for inventory levels, wastage, available staff hours and production facility hours, etc.

2.4 **Calculate budgets for different types of cost** 4,5

Students need to be able to calculate budgets for the following types of cost:

- direct

- indirect

- fixed

- variable

- semi-variable

- stepped

- capital

- revenue

- Operational costs (materials, production labour, direct expenses and production overhead)

- Staff costs

- Core costs (non-operational overheads)

The creation of an appropriate accountability structure (investment centres, profit centres and cost centres) is fundamental to planning, coordination and control. Students must be able to classify and allocate cost and revenue data accordingly.

Indirect costs (overheads) are attributed to production through apportionment to departments and the use of overhead recovery rates, or through activity based costing, etc. The budget needs to be consistent with the method of attribution that will be employed to calculate the actual results. In a multiple-choice task, candidates are required to identify methods of attribution appropriate to various types of indirect cost.

2.5	**Prepare draft budgets from historical data, forecasts and planning assumptions**	3,5

Students need to be able to prepare the following budgets:

- sales revenue
- material usage and purchases
- labour (employee and other resources)
- production facilities
- other overheads
- operating statement (profit and loss account down to operating profit)
- capital expenditure budget
- master budget
- operating budget
- financial budget
- static budget (also called fixed or non-flexed budget
- flexible budget

Candidates are required to prepare budgets for sales revenue, material costs, labour (employees and other manpower), production facilities, other overheads (including depreciation) and capital expenditure and assemble these results into a master budget. They also break down budgets into weeks, months, quarters or other timeframe to facilitate regular reporting and monitoring of performance.

| 2.6 | **Prepare cash flow forecasts** | 5 |

Students need to be able to:

- prepare a cash flow forecast from budget data, making due allowance for time lags or assumptions about changes in debtor, creditor and inventory balances

- analyse a cash flow forecast into shorter control periods, allowing for time lags.

Cash flow forecasts must be consistent with all other aspects of the budget. Candidates are required to prepare a cash flow forecast from budget data and update it as actual performance results become available.

| 3 | **Demonstrate how budgeting can improve organisational performance** | |

| 3.1 | **Discuss how budgeting can promote effective, ethical and focused management** | 1,8 |

Students need to be able to:

- create an effective budget system, built on honesty and transparency

- use budget planning and control to motivate the management team

- use budget planning and control to create a cycle of continuous improvement

- coordinate budgets to achieve goal congruence

- recognise the behaviours that threaten effective budgetary control by crating budgetary slack, rivalry and suboptimal performance

- discuss the benefits and risks of linking remuneration to budget achievement.

3.2 **Discuss the use of budgeting for planning, coordinating, authorising and cost control** 1,5

Students need to know:

- how budgeting fulfils these four apparently diverse functions

- why a balance must be maintained (for example, overemphasis on cost control is likely to constrain business growth and high level planning targets can conflict with detailed coordination activity)

- The potential for conflict between these functions.

Budgetary control fulfils these four apparently diverse functions and a balance must be maintained. For instance, over-emphasis on cost control is likely to constrain business growth. Also, high level planning targets can conflict with detailed coordination activity.

Candidates are required to describe these functions and explain their potential for conflict.

3.3 **Break a budget down into control periods** 5

Students need to be able to:

- split the elements of an operating statement budget into appropriate time periods to facilitate regular reporting

- ensure that the planning assumptions and cost behaviours in the budget are correctly reflected in the split into control periods.

Candidates are required to break down budgets into weeks, months, quarters or other timeframe to facilitate regular reporting and monitoring of performance.

Chapter

3.4 **Recommend appropriate performance measures to support budgetary control**

8

Students need to be able to:

- suggest suitable physical and financial performance measures, consistent with key planning assumptions to aid budgetary control

- calculate these measures for budget and for actual performance

- provide constructive advice to assist the achievement of targets and budgets.

Examples of physical measures include quality indicators such as reject rates; efficiency indicators such as the number of products made per labour hour or idle time ratios, and capacity measures such as machine utilisation ratios. Simple financial measures include average selling price, profit percentage of sales revenue, material cost per unit of purchase, labour rate per hour, cost per unit of production and sales and cost variances.

Candidates are required to identify suitable physical and financial measures, consistent with the key planning assumptions, to use as performance measures. They calculate these measures for the budget and for actual performance and provide advice to enable budgets to be achieved.

3.5 **Integrate standard costing into budgetary control**

7,8

Students need to be able to:

- incorporate standard costs into budget calculations

- use standard costing methodology to split the total material and the total labour variances into price and efficiency variances

- explain how the use of standard costing can complement budgetary control.

Candidates are required to calculate variances in absolute and percentage terms, accurately comparing like with like, and present the results clearly. Variance percentages should be based on the budget, not the actual result.

Variances can be caused by better or worse than expected performance within the organisation or by unforeseen external factors. They can also be due to unrealistic or inaccurate budgeting. A significant variance requires a management response. This could be, for example, to investigate poor performance and take corrective action.

Candidates are required to analyse variances, in the context of the operational information provided in the assessment, to identify possible causes and to offer suitable management advice. This advice might explain how performance could be improved or suggest appropriate further investigation.

| 3.6 | **Prepare and explain a flexed budget** | 8 |

Students need to be able to:

- flex budgets, adjusting each element of the budget correctly according to the original budget assumptions about cost behaviour

- explain the purpose of budget flexing

- discuss the limitations of flexing in the context of a given scenario.

Candidates are required to flex a budget, adjusting each element of the budget correctly according to the original budget assumptions about cost behaviour.

Chapter

**3.7   Calculate variances between budget and   8
actual income and expenditure**

Students need to be able to:

- calculate variances in absolute and percentage terms

- calculate backward variances (use variance data to calculate underlying budget or actual performance)

- identify favourable and adverse variances

- compare like with like and present the results clearly.

Candidates are required to calculate variances in absolute and percentage terms, accurately comparing like with like, and present the results clearly. Variance percentages should be based on the budget, not the actual result.

Variances can be caused by better or worse than expected performance within the organisation or by unforeseen external factors. They can also be due to unrealistic or inaccurate budgeting. A significant variance requires a management response. This could be, for example, to investigate poor performance and take corrective action.

**3.8   Review and revise budgets to reflect   5
changing circumstances**

Students need to be able to:

- identify when a budget revision is appropriate

- calculate the impact of changes to planning assumptions and forecasts

- recalculate budgets accordingly.

Budgets have to be based on what is practically possible. Every business has a budget factor (limiting factor), which could, for instance, be a production bottleneck, possible market share or access to finance.

Chapter

Candidates are required to identify budget limiting factors (constraints in capacity and limitations on costs and sales) and to prepare or revise a budget to fit within such a constraint.

Budgets need to be reviewed regularly in the light of actual and forecast performance. Volume changes can often be dealt with by budget flexing but significant changes in business strategy must be evaluated and the budget amended accordingly.

Candidates are required to recalculate a budget to reflect changed planning assumptions, This requires an understanding of cost behaviour.

4   Report budgetary information to management in a clear and appropriate format

**4.1   Discuss the basic methods of budgeting and   5
make recommendations for their use**

Students need to know:

- The features of the basic methods:

   – incremental (historical)

   – zero based

   – priority based

   – activity based

   – Top down

   – Bottom up

   – Participatory

   – Rolling

   – Contingency

   – Resource restricted

   – the comparative advantages of each method

   – the circumstances in which each method should be recommended.

Chapter

4.2 **Plan and agree draft budgets with all parties involved**   2,5

Students need to be able to:

- describe the sources of information and the validity of those sources when submitting draft budgets to management

- identify the key planning assumptions in a prepared budget

- identify the potential threats to budget achievement

- identify the responsibilities of relevant managers

- quantify the impact of the budget on the organisation

- submit the budget for approval.

Candidates are required to identify critical factors affecting costs and revenues, such as market conditions, staffing levels, material availability, etc., and explain their impact on the budget. This is part of an email report task.

4.3 **Analyse variances and explain their impact on the organisation**   8

Students need to be able to:

- Calculate backward variances (use variance data to calculate underlying budget or actual performance)

- identify significant variances

- use operational information provided to explain the likely causes of variances

- provide suitable advice to management

- explain the impact of variances on overall organisation performance

- identify where further investigation is needed

- make recommendations to improve operational performance.

Chapter

Candidates are required to analyse variances, in the context of the operational information provided in the assessment, to identify possible causes and to offer suitable management advice. This advice might explain how performance could be improved or suggest appropriate further investigation.

4.4   **Effectively present budgetary issues to**   9
management

Students need to be able to:

- identify and describe important budgetary planning and control issues

- make relevant and focused recommendations to initiate management action.

Candidates are required to analyse variances, in the context of the operational information provided in the assessment, to identify possible causes and to offer suitable management advice. This advice might explain how performance could be improved or suggest appropriate further investigation.

Delivering this unit

This unit has the following links across the AAT Professional Diploma in Accounting.

Unit name	Content links	Suggested order of delivery
Management Accounting: Decision and Control Cash and Treasury Management	This unit and Management Accounting: Decision and Control are complementary, forming the management accounting element of the level 4 qualification. Some criteria appear in both units, such as statistical techniques, performance measures and writing management reports. The application of these is broader in Management Accounting: Decision and Control than in Management Accounting: Budgeting. There is also a small overlap with the optional unit Cash and Treasury Management. However, preparation of a cash flow forecast from budget data only appears in Management Accounting: Budgeting.	Students may find it useful to study Management Accounting: Decision and Control and Management Accounting: Budgeting concurrently, as there are many overlapping concepts.

THE ASSESSMENT

Test specification for this unit assessment

Assessment type	Marking type	Duration of exam
Computer based assessment	Partially computer/ partially human marked	2.5 hours

The assessment for this unit consists of 8 compulsory, independent, tasks.

The competency level for AAT assessment is 70%.

Learning outcomes		Weighting
1	Prepare forecasts of income and expenditure	10%
2	Prepare budgets	35%
3	Demonstrate how budgeting can improve organisational performance	35%
4	Report budgetary information to management in a clear and appropriate format	20%
Total		100%

UNIT LINK TO SYNOPTIC ASSESSMENT

AAT AQ16 introduced a Synoptic Assessment, which students must complete if they are to achieve the appropriate qualification upon completion of a qualification. In the case of the Professional Diploma in Accounting, students must pass all of the mandatory assessments and the Synoptic Assessment to achieve the qualification.

As a Synoptic Assessment is attempted following completion of individual units, it draws upon knowledge and understanding from those units. It may be appropriate for students to retain their study materials for individual units until they have successfully completed the Synoptic Assessment for that qualification.

With specific reference to this unit, the following learning objectives are also relevant to the Professional Diploma in Accounting Synoptic Assessment

LO3 Demonstrate how budgeting can improve organisational performance

STUDY SKILLS

Preparing to study

Devise a study plan

Determine which times of the week you will study.

Split these times into sessions of at least one hour for study of new material. Any shorter periods could be used for revision or practice.

Put the times you plan to study onto a study plan for the weeks from now until the assessment and set yourself targets for each period of study – in your sessions make sure you cover the whole course, activities and the associated questions in the workbook at the back of the manual.

If you are studying more than one unit at a time, try to vary your subjects as this can help to keep you interested and to see the relationships between subjects.

When working through your course, compare your progress with your plan and, if necessary, re-plan your work (perhaps including extra sessions) or, if you are ahead, do some extra revision/practice questions.

Effective studying

Active reading

You are not expected to learn the text by rote, rather, you must understand what you are reading and be able to use it to pass the assessment and develop good practice.

A good technique is to use SQ3Rs – Survey, Question, Read, Recall, Review.

1   **Survey the chapter**

    Look at the headings and read the introduction, knowledge, skills and content, so as to get an overview of what the chapter deals with.

2   **Question**

    Whilst undertaking the survey ask yourself the questions you hope the chapter will answer for you.

KAPLAN PUBLISHING

3   Read

Read through the chapter thoroughly working through the activities and, at the end, making sure that you can meet the learning objectives highlighted on the first page.

4   Recall

At the end of each section and at the end of the chapter, try to recall the main ideas of the section/chapter without referring to the text. This is best done after short break of a couple of minutes after the reading stage.

5   Review

Check that your recall notes are correct.

You may also find it helpful to reread the chapter to try and see the topic(s) it deals with as a whole.

Note taking

Taking notes is a useful way of learning, but do not simply copy out the text. The notes must

- be in your own words
- be concise
- cover the key points
- well organised
- be modified as you study further chapters in this text or in related ones.

Trying to summarise a chapter without referring to the text can be a useful way of determining which areas you know and which you don't.

Three ways of taking notes

1   Summarise the key points of a chapter

2   Make linear notes

A list of headings, subdivided with sub-headings listing the key points.

If you use linear notes, you can use different colours to highlight key points and keep topic areas together.

Use plenty of space to make your notes easy to use.

3   Try a diagrammatic form

The most common of which is a mind map.

To make a mind map, put the main heading in the centre of the paper and put a circle around it.

Draw lines radiating from this to the main sub-headings which again have circles around them.

Continue the process from the sub-headings to sub-sub-headings.

Annotating the text

You may find it useful to underline or highlight key points in your study text – but do be selective.

You may also wish to make notes in the margins.

Revision phase

Kaplan has produced material specifically designed for your final examination preparation for this unit.

These include pocket revision notes and a bank of revision questions specifically in the style of the new syllabus.

Further guidance on how to approach the final stage of your studies is given in these materials.

Further reading

In addition to this text, you should also read the 'Student section' of the 'Accounting Technician' magazine every month to keep abreast of any guidance from the examiners.

TERMINOLOGY

There are different terms used to mean the same thing – you will need to be aware of both sets of terminology.

UK GAAP IAS

Profit and loss	Income statement
Sales	Revenue
Balance sheet	Statement of financial position
Fixed assets	Non-current assets
Stock	Inventory
Trade debtors	Trade receivables
Trade creditors	Trade payables
Capital	Equity
Profit	Retained earnings

Responsibility centres and the behavioural aspects of budgeting

1

Introduction

This chapter provides general background information to the context of budgeting as a key element of management accounting. It is essential background knowledge and should be useful in answering tasks in the exam.

ASSESSMENT CRITERIA
• Identify budgetary responsibilities and accountabilities (Element 2.1)
• Discuss how budgeting can promote effective, ethical and focused management (Element 3.1)
• Discuss the use of budgeting for planning, coordinating, authorising, and cost control (Element 3.2)

CONTENTS
1 Planning, budgeting and forecasting
2 Responsibility accounting
3 Participation in budget setting

1 Planning, budgeting and forecasting

1.1 Introduction

Given the increasing complexity of business and the ever-changing environment faced by firms it is doubtful whether any firm can survive by simply continuing to do what it has always done in the past. If the firm wishes to earn satisfactory levels of profit in the future, it must plan its course of action in order to attempt to improve its performance.

In a management accounting context, the budgeting process is part of the overall planning process.

1.2 The concept of corporate planning

Planning is an important concept in all walks of life, including your preparation for examinations. A **plan** is a series of actions to be carried out if objectives and goals are to be met.

In a business context, the term corporate planning is often used. **Corporate planning** is a long run, on-going activity which seeks to determine the direction in which the firm should be moving in the future:

'Where do we see ourselves in ten years time?'

Frequently asked questions in formulating the corporate plan are:

(a)   the reason why the company exists (its **mission**)

(b)   what it wants to achieve (its corporate **objectives**)

(c)   how it intends to get there (its business **strategy**)

(d)   what resources will be required (its **operating plans**)

(e)   how well it does in comparison to the plan (**control**).

These areas are discussed below.

Mission is a broad statement of the overall aims of the organisation.

A clearly defined mission, which is widely publicised within and outside the organisation, will guide it in its decision making. Most organisations now prepare and publish their mission in a document known as a mission statement.

Examples of real world mission statements are:

- 'To be the industry leader in the vehicle interior trims market by offering excellent quality, flexibility and value, by proactively partnering our customers in a joint mission to create a world class service.'

- Our mission: 'To make Hampshire safer' (Hampshire Fire Brigade).
- 'Our Corporate Mission Statement is for Fly Magic to become the largest pleasure flying organisation in the UK.'

Note that mission statements give an overall aim or goal which is not time specific and not quantified. You should contrast this with the concept of objectives dealt with below.

Corporate objectives are quantified, time-limited statements of what a firm wishes to achieve. Traditionally it was assumed that all firms were only interested in the maximisation of profit (or the wealth of their shareholders). Nowadays it is recognised that for many firms profit is only one of many objectives pursued.

Examples of other objectives include:

(a) maximisation of sales (whilst earning a 'reasonable' level of profit)

(b) growth (in sales, asset value, number of employees, etc.)

(c) survival

(d) research and development leadership

(e) quality of service

(f) contented workforce

(g) respect for the environment.

For corporate planning purposes it is essential that the objectives chosen are quantified and have a timescale attached to them. It has been suggested that objectives should be SMART:

- **S**pecific
- **M**easurable
- **A**chievable
- **R**elevant
- **T**ime limited

A statement such as maximise profits and increase sales would be of little use in corporate planning terms. The following would be far more helpful:

(a) achieve a growth in profit of 5% per annum over the coming ten-year period

(b) obtain a revenue of $x million within six years

(c) launch at least two new products per year, etc.

Some objectives may be difficult to quantify (e.g. contented workforce) but if no attempt is made there will be no yardstick against which to compare actual performance.

Strategy is the course of action, including the specification of resources required, that the company will adopt to achieve its specific objective.

Strategy formulation usually involves:

(a) an analysis of the environment in which the firm operates, a review of the strengths and weaknesses of the company and a consideration of the threats and opportunities facing it

(b) the results of the firm's existing operations are then projected forward and compared with stated objectives

(c) any differences between projected performance and objectives ('gaps') are identified.

To bridge these gaps the firm will either change its objectives (because they are too optimistic) or attempt to change the firm's direction to improve performance. This change of direction is strategy formulation.

Formulation of strategy is largely a creative process, whereby the firm will consider the products it makes and the markets it serves. Typical strategies include:

- market penetration (sell more of existing products to existing customers)

- product development (new products sold to existing customers)

- market development (continue in existing markets, develop new ones)

- diversification (develop new products and sell them to new customers).

These strategies might be followed either:

- internally – for example, the company develops its own products

- by acquisition – the company buys another which currently has the product range it wants.

Operating plans are the short-term tactics of the organisation.

A strategic plan might call for expansion in a particular market; whereas the operating plan will detail how the extra products are to be made and how much is to be spent on advertising. Military analogy is useful here – strategy is how to organise to win the war, operating plans (or tactics) are how to fight individual battles.

Control is the comparison of the results of the plans and the stated objectives to assess the firm's performance, and the taking of action to remedy any differences in performance.

This is an essential activity as it highlights any weakness in the firm's corporate plan or its execution. Plans must be continually reviewed because as the environment changes so plans and objectives will need revision. Corporate planning is not a once-in-every-ten-years activity, but an 'on-going' process which must react quickly to the changing circumstances of the firm.

Overview of the planning process

The overall planning and control process is summarised in the diagram that follows.

You will note that the bottom section of the diagram introduces the word budget.

We saw earlier the concept of a plan and mentioned the example of students having a plan to help them to achieve their objective of passing examinations. You, as an individual, might take the view that you can afford to buy this (essential and invaluable) textbook, but you may not be able to afford to attend a series of expensive seminars held in upmarket hotels where leading experts discuss management accounting topics in great detail. By taking this view, you are, in effect turning your plan to pass the examination into a budget.

The classic concept of a budget is that it takes a plan, which might be in terms of, say hours, number of units of sales etc. and turns it into MONEY terms.

A budget is a plan in monetary terms.

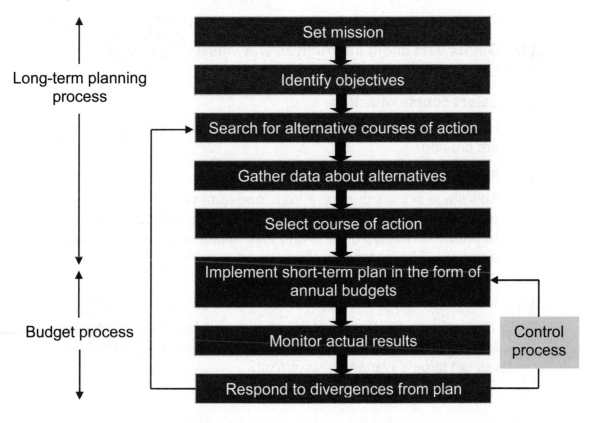

The eight stages are explained below:

(a) **Set mission**

This involves establishing the broad overall aims and goals of the organisation – these may be both economic and social.

(b) **Identify objectives**

This requires the company to specify objectives towards which it is working. These objectives may be in terms of:

- economic targets
- type of business
- goods/services to be sold
- markets to be served
- market share
- profit objectives
- required growth rates of sales, profits, assets.

(c) **Search for possible courses of action**

A series of specific strategies should be developed dealing particularly with:

- developing new markets for existing products
- developing new products for existing markets
- developing new products for new markets.

(d) **Gather data about alternatives and measuring pay-offs**

This is an information-gathering stage.

(e) **Select course of action**

Having made decisions, long-term plans based on those decisions are created.

(f) **Implement of short-term plans**

This stage signals the move from long-term planning to short-term plans in the form of annual budgeting. The budget provides the link between the strategic plans and their implementation in management decisions. The budget should be seen as an integral part of the long-term planning process.

(g) **Monitor actual outcomes**

This is the particular role of the cost accountant, keeping detailed financial and other records of actual performance compared with budget targets (variance accounting).

(h) **Respond to divergences from plan**

This is the control process in budgeting, responding to divergences from plan either through budget modifications or through identifying new courses of action.

Before we leave this section we should relate together some of the most important features of management accounting, and of your examination syllabus, which we have now seen:

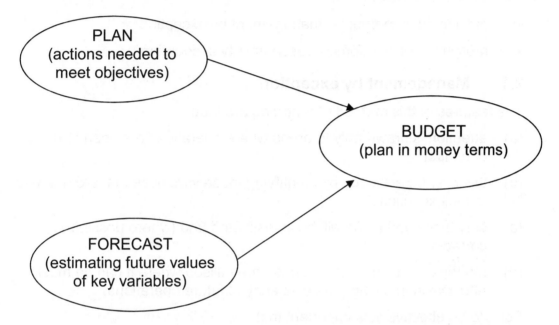

This indicates that the preparation of a budget, the subject matter of this and the next few chapters in this book needs a plan to be in place AND requires relevant forecast information to be available. Planning and forecasting are seen to be essential preliminary steps in the budgetary process.

1.3 Influences on planning and control systems

The planning and control system in all organisations should follow the general structure set out above. However, the detail of the process will be influenced by a number of factors and therefore will vary from one organisation to another.

The principal factors which will influence the process in a given organisation will include:

- organisational structure
- corporate objectives
- administrative procedures
- the nature of the activities of the business.

2 Responsibility accounting

Examinations frequently require a discussion on whether the budgeting procedures used within an organisation are likely to achieve their aims.

These aims, and the methods used to achieve them, can be broadly categorised as follows:

- efficient management – management by exception
- motivation of workforce – responsibility accounting.

2.1 Management by exception

The features of this method of reporting are that:

(a) attention is drawn only to areas where operations are seen to be 'out of control'

(b) this may be achieved by identifying those variances that are deemed to be 'exceptional'

(c) only these variances will be investigated and (where possible) corrected

(d) management time and expertise are utilised where it can be most effective in improving the efficiency of future operations.

For it to be effective, it is important that:

- exceptional variances are correctly isolated
- only such variances owing to factors capable of correction be considered for investigation
- costs and benefits of investigation are assessed.

2.2 Responsibility accounting

The aim of a responsibility accounting system is to motivate management at all levels to work towards the company's objectives with the minimum of direction.

What is involved?

(a) The use of budgets as 'targets' against which management performance may be measured and (often) rewarded.

(b) The presentation of 'performance reports' relating to particular responsibility centres. These centres fall into four categories as follows.

    (i) **Cost centre** or **expense centre** where a manager is held responsible for control of expenditure.

(ii)   A **revenue centre** is a part of the organisation that earns sales revenue. It is similar to a cost centre, but only accountable for revenues, and not costs.

(iii)   **Profit centre** where a manager is held responsible for control of sales revenue and expenditure.

(iv)   **Investment centre** where a manager is held responsible for investment decisions as well as the control of sales revenue and expenditure.

(c)   The requirement that the person deemed responsible for that area should give explanations of significant variances shown therein.

Examinations on this subject tend to concentrate on a practical application of the principles necessary for a system of responsibility accounting to work effectively, and often require the preparation of a draft performance report, or the criticism of such a report. An in-depth theoretical knowledge of the work carried out in this field is not needed; a common sense approach to a practical problem suffices.

2.3   Budgets and motivation

Motivation is the drive or urge to achieve an end result. Motivation can be as a force operating within an individual which drives that individual on to attain some goals or objectives. The word motivation comes from the Latin word meaning to move – this shows the key idea involved. An individual is motivated if they are moving forward to achieving goals or objectives.

Motivation may affect many aspects of the life of an individual. You have to be motivated to pass your examinations and to gain a recognised accounting qualification. At work you are motivated to achieve promotion and to gain a position of greater authority and responsibility within the organisation.

In a business context, if employees and managers are not motivated, they will lack the drive or urge to improve their performance and to help the organisation to achieve its goals and move forward. This is the importance of motivation in a business.

Three main areas need to be examined in relation to the use of budgets in responsibility accounting:

(a)   participation in budget setting

(b)   budgets as motivational targets

(c)   performance evaluation and reward.

The conclusions under each of these headings are largely common sense – you should try to think up practical examples in relation to your own position in study or at work to help you remember them.

3 Participation in budget setting

Conventional wisdom suggests that managers should be encouraged to participate in the budget setting process and that the budget should be built up from the lower rungs of management ('bottom up' budgeting) rather than imposed from above ('top down' budgeting).These are the advantages:

- Managers will then feel that they 'own' the budget and will therefore be more committed to the targets and motivated to achieve them.

- Operating managers are often the only people with sufficient detailed knowledge to develop a meaningful budget.

3.1 Disadvantages of participation

However, there are disadvantages to participation.

- The objectives of the managers and the objectives of the organisation may not be the same. 'Goal congruence' does not automatically result from empowering managers to develop their own budgets.

- Operating management may use their knowledge to manipulate the budget. They may deliberately set targets that they cannot fail to achieve, particularly if bonuses are awarded for meeting the budget.

- Managers may not wish to participate in the budget setting process. This may be because:

  (i)   they simply want to know what their targets are

  (ii)   they do not have the technical expertise to participate in budget setting

  (iii) they do not have the necessary commitment to the organisation

  (iv) they feel that the budget will be 'used against them'.

3.2 Budgets as motivational targets

In general, it is accepted that corporate objectives are more likely to be met if they are expressed as quantified targets, often in the form of budgets.

If a target is to have any influence on performance:

- the recipient must be aware of its existence and feel committed to achieving it

- it must be set at the right level of difficulty to act as a motivator; both unrealistic and over-generous targets will be demotivational.

In theory, there may be a need for two budgets to be prepared for the same area.

- One should be a challenging (aspirations) budget to motivate the manager.

- The second should be a lower, and more realistic, expectations budget for planning and decision purposes.

Care should be taken to reward success as well as penalising failure, in order that a benefit is perceived in bettering rather than just achieving the target.

Budgets become stronger motivators as they become tighter up to a point, but thereafter motivation declines. The optimal degree of tightness depends on both the situation and the personality of the individuals concerned.

Empirical evidence suggests that if a budget target is set that is too easy, then actual performance will be a little better than the budget but it will not be optimised. In other words, managers do not usually work to their full potential if they know that a lower level of performance will still meet the budget – human behaviour will tend to lead to individuals putting in the minimum possible effort to achieve a set target. If greater effort were applied, a higher target may be achieved.

On the other hand, if the budget is too difficult, because it is based on ideal levels of performance, managers become discouraged at what they regard as an unattainable standard. This may de-motivate and as a result, actual performance falls short of what might reasonably have been expected.

You can apply these points to your own position in the context of examinations. If the pass mark for an examination is very low – say 10% – you know you can pass with little effort and you will (perhaps) not work to your full potential. On the other hand, if the pass mark were 99% you would, probably, view that as impossible to achieve and decide not to try at all!

The aim should be to agree a budget that falls between these two extremes and therefore incorporates just the right degree of difficulty which will lead to the optimal level of performance. At this level the budget should be challenging enough to motivate a manager to optimise his performance without being too ambitious. Authors writing on this subject have used the phrase 'tough but attainable' for the targets to be set.

The right level of difficulty is that which is acceptable to that individual manager. This level of acceptability will differ from manager to manager, as each individual behaves and reacts in a different way in similar circumstances.

This concept of budget difficulty can be demonstrated diagrammatically as follows:

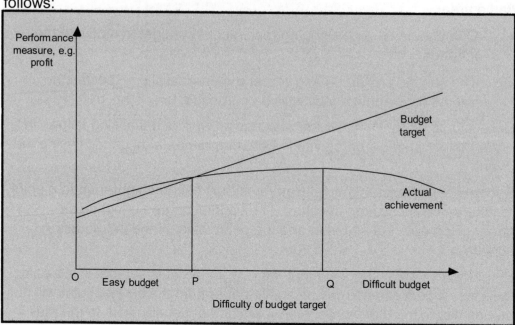

- A budget set at the degree of difficulty represented by point P is referred to as an 'expectations budget' as budget target and actual achievement are likely to coincide. The target level of performance has been met.

- However, a relatively easy-to-achieve budget, (set to the left of point P), is likely to lead to sub-optimal actual performance in that, although the budget has been met, the ACTUAL performance is at a relatively low level.

- In order to achieve a higher actual performance a more difficult budget needs to be set (an 'aspirations budget') at some point between P and Q. A budget set where point Q represents the degree of difficulty should lead to optimal performance (highest point on the 'actual' performance curve). However, it should be noted that this would give rise to an adverse variance compared with budget. If this target is set, senior management should not penalise the manager for the adverse variance, which may be unavoidable.

The diagram brings out one of the most fundamental points in budgeting:

How the degree of difficulty, represented by point Q, is determined is not at all easy in practice because it involves a knowledge of how each individual manager will react and behave. Attempts to quantify the degree of difficulty using work study assessments are a highly simplified approach to a very complex problem.

Furthermore, attempts to use the budget as a motivating tool in the manner described may in fact lead to the need for two budgets.

- One is the total of what all the individual managers have agreed to achieve (with the different degrees of budget difficulty incorporated into them).

- The second may recognise that actual performance is likely to fall short of aspiration and is, therefore, a more realistic basis for planning purposes.

 Test your understanding 1

World History Museum

The World History Museum has an Education Department which specialises in running courses in various subjects.

You have recently started work as the assistant management accountant for the museum. During a discussion with Chris Brooks, the general manager, she expresses to you that her interest in the control aspects of budgeting has been sparked by her attendance on a course entitled 'Budgetary control for managers'. She has shown you the following extract from the course notes she was given:

> 'A system of participative budgeting involves managers in the process of setting their own budgets. Participative systems are likely to be more successful in planning and controlling the activities of an organisation.'

Write a brief memo to Chris Brooks which explains the advantages and disadvantages of participative budgeting as a part of the budgetary planning and control process.

3.3 Performance evaluation and reward

Managers should only be held accountable for items over which they have control, and measures of performance should be devised that promote decisions in line with corporate objectives.

Thus a manager of a profit centre may be judged by variances affecting sales and direct costs (before allocated fixed costs); the performance of the centre itself will be measured by direct controllable contribution (having accounted for costs that are directly attributable to that centre, but not necessarily all controlled by the manager).

There are three main styles of management in the use of budget performance reports:

(a)   The budget-constrained style, which lays particular emphasis on results being closely in accordance with the budget plan.

(b)   The profit-conscious style, which is less concerned with current deviations from budget than with a manager's ability to achieve a trend of results which is acceptable in relation to changing conditions.

(c)   The non-accounting style, which tends to disregard accounting reports as a means of measuring management performance and instead looks at factors such as:

- the number of customer complaints or substandard items produced

- staff turnover

- morale in the department

- other qualitative measures.

Of the three styles, the middle is probably the most successful in achieving the company's long-term goals. The first creates good cost consciousness but also a great deal of tension between a manager and his subordinates, and manipulation of accounting information. The last promotes general good morale, but managers have a low involvement with costs.

Managers may receive financial rewards (for example, bonuses) and non-financial rewards (for example, promotion or greater responsibility) based on their ability to meet budget targets.

In the previous section the motivating effect of budgets was considered, but it should be remembered that the budgets by themselves have a limited motivational effect. It is the reward structure that is linked to achieving the budget requirements, or lack of reward for non-achievement, which provides the real underlying motivational potential of budgets.

A manager will need to regard the reward as being worthwhile if his behaviour is to be influenced so that he/she strives actively towards the achievement of the budget.

It is a common practice to attempt to assess the performance of a manager by a comparison of budgeted and actual results for his area of responsibility in the organisation. The choice of which particular measures to use is important to ensure that the individual manager sees the attainment of his targets as worthwhile for himself and at the same time in the best interests of the organisation as a whole – this is the concept of goal congruence which we saw in the chapter on responsibility accounting and which we shall cover again later in this chapter. In practice, conflicts can and often do arise between individual managers' personal objectives and those of the organisation as a whole.

The way in which the information in budget reports is used in the assessment of managerial performance has to be considered. Different degrees of emphasis on the results of budget versus actual comparisons can lead to different attitudes and feelings among managers. There is a need to achieve the correct balance between on the one extreme, an over-emphasis on results leading to pressure and feelings of injustice from the system; and on the other, too little stress on results leading to a budget irrelevancy attitude and low morale.

In general, we can summarise the characteristics of a sound employee reward system as follows:

- Fairness – the system should reward effort which helps the organisation achieve its objectives.

- Motivational – it should motivate the managers and employees to behave congruently i.e. in a way which assists the organisation to achieve its objectives.

- Understandability – the system should be such that it is clear to managers what they need to do to achieve the rewards. Unduly complex reward systems, perhaps based on complex bonus formulae are unlikely to be effective in generating improved performance.

- Consistently applied – the system should operate in the same way for all employees or, if not possible, for all employees at a given level in the organisation.

- Objective – the system should be based on measurable criteria with a minimum of subjectivity. It should also be such that it is not open to manipulation by managers in their own interests.

- Universal – all employees and managers at all levels in the organisation should be subject to an appraisal and reward system.

'Performance-related pay' is a method of rewarding employees in the form of bonuses, options to buy shares or other incentives, with a view to motivating them to improve their own performance or, in the case of managers, the performance of the part of the organisation which they manage.

Linking remuneration to budget achievement like this has his benefits: it can be a successful method of motivating managers to meet their budgetary targets. However, this only works when there is a short timescale between the target being met and the reward; and the risk is that managers start to focus on meeting short-term goals, rather than looking at the strategic, long-term objectives of the company.

3.4 The top down approach to budgeting

The top down approach is where budgets are set by higher levels of management and then communicated to the lower levels of management to whose areas of responsibility they relate. This is also known as an imposed budget.

In this approach lower-level managers are not allowed to participate in the budget-setting process.

The main problem with this approach is that those responsible for operating the budget will see it as something in which they have had no say. They lack ownership of the budget and as such they will be reluctant to take responsibility for it. It is unlikely to motivate the employees to achieve the budgetary targets set for them.

However, it can be argued that this top down approach may be the only approach to budgeting which is feasible if:

- lower level employees have no interest in participating in the process

- they are not technically capable of participating in budget setting

- only top level management have access to information which is necessary for budgeting purposes – perhaps information which is commercially sensitive.

3.5 The bottom up approach to budgeting

The bottom approach to budgeting is where lower level managers are involved in setting budget targets. This is known as a participative budget.

The more that individual managers are involved in setting budget targets, the more likely it is that they will accept those targets and strive actively towards the attainment of them. Employees are more likely to internalise the budget – accept it as part of themselves.

In this way actual performances should be improved by the motivational impact of budgets.

The main problem is:

- If budgets are used both in a motivational role and for the evaluation of managerial performance, then the problem of budgetary bias may arise.

Budgetary bias is where a manager deliberately sets a lower revenue target or a higher cost target.

By lowering the standard in the budget the target will be easier to achieve and performance will appear to be better. There is evidence to show that this tends to occur where a manager is actively seeking progression within an organisation or where financial rewards are based on ability to beat the budget. The effects of this sort of bias can be minimised by careful control, at the budget setting stage, and over any changes in the budget from one year to the next which are not due to external factors.

- Some people in organisations, by the very nature of their personality, do not wish to participate in the wider aspects of their jobs. They prefer an authoritarian style of leadership and do not strive for independence. Participative approaches to budget-setting will be very limited in their effect in such circumstances.

- Participation will be less effective in organisational situations where a manager or employee feels that he has little scope to influence the actual results for the budgeted area of responsibility. The lower down in the organisation structure the budget holder is, the more constrained is he by factors imposed from above. For example, objectives, strategies and policies, as well as the sales forecast and budget, limit the extent that a subordinate manager in the production function has for real participation in the setting of the budget for his area of responsibility.

- An important point to recognise is the difference between actual and perceived participation. It is the extent to which an individual manager perceives that he has influenced the budget that is crucial in that manager's acceptance of it.

An extension of this bottom up approach is the concept of budget challenging – employees are given the chance to question a budget presented to them (in a positive way!) before it is finalised.

3.6 Goal congruence

The principle of goal congruence involves ensuring that all members of the organisation pull in the same direction towards helping the organisation to achieve its overall goals and objectives.

If individuals in an organisation fail to demonstrate congruent behaviour, decisions taken may benefit that individual personally or the division which that individual works for, but may not benefit the organisation as a whole – this is known as dysfunctional behaviour.

We saw in the earlier chapter that an appropriate choice of performance evaluation methods is important in this context. The way the budgetary control system is operated can also be significant.

There may be a general fear and misunderstanding about the purpose of budgetary control. It is often regarded as a penny-pinching exercise by top management rather than recognised as a tool of management at all levels in an organisation structure. If this tends to be the attitude, a carefully planned campaign of education and training should be undertaken. Managers should be encouraged to discover how the budgetary control system can be of benefit to them personally as well as how it may benefit the organisation.

Employees may become united against management and devote their energies to finding excuses for not meeting targets. Targets that are realistic, and are seen by the employees as being realistic, are what is required. Good communications involving consultation and participation should help to minimise this problem.

One of the key roles in any organisation is at the supervisor/foreman level where the continual interface between management and employees exists. The leadership and motivational function of a supervisor or foreman is very important if the work is to be done and targets are to be achieved.

Conclusion

The main point to appreciate is that a budgetary control system should have the effect of motivating employees to work in the best interests of the organisation as a whole – the concept of goal congruence.

Participation (the 'bottom-up' approach) and education play important roles in encouraging a positive approach to budgeting in the mind of employees.

Test your understanding answers

Test your understanding 1

World History Museum

MEMORANDUM

To: Chris Brooks

From: Assistant Management Accountant

Date: 13 June 20X4

Subject: Participative budgeting

As requested, I enclose brief explanations of the advantages and disadvantages of participative budgeting.

Advantages

(i) Managers are likely to be demotivated if budgets are imposed on them without any prior consultation. If they are consulted, they are more likely to accept the budgets as realistic targets.

(ii) If managers are consulted, then the budgets are more likely to take account of their own aspiration levels. Aspiration levels are personal targets which individuals or departments set for themselves. If budget targets exceed aspiration levels, then the budgets can have a negative motivational impact because they will be perceived as unachievable. However, if the targets fall too far below aspiration levels, then the performance of the individuals or departments may be lower than might otherwise have been achieved.

(iii) Managers who are consulted may be motivated by the feeling that their views are valuable to senior management.

(iv) Managers who are closely involved with the day to day running of operations may be able to give very valuable input to the forecasting and planning process.

Disadvantages

(i) If too many people are involved in budgetary planning, it can make the process very slow and difficult to manage.

(ii) Senior managers may need to overrule decisions made by local managers. This can be demotivating if it is not dealt with correctly.

(iii) The participative process may not be genuine. Managers must feel that their participation is really valued by senior management. A false attempt to appear to be interested in their views can be even more demotivating than a system of imposed budgets.

(iv) Managers may attempt to include excess expenditure in their budgets, due to 'empire-building' or to a desire to guard against unforeseen circumstances.

KAPLAN PUBLISHING

Sources of data

2

Introduction

Budget data is drawn from a variety of sources, within the organisation and externally. This chapter highlights the importance of appropriate, reliable sources for each piece of information required in budget construction.

The external environment has a direct impact on sales demand, prices, availability of resources and costs. Some costs, including taxes, are not within the organisation's control. Even material and labour costs are subject to economic pressures that may not be quantifiable when budgets are constructed; realistic budgets have to be prepared in this context.

ASSESSMENT CRITERIA
• Identify internal and external sources of information used to forecast income and expenditure (Element 1.1)
• Discuss the purpose of revenue and cost forecasts and their link to budgets (Element 1.3)
• Identify the impact of internal and external factors on income and expenditure forecasts (Element 1.4)
• Identify budgetary responsibilities and accountabilities (Element 2.1)
• Plan and agree draft budgets with all parties involved (Element 4.2)

CONTENTS

1 Sources of information
2 Internal sources of information
3 External sources of information

1 Sources of information

When producing a budget in accordance with guidelines drawn up by the senior management of an organisation the usual starting point is the previous year's actual results. In some cases the budgeting process merely takes the form of adding to last year's income statement a general allowance for changes in volume and prices. This 'incremental' approach to budgeting is not regarded as an effective means of providing useful information for planning and control. Any inefficiency that has occurred in the current year will be perpetuated in future years. Nevertheless, the current income statement provides useful information.

In addition to previous year information, figures in budgets can come from three other sources.

Other internal sources

Information about the state of repair of non-current assets, training needs of staff, long-term requirements of individual large customers, etc. can be obtained by talking to individual junior managers. Likely costs of new products or services can be estimated using work study techniques or the services of the research and development team, quantity surveyors or the sales team.

Statistical techniques

Figures such as sales forecasts or estimates of the fixed and variable elements of semi-variable costs can be produced with the aid of techniques such as linear regression. Other techniques can help determine optimal inventory levels and optimal ways of organising large construction projects.

External sources

The obvious external source of budgetary information will be suppliers' price lists both for materials and for services. It is important for a firm to try to establish how long those prices are likely to last and the size of any price rises. In addition external market rates of pay should be established to determine a sensible level of wage rises.

The production of an annual budget is not a precise science. Figures are always subject to uncertainty. It is said that a budget is more than just a forecast of future costs and revenues that may be incurred or received, it is a statement of what management feels should be paid or received. Nevertheless, firms operate in an uncertain economic climate.

1.1 Budget committee

A **budget committee** is a group of managers and employees drawn from a range of departments within the organisation with responsibility for the budgetary process.

A typical budget committee comprises the chief executive, the management accountant (acting as budget officer) and functional heads. Its role is to agree planning assumptions for budget preparations, so the functions of the committee are to:

(a) agree policy with regard to budgets

(b) co-ordinate budgets

(c) suggest amendments to budgets (e.g. because there is inadequate profit)

(d) approve budgets after amendment, as necessary

(e) examine comparisons of budgeted and actual results and recommend corrective action if this has not already been taken.

The budget officer (usually a management accountant) is secretary to the committee and is responsible for seeing that the timetables are adhered to and for providing the necessary specialist assistance to the functional managers in drawing up their budgets and analysing results.

1.2 Budget manual

A budget manual is a document which sets out standing instructions governing the responsibilities of persons, and the procedures, forms and records relating to the preparation and use of budgets. It sets out the procedures to be observed in budgeting, the responsibilities of each person concerned, and the timetable to be observed.

Nowadays much of the budget manual is likely to be distributed as blank computer files (particularly spreadsheet files) for managers to complete. In this way the management accountant or the finance director can ensure that information is received from the various sources in a form that is easy to consolidate into a master budget.

2 Internal sources of information

Internal information may come from various sources.

2.1 Accounting system

The accounts system will collect data from source documents such as invoices, timesheets and journal entries. The data will be sorted and analysed by the coding system by type of expense, department, manager and job. Reports of direct and indirect costs compared to budgets may be produced at regular intervals to help managers plan and control costs. Ad hoc reports may be produced to help managers make specific decisions.

Consider the examples listed below – you can probably think of many others from your own experience.

- Sales analysed by product will help management to assess the patterns of demand for each product.

- This same information will help plan production and inventory levels.

- In turn, production information will enable the organisation to plan its requirements for raw materials, labour and machine hours.

- Information on material, labour and other costs will allow the organisation to set estimated costs for its products. This will be the basis for a budgetary control and standard costing system, as we shall see in a later chapter.

- In the context of long-term, strategic decision making, the sales analysis given above may help management to assess future product strategies – expand output of those for which demand is increasing, reduce output of those for which demand is falling.

- An aged receivables report would provide the basis for debt collection decisions taken by a credit control manager.

- Figures for wastage rates or product reject rates may allow management to reach decisions on the product quality aspect of the organisation's operations.

2.2 Payroll system

The payroll system may provide information concerning detailed labour costs. Hours paid may be analysed into productive work and non-productive time such as training, sick, holiday and idle time. Labour turnover by department or manager may be analysed and may help management to assess the employment and motivation policies.

2.3 Strategic planning system

The strategic planning system may provide information relating to the organisation's objectives and targets. Assumptions relating to the external environment may be detailed. Details of the organisation's capital investment programme and product launch programme may also be recorded here. Some of this information will be very commercially sensitive and only accessed by very senior managers in the organisation.

A Customer Relationship Management System will provide information on customers, and its objective is to increase customer loyalty (in order to increase profitability).

3 External sources of information

Businesses are finding it increasingly difficult to succeed if they ignore the external environment which will influence their activities. The process known as environmental scanning or environmental monitoring is becoming a more important part of the role of the management accountant. These terms are used to describe the process whereby data is collected from outside, as well as from inside, the organisation and used in the decision-making process.

The main sources of external information which we shall consider here are:

- government sources
- business contacts – customers and suppliers
- trade associations and trade journals
- the financial and business press and other media.

These are dealt with in more detail below. A word of warning first, however. Internal information is produced by the company itself so managers are aware of any limitations in its quality or reliability. External information is not under the control of the organisation – staff may not be aware of any limitations in its quality – this point should always be considered. Even government-produced statistics have been known to contain inaccuracies!

3.1 Government sources

There is a wealth of published statistical data covering many aspects of the nation's economy: population, manpower, trade, agriculture, price levels, capital issues and similar matters. Most, but not all of this is produced by national governments.

The primary purpose of this data is to provide information for economic planning at the national level. The data serves the secondary purpose of providing industry with useful background information for deciding on future policies such as raising new finance or recruiting specialised labour. The data is only published in general terms (e.g. for a particular industry or geographical area).

The following list shows some (there are many others) of the main sources of this type of information in the UK. Other countries will usually have similar information available. Copies are generally available in reference libraries and on government websites – have a look to see the type of data published.

Title	Frequency of publication	Main topics covered
Employment Gazette	Monthly	Earnings, basic wage rates, unemployment, indices of wholesale and retail prices.
British Business	Weekly	Wholesale and retail prices, production for specific sectors of industry, capital expenditure.
National Income and Expenditure Blue Book	Annually	Personal income and expenditure, gross national product.
Financial Statistics	Monthly	Money supply, interest rates, hire purchase liabilities, building societies.
Bank of England Quarterly Bulletin	Quarterly	Both summarise many of the above statistics.
Monthly Digest of Statistics	Monthly	
Economic Trends	Monthly	Similar coverage to Monthly Digest, but given information stretching back over a long period.
Annual Abstract of Statistics	Annually	
Price Indices for Current Cost Accounting	Annually, but updated by monthly supplement	Retail price index, also industry specific and asset specific price indices.

All the above publications relate to the UK. Publications concerned with statistics relating to the European Union include *European Economy Annual Statistical Yearbook*, *Eurostat* (monthly) and *OECD Main Economic Indicators* (monthly). Information on the World Economy is available from the United Nations (*Demographic Yearbook* and *Statistical Yearbook*), the International Labour Organisation (*Yearbook of Labour Statistics*) and UNESCO (*Statistical Yearbook*).

3.2 Business contacts

Government produced information will be broadly based and general, dealing with the economy as a whole or particular sectors or industries. An organisation may be looking for information more focused on its own position. Its day-to-day business contacts, customers and suppliers, can be a useful source of this information – and often it is available free.

Customers can provide information on such matters as:

– the product specification which they require

– their quality requirements

– requirements for delivery periods

– their preference for packaging and distribution methods

– feedback on the above and on general aspects of customer service.

Suppliers may be able to provide information on:

– quantity discounts and volume rebates which may help the organisation to decide on order size

– availability of products and services

– alternative products or services which may be available or may become available

– technical specifications of their product.

3.3 Trade associations and trade journals

Most major industries have their own trade association. The role of these organisations includes:

• representing their member firms in legal and other disputes

• providing quality assurance schemes for customers of member organisations

• laying down codes of practice to be followed by their member organisations

• publishing trade journals and other information useful for the management and development of their businesses.

There follows a very brief list of just a small selection of trade associations operating in the UK – it is taken from an alphabetical listing of associations and shows the first few starting with the letter A. There are hundreds more!

- *Agricultural Industries Confederation*
- *Airport Operators Association*
- *Association for Payment Clearing Services APCS*
- *Association for Road Traffic Safety & Management*
- *Association of Art and Antique Dealers*
- *Association of British Fire Trades Ltd.*

Many of these organisations publish their own industry or trade journals which will contain useful news and other information for organisations operating in that industry. Trade journals are also published by many publishing organisations. In the UK one of the best known of these journals is *The Grocer* aimed at the food and drink retail sector. Again, many others exist.

3.4 The financial press, business press and other media

In the UK, *The Financial Times*, the *Guardian*, *The Times* and the *Daily Telegraph* together with some regional newspapers provide statistics and financial reviews as well as business and economic news and commentary. These include:

- the FTSE 100 Index, the stock market index of the 100 leading shares

- the FT Actuaries All-share Index – an index of all share prices quoted on the stock exchange.

Such information is now also widely available via electronic media. Digital television services available on satellite or cable systems carry specialist business and financial channels and programmes (such as Bloomberg TV) which give both national and world-wide coverage. There is also the internet as a widely available source of up-to-date financial information.

KAPLAN PUBLISHING

Test your understanding 1

Match the data in the first column with the appropriate source in the second column (only 1 source possible):

Data	Source
Currency exchange rates	A website for a leading business news and information organisation (e.g. The Financial Times' website)
TV licence fee cost	Office for National Statistics
Cost of electricity generated by wind power	BBC Website
Inflation trends in the UK	HMRC publications
	Gross National Product
	The Environment Agency

 Test your understanding 2

Who would you contact in each of the following situations?

- You want to identify the production capacity of the firm.

- You want to forecast the price of raw materials.

- The draft budget has been reviewed by the Budget Committee and is ready to be submitted for final approval.

Choose from:

- Trade union representative

- Managing Director

- Buyer

- Board of Directors

- Production Planning Manager.

4 Summary

The cost accountant is mainly concerned with the proper recording and analysis of costs incurred in a business in a manner that will enable management to control current operations and plan and make decisions for the future.

Effective communication with the workforce and management is vital and will be achieved via the following:

(a)   a suitable organisational structure

(b)   reports produced on a timely basis.

This chapter considers internal and external information which affects forecasts.

Forecasts of future events are normally based on historical information. Information may be available from a wide variety of sources both internal and external to the business.

Test your understanding answers

Test your understanding 1

Data	Source
Currency exchange rates	A website for a leading business news and information organisation (e.g. The Financial Times' website)
TV Licence fee	BBC website
Cost of electricity (wind power)	The Environment agency
Inflation trend in the UK	Office for National Statistics

Test your understanding 2

Who would you contact in each of the following situations?

- You want to identify the production capacity of the firm
- Production Planning Manager

- You want to forecast the price of raw materials
- Buyer

- The draft budget is ready for final approval
- Board of Directors

Forecasting techniques and the product lifecycle

Introduction

Using time series analysis in order to forecast future figures in a budget is a favourite examination topic. You only need to use the time series techniques to forecast future trends.

You should be able not only to use the time series techniques to forecast future trends and seasonal variations but also understand the weaknesses of time series analysis and the problems of using historical data to predict the future.

Sampling and index numbers are also important topics and are covered in this chapter.

ASSESSMENT CRITERIA	CONTENTS
• Use statistical techniques to forecast income and expenditure (Element 1.2)	1 Forecasting techniques: time series
• Discuss the purpose of revenue and cost forecasts and their link to budgets (Element 1.3)	2 Forecasting with time series analysis
• Identify the impact of internal and external factors on income and expenditure forecasts (Element 1.4)	3 Forecasting techniques: sampling
	4 Forecasting techniques: index numbers
	5 Forecasts and plans
• Prepare draft budgets from historical data, forecasts and planning assumptions (Element 2.5)	6 Dealing with uncertainty

1 Forecasting techniques: time series

The process of forecasting will inevitably involve some analysis of historic data (sales, costs, share prices, etc.) in order that future values may be predicted.

The data may concern the economy as a whole, the particular industry with which the organisation is involved (or wants to be) or the organisation itself.

🔍 Definitions

A **time series** is a set of values for some variable (e.g. monthly production) which varies with time. The set of observations will be taken at specific times, usually at regular intervals. Examples of figures which can be plotted as a time series are:

- monthly rainfall in London
- daily closing price of a share on the Stock Exchange
- monthly sales in a department store.

Time series analysis takes historic data and breaks it down into component parts that are easier to extrapolate (predict future values of). In particular, it will isolate the underlying trend.

1.1 Plotting the graph of a time series

The basic pattern of a time series can be identified by plotting the recent points of the values on a graph, such as below.

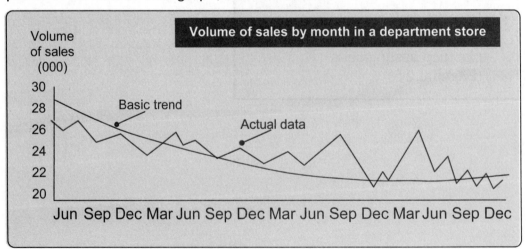

In such a graph time is always plotted on the horizontal x axis. Each point is joined by a straight line hence the typically 'jagged' appearance. Don't try to draw a smooth curve which will pass through all the points on a time series graph. You will find it practically impossible and, in any case, it is incorrect to do so. The only reason for joining the points at all is to give a clearer picture of the pattern, which would be more difficult to interpret from a series of dots.

On the graph above you will see that, having completed the time series graph, we have sketched in a 'basic trend' line. But what does it tell us? We need to look in more detail at what factors are at play in a time series.

1.2   Characteristic time series components

Analysis of time series has revealed certain characteristic movements or variations: the components of the time series. Analysis of these components is essential for forecasting purposes.

The four main types of component are as follows:

- basic trend (long-term)
- cyclical variations (not so long-term)
- seasonal variations (short-term)
- irregular or random variations (short-term).

1.3   Basic trend

The basic trend refers to the general direction of the graph of a time series over a long interval of time once the short-term variations have been smoothed out. This movement can be represented on the graph by a basic trend curve or line.

1.4   Cyclical variations

Cyclical variations refer to long term oscillations or swings about the basic trend. These cycles may or may not be periodic; they do not necessarily follow exactly similar patterns after equal intervals of time. In business and economic situations movements are said to be cyclical if they recur after time intervals of more than one year. A good example is the trade cycle, representing intervals of boom, decline, recession, and recovery.

1.5   Seasonal variations

Seasonal variations are the identical, or almost identical, patterns which a time series follows during corresponding intervals of successive periods. Such movements are due to recurring events such as the sudden increase in department store sales before Christmas. Although, in general, seasonal movements refer to a period of one year, this is not always the case and periods of hours, days, weeks, months, etc. may also be considered, depending on the type of data available.

Having isolated the trend we need to consider how to deal with the seasonal variations. We will look at two models – the additive model and the multiplicative model.

The additive model is the simplest model and is satisfactory when the variations around the trend are within a constant band width. If, as is more usual, the variations around the trend increase as the trend itself rises, it is better to use the multiplicative model.

The additive model – finding the seasonal variations

The additive model we will use expresses variations in absolute terms with above and below average figures being shown as positive or negative.

The four components of a time series (T = trend; S = seasonal variation; C = cyclical variation; R = random variation) are expressed as absolute values which are simply added together to produce the actual figures:

$$\text{Actual data (time series)} = T + S + C + R$$

For unsophisticated analyses over a relatively short period of time cyclical variations (C) and random variations (R) are ignored. Random variations are ignored because they are unpredictable and would not normally exhibit any repetitive pattern, whereas cyclical variations (long-term oscillations) are ignored because their effect is negligible over short periods of time. The model therefore simplifies to:

$$\text{Actual data} = T + S$$

The seasonal variation+ is therefore the difference between the computed trend figure and the original time series figure. Thus:

$$S = \text{Actual} - T$$

Example 1

TS Limited

The seasonal variations can be extracted by subtracting each trend value (using the moving averages method) from its corresponding time series value.

Solution

Quarter	Original time series	Underlying trend	Seasonal variation (S)
	(a)	(b)	(a) – (b)
3	94	100	(6)
4	127	102	25
1	84	106	(22)
2	106	111	(5)

 Test your understanding 1

Eastoft Feeds and Fertilisers Ltd uses a number of standard raw materials for its product range. Product F4's main raw material is 'EF1'. The average price per tonne for this material, which is subject to seasonal change, for each quarter during 2015 is given below. The material is in short supply.

2015	Q1	Q2	Q3	Q4
Average price per tonne	£40	£44	£64	£76
Seasonal variation	–£4	–£8	+£4	+£8

Complete the following calculations of the seasonally adjusted price of raw material 'EF1'. Assuming a similar pattern of price movements was to continue, determine the likely purchase price per tonne for each of the 4 quarters of 2016.

2015	Q1	Q2	Q3	Q4
Actual price per tonne				
Seasonal variation				
Trend				
2016				
Trend				
Seasonal variation				
Forecast price per tonne				

1.6 Random variations

Random variations are the sporadic motions of time series due to chance events such as floods, strikes, elections, etc.

By their very nature they are unpredictable and therefore cannot play a large part in any forecasting, but it is possible to isolate the random variations by calculating all other types of variation and removing them from the time series data. It is important to extract any significant random variations from the data before using them for forecasting.

Random variations will not concern you in your examination.

1.7 Isolating the trend

There are three ways of isolating the trend:

• drawing a scattergraph

• using moving averages

• using linear regression.

Scattergraph – sketching a basic trend line

A basic trend line was drawn in on the time series graph shown earlier in this chapter. Indeed one way of isolating the trend is simply to draw it in freehand on the graph. This is called a 'scattergraph'.

This is actually a very helpful method. Once a time series has been prepared as a graph, it is usually a fairly simple matter to sketch in a basic trend line which manages to echo the overall long-term trend of the time series. There are some advantages to doing it this way:

• It is quick and easy.

• It allows one to interpolate a value easily. If you have monthly data for, say, Months 1, 3, 5, 7, 9 and 11 only, plotting those values and sketching a trend line will allow you to see what the likely value for the even-numbered months might have been. On the graph below you will see that we have interpolated the values of £125,000 for Month 6 of 20X4, and £175,000 for Month 12 of 20X4.

• It is possible to extrapolate a figure past the end of the data available (see the dotted line on the graph below). It is always worth bearing in mind, however, that data cannot be extrapolated very far ahead. Common sense suggests, for instance, that the trend line in the graph below is unlikely to continue in a horizontal line for very long – it is bound either to rise or fall. So the extrapolation of £175,000 for Month 7 in 20X5 is not unreasonable, but it would not be helpful to extrapolate the line and make the same prediction for, say, Month 1 of 20X6.

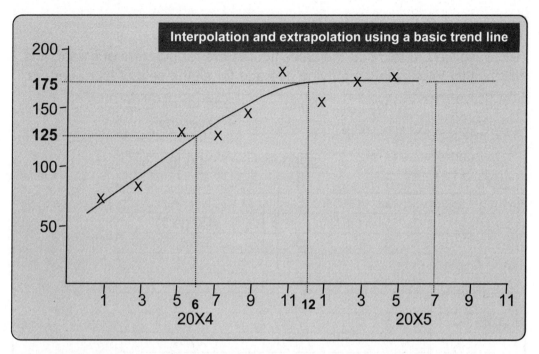

Two other common methods for isolating the trend are as follows:

Moving averages

By using moving averages, the effect of any seasonal variation in a time series can be eliminated to show the basic trend. This elimination process will only work if the moving average is calculated over the correct number of values (being the number of values in one complete cycle). For instance, if a seasonal variation present in a time series is repeated every fourth period, then moving averages with a cycle of four should be used.

This will become clearer as you follow through this simple example.

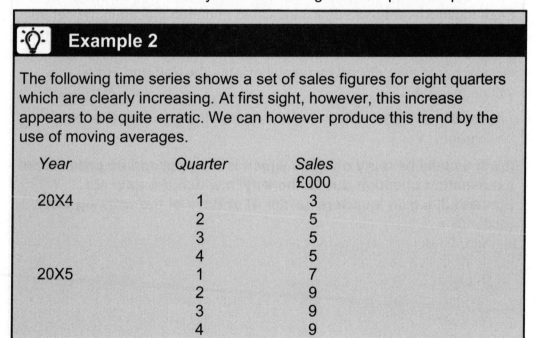

Example 2

The following time series shows a set of sales figures for eight quarters which are clearly increasing. At first sight, however, this increase appears to be quite erratic. We can however produce this trend by the use of moving averages.

Year	Quarter	Sales £000
20X4	1	3
	2	5
	3	5
	4	5
20X5	1	7
	2	9
	3	9
	4	9

Solution

Because we are told that the sales figures are for quarters of a year, it is necessary to calculate a moving average for all the sets of four quarters.

Year	Quarter	Sales	4-quarter moving average
		£000	£000
20X4	1	3	
	2	5	
			4½ (W1)
	3	5	
			5½
	4	5	
			6½
20X5	1	7	
			7½
	2	9	
			8½
	3	9	
	4	9	

Workings

The moving average for the first four quarters is calculated as

$$\frac{3 + 5 + 5 + 5}{4} = 4\frac{1}{2}$$

Each moving average value is calculated and then placed in the centre of the numbers that were used in the calculation. For example, the first 4-value moving average is calculated as the average of the first four numbers, and then placed mid-way between the 2nd and 3rd quarter values of 2004.

The moving average of four values captures the steadily increasing basic trend.

It will usually be fairly obvious which is the appropriate order in an examination question due to the way in which the data are presented, e.g. in 'quarters' (order 4) or days of the working week (order 5).

Be sure that you have understood the positioning of the moving averages in the above table. Each average has been written exactly opposite the middle of the figures from which it has been calculated. This results in the moving averages for even numbers of values (four in this case) being suspended halfway between two of the original figures.

Where you have a moving average for an even number of values, it is necessary to realign the moving averages so that they fall opposite the original values by calculating a centred moving average for every two moving average values.

Year	Quarter	Original time series	Moving average (4 values)	Centred moving average order 4
20X4	1	3		
	2	5		
			4½	
	3	5		5 (W)
			5½	
	4	5		6
			6½	
20X5	1	7		7
			7½	
	2	9		8
			8½	
	3	9		
	4	9		

As you can see by the centring process, the centred moving average is the basic trend.

(W) (4½ + 5½) ÷ 2 = 5

Example 3

TS Limited (continued)

The following data represents the sales for TS Limited for the eight quarters shown.

		Quarter		
	1	2	3	4
Year 1	74	100	94	127
Year 2	84	106	120	141

Calculate the trend using moving averages.

Solution

Year	Qtr	Value	4-quarter moving total	4-quarter average	Trend
1	1	74			
	2	100			
			395	99	
	3	94			100
			405	101	
	4	127			102
			411	103	
2	1	84			106
			437	109	
	2	106			111
			451	113	
	3	120			
	4	141			

Disadvantages of moving averages

- Values at the beginning and end of the series are lost – therefore the moving averages do not cover the complete period.

- The moving averages may generate cycles or other variations that were not present in the original data.

- The averages are strongly affected by extreme values. To overcome this a 'weighted' moving average is sometimes used giving the largest weights to central items and small weights to extreme values.

Linear regression

The third way of isolating a trend is to use a mathematical technique called 'linear regression'. Only a broad understanding of linear regression is required in the context of producing a trend for a time series.

Regression analysis is a technique for estimating the line of best fit, given a series of data. It is essentially a statistical technique, and the description that follows is only a working guide for applying the technique.

Regression analysis is based on the concept of 'drawing the line that minimises the sum of the squares of the deviations of the line from the observed data' (so it is sometimes referred to as the least squares method). The regression line of y on x is used when an estimate of y (the **dependent** variable) is required for a given value of x (the **independent** variable).

The general equation for the regression line is given as:

$$y = a + bx$$

Where:

x is the independent variable

y is the dependent variable

a is the fixed element

b is the variable element

You do not have to understand how this equation is calculated, but you do need to be able to use it.

In particular, you must understand that the independent variable (x) in some way causes the dependent variable (y) to have the value given by the equation.

Thus, if we were calculating the value of umbrellas sold for given amounts of monthly rainfall, the rainfall would be the independent variable (x) and the sales value would be the dependent variable (y) (rainfall causes umbrella sales and not vice versa).

Example 4

X Ltd is forecasting its sales for the four quarters of 20X5. It has carried out a linear regression exercise on its past sales data and established the following:

a = 20

b = 0.7

The equation of the regression line is therefore:

y = 20 + 0.7x

When x is number of the quarter and y is the sales value in £000s. Calculate the sales for each of the quarters in 20X5.

Solution

		£000
Quarter 1	y = 20 + (0.7 × 1) =	20.7
Quarter 2	y = 20 + (0.7 × 2) =	21.4
Quarter 3	y = 20 + (0.7 × 3) =	22.1
Quarter 4	y = 20 + (0.7 × 4) =	22.8

Regression analysis is based on sample data and if we selected a different sample it is probable that a different regression line would be constructed. For this reason, regression analysis is most suited to conditions where there is a relatively stable relationship between the variables.

Assumptions we are making:

- The relationship is a linear one.

- The data used is representative of future trends.

 Test your understanding 2

Regression line

A regression line has been calculated as y = 192 + 2.40x, where x is the output and y is the total cost. You are required to:

(a) Explain this formula.

(b) Use it to predict the total cost for (i) 500 units and (ii) 1,500 units.

2 Forecasting with time series analysis

Earlier we noted that the analysis of a time series into its component parts would make extrapolation easier for forecasting future values for planning purposes.

In general, for short-term forecasts, only the trend and seasonal variations will be used; the cyclical variations will only have a significant effect over quite a long period of time and the random variations are, by their *very* nature, unpredictable.

Thus the approach to forecasting will be to:

- extrapolate the trend to the appropriate future time and

- adjust the extrapolated trend value by the appropriate seasonal variation.

2.1 Extrapolating the trend

There is no unique method for extrapolation of the basic trend, as it will very much depend upon its particular shape (if, indeed, it has a discernible one).

In practice, computers will be of great help in producing various possible equations for the trend, which can be rapidly tested against the data available to determine which fits best.

If the moving averages method has been used, a certain amount of judgement will be necessary. Possible approaches include the following:

- Plot the trend values on a graph and extrapolate by eye. (In fact, an initial sketch graph can be useful anyway to get a visual impression of the trend, before using one of the following methods to predict it.)

- Look at the increments between each trend value for any approximate pattern (e.g. roughly equal, which makes the trend approximately linear, or steadily increasing) and continue this pattern to the future time required.

- If the increments appear to vary randomly, an average increment for the period may be calculated and used in the forecast.

- If the pattern of the trend appears to change significantly over the period, you may restrict your prediction technique to later data values only, as being more representative of future values.

Example 5

We will now use the time series analysis from the 'TS Limited' example above to forecast the sales value for quarter 4 of year 3, given that the time series figures are the quarterly sales in £000.

Solution

The trend values obtained by moving averages have been plotted on a graph (unless specifically required, it is unlikely that you would have time to do this in an examination).

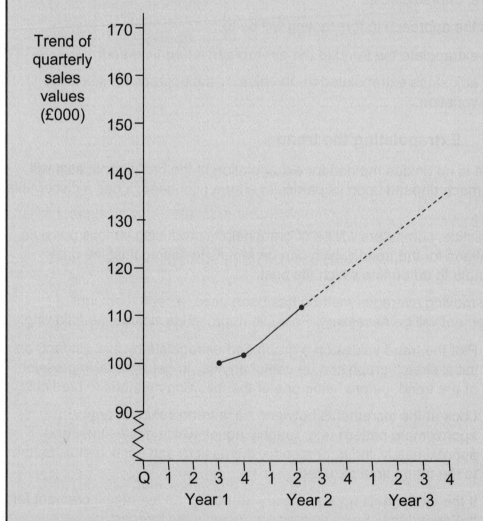

The graph shows an upward sloping trend, very approximately linear, but which becomes increasingly steep.

If we were to use the graphical approach to extrapolation, one approach would be to extend the line using the later, steeper gradient (although it should be noted that the earlier part of the curve shows that this may, in fact, revert to a shallower gradient). This approach may be over-optimistic. Perhaps it would be more prudent to assume that the earlier gradient will continue. The dashed line on the above graph shows a compromise between the two and produces a forecast for Q4 of Year 3 of approximately 135, indicating a trend value for sales of £135,000.

Now consider the increments (the differences between each successive pair of trend values). Note that you do not need to work these out exactly; they will just be used to detect any pattern or change.

From previous quarter to		Trend	Approximate increment
Year	Quarter		
1	3	100	–
	4	102	2
2	1	106	4
	2	111	5

There is no clear pattern, so some average increment may be used. The average increment over the whole period is $(111 - 100)/3 \cong 3.67$

(Note that we divide by the number of increments (3), not the number of trend values; we are averaging the 'gaps'.)

This would result in a forecast trend value for year 3, quarter 4 (which is six increments on from the last trend value) of 111 (the last trend value) + (6 × 3.67) = 133, or trend sales of £133,000.

Now we must adjust the trend value for the expected seasonal variation.

This is a lot more straightforward! Earlier, we calculated the seasonal variations for each quarter, and found that for quarter 4 the value was +25. pg 37.

This means that we expect quarter 4 values to be £25,000 above the trend value. Thus, seasonally-adjusted predictions for quarter 4, year 3 would be:

£133,000 + £25,000 = £158,000 (using the incremental method) or

£135,000 + £25,000 = £160,000 (using the graphical method)

depending upon which trend value was used.

In an examination, you should only make one prediction, justifying the approach used. There will rarely be one 'correct' way, so do not spend too long deciding how you are going to do it.

2.2 Seasonal variations and the multiplicative model

In some examinations you may be given the trend figures and seasonal variations but, instead of the seasonal variations being given in absolute figures as in the additive model that we have used so far, the seasonal variations may be given as percentage figures. This is the case if the multiplicative model is used for the time series analysis.

In order to find the forecast figures in this case, simply multiply the trend figure by the seasonal variation percentage and either add it to the trend or deduct it from the trend.

 Example 6

Given below are the estimated trend figures for a company's sales for the next four quarters:

20X3	Trend
	£
Quarter 1	560,000
Quarter 2	580,000
Quarter 3	605,000
Quarter 4	632,000

The seasonal variations using the multiplicative model have been calculated as:

Quarter 1	+ 15%
Quarter 2	+ 10%
Quarter 3	− 5%
Quarter 4	− 20%

Calculate the forecast sales figures for each of the next four quarters.

Solution

Quarter 1	£560,000 + (560,000 × 0.15) =	£644,000
Quarter 2	£580,000 + (580,000 × 0.10) =	£638,000
Quarter 3	£605,000 − (605,000 × 0.05) =	£574,750
Quarter 4	£632,000 − (632,000 × 0.20) =	£505,600

Test your understanding 3

From the following data, revise the income forecast.

Next year's income is forecast at £5,974,000. This assumes a 3% increase in selling price.

In the light of increasing competition the marketing manager has decided not to make the increase.

The forecast should be revised to _____

Select from:

- £5,626,000
- £5,800,000
- £5,974,000
- £6,153,000

Test your understanding 4

In IST Ltd, this year sales amount to £1,325,000. Analysis of recent years show a growth trend of 2% per annum. The seasonal variation has been:

- Quarter 1 + £12,000
- Quarter 2 +£18,000
- Quarter 3 –£25,000
- Quarter 4 –£5,000

You have been asked to forecast the income for each quarter of next year:

Quarter	£
1	
2	
3	
4	
Year	

2.3 Problems with forecasting

There are a number of problems with using time series analysis in order to estimate or forecast future results.

- The main problem is the inherent weakness of extrapolation. In order to estimate the trend for the future the trend line is extended on the graph and the figures read off. However, although the time series has moved in that particular manner in the past, it does not necessarily mean that it will continue to do so in the future.

- The seasonal adjustments used to find the forecast for the future are again based upon historic figures that may well already be out of date. There is no guarantee that the seasonal variations will remain the same in the future. If the time series has a large residual or random variation element, then this will make any forecasts even less reliable.

3 Forecasting techniques: sampling

As we have seen, the purpose of the management information system and the management accountant is to provide useful information to the management of the business. In order to do this the management accountant will have to collect the information in the first place. However, before collecting information, it will be necessary to determine what population we are interested in.

Definition

The population is simply all of the items of information that the collector is interested in. For example, if the management accountant wanted to know the proportion of defective units produced by a machine in a day then the population would be all of the units of product produced by the machine in the day.

3.1   Census or sampling approach

If information is required about a particular topic then there are two main approaches to obtaining the information, the census approach or the sampling approach.

The question here is whether we examine every item in the population, the census approach, or take a sample of the population. In business contexts it is rare to use the census approach so some form of sampling technique will be used. When sampling is used only a small number of items in the population are examined or tested.

Care must be taken when selecting a sample as the reliability of the results will be dependent upon how unbiased the sample is.

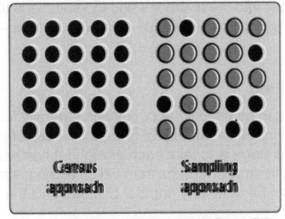

The census approach examines every item in the population

3.2   Random sampling

Random sampling is the best method of producing a totally unbiased sample; each item in the population has an equal chance of being included in the sample. In order for random sampling to be used each item in the population must be known and must have a consecutive number assigned to it. The sample is then chosen using random numbers taken from random number tables or a random number generator.

It is rare in practice for all items of the population to be known and for pure random sampling to be used. Therefore there are a number of other quasi-random methods of sampling that could be used:

* systematic sampling

* stratified sampling

* multi-stage sampling.

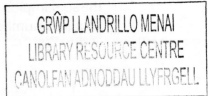

3.3 Systematic sampling

Systematic sampling is a simpler method of random sampling where again all of the items in the population must be known and each item must have a consecutive number assigned to it. Under systematic sampling the first item in the sample is chosen using a random number. Thereafter, every nth item in the population is taken to make up the sample. For example, the 14th item followed by every 50th item would produce a sample of 20 items from a population of 1,000 items.

3.4 Stratified sampling

Stratified sampling can be used if the population falls into distinct layers or groups. The population is split into these groups and the sample is then chosen from each group in proportion to the size of the group compared to the total population.

3.5 Multi-stage sampling

Again this is a method that can be used if the population naturally fall into fairly large groups or areas. Initially a number of groups or areas are selected randomly. The next stage is to take each group that has been selected and to split them into smaller groups from which again a sample is chosen randomly. This can be done any number of times until the final sample has been chosen.

3.6 Non-random sampling methods

In some instances it may not be cost effective to carry out random sampling techniques and therefore some form of non-random sampling is used. These methods will not produce such accurate results as the random sampling methods but the information collected can still be useful. Typical non-random sampling methods that can be used are:

- quota sampling
- cluster sampling.

3.7 Quota sampling

This is particularly useful when market research is being carried out. Quota sampling can be used when there are a number of different groups in the population, for example men under 30, women over 30, etc. The number of sample members required from each group is determined and these samples are taken on a non-random basis from the group until the required number has been reached.

3.8 Cluster sampling

Cluster sampling is where one or more areas of the population are determined to be representative of the population as a whole and therefore the sample is taken from that group alone. For example, if a business was carrying out market research into the buying habits of supermarket shoppers countrywide then it may be decided that customers shopping at three different supermarkets in Birmingham are representative of nationwide supermarket shoppers and the sample can then be taken from shoppers at these three supermarkets only.

4 Forecasting techniques: index numbers

We have seen that the trend of income or costs can be estimated using time series analysis. However, this method is quite complex and time-consuming. There are other methods of indicating the trend of figures for income or costs and one of these is to use index numbers.

4.1 Use of index numbers

A time series of figures for costs or income can be easily converted into an index. This is done firstly by choosing a base year and allocating to this year's figure an index of 100. Each subsequent period's figure is then converted into a relevant index number using the formula:

$$\text{Index} = \frac{\text{Current year's figures}}{\text{Base year figure}} \times 100$$

 Example 7

The materials costs for a business for the last six months have been as follows:

	£
March	427,000
April	442,000
May	460,000
June	433,000
July	447,000
August	470,000

If the index for March is 100, what are the index numbers of the costs for each of the subsequent months and what do these index numbers tell us?

Solution

Month		Index
March		100.0
April	$\dfrac{442,000}{427,000} \times 100$	103.5
May	$\dfrac{460,000}{427,000} \times 100$	107.7
June	$\dfrac{433,000}{427,000} \times 100$	101.4
July	$\dfrac{447,000}{427,000} \times 100$	104.7
August	$\dfrac{470,000}{427,000} \times 100$	110.1

The index shows that the materials costs are generally rising although there is a fall back in June which has been made up for by the highest level yet in August.

4.2 Indices to measure inflation

Published indices that can be useful to the management accountant are the Consumer Price Index (CPI) and the Retail Price Index (RPI). These indices published on a monthly basis by the Government and are used as measures of general price changes and inflation.

If we have a series of cost or income figures measured over a fairly long time period then they could have been distorted by price changes over the period and may not necessarily show the correct position.

We can use the RPI to adjust all of the figures in the time series into current day prices by using the formula:

$$\text{Current price adjusted figure} = \text{Actual sales} \times \frac{\text{RPI in current year}}{\text{RPI in year of sales}}$$

Example 8

Suppose that a company has recorded annual sales over the last six years as follows:

	£
	£
20X0	735,000
20X1	764,000
20X2	791,000
20X3	811,000
20X4	833,000
20X5	856,000

The average RPI for each of those years was as follows:

	RPI
20X0	144.3
20X1	149.8
20X2	153.0
20X3	157.2
20X4	161.9
20X5	170.0

Show the sales for the last six years in terms of current year (20X5) prices and explain what this shows.

Solution

	Actual sales	RPI adjustment	Price adjusted sales
	£		£
20X0	735,000	× 170.0/144.3	865,900
20X1	764,000	× 170.0/149.8	867,000
20X2	791,000	× 170.0/153.0	878,900
20X3	811,000	× 170.0/157.2	877,000
20X4	833,000	× 170.0/161.9	874,700
20X5	856,000		856,000

Whereas the original, unadjusted figures indicated a fairly substantial increase in sales over the period, once the sales are adjusted to current day prices, a different picture appears. In fact the sales increased very gradually until 20X2 and have been in decline for the last three years.

When comparing costs or income over time the management accountant should consider the effects of either general inflation by using the RPI or more specific price changes that affect the cost or income by using a price index specifically related to that cost or income.

Test your understanding 5

Price indices

A product which cost £12.50 in 20X0, cost £13.65 in 20X1. Calculate the simple price index for 20X1 based on 20X0.

 Test your understanding 6

Forecast for energy costs

Next year, energy costs are forecast at £2,970,000. This assumes a 4% increase in energy consumption, as well as a 4% increase in gas and electricity tariffs.

However, energy saving measures are being proposed. Instead of increasing, consumption should be reduced by 10%.

The energy budget should be:

- £2,566,080

- £2,570,192

- £2,745,931

- £2,855,770

 Test your understanding 7

The budget committee has set the sales volume growth and pricing assumptions for years 2, 3, 4 and 5 in the form of indices. Complete the sales revenue forecast below.

Do not show decimals. Round each figure to the nearest whole number.

	Year 1	Year 2	Year 3	Year 4	Year 5
Sales volume index	130	131	132	133	134
Sales price index	112	115	120	125	130

Sales revenue	Actual Year 1 £	Forecast Year 2 £	Forecast Year 3 £	Forecast Year 4 £	Forecast Year 5 £
At Year 1 prices	250,000				
At expected prices					

5 Forecasts and plans

Although the words are often used interchangeably, there is a distinction between a forecast and a plan. The key difference between a budget and a forecast is that the budget is a plan for where a business wants to go, while a forecast is the indication of where it is actually going.

A forecast is an expectation of or estimate of what might happen in the future based on historical data and analysis using various assumptions, whereas a plan is a deliberate commitment or intent.

A budget is a plan but it takes into account forecasts of factors over which the organisation does not have control.

6 Dealing with uncertainty

Because data produced from forecasts is inherently uncertain, organisations must use techniques to minimise the risks of basing budgets on inaccurate forecasts. There are several methods available, and managers may use one or more of them.

One method is to use 'sensitivity analysis' to model the impact of using different forecasts. This is closely allied to the scenario planning or 'what-if analysis' technique that you may have studied in other units. For example, if the employees pay level is not yet determined for the budget period, then alternative budgets based on (say) current pay levels, increases of 2%, or increases of 4% could be drafted to evaluate the impact.

Another method could be to update forecasts regularly to ensure that recent events are taken into account. As the initial forecasts may be completed well in advance of the budget period, it would make sense to see if they are still valid as the budget period approaches. For example a sales forecast based on trend analysis may initially be developed using historical data that ceases a year before the budget period. By re-forecasting using more recent sales data as it becomes available, the managers can reassure themselves that the forecast being used is still valid, or if not they can make appropriate changes to their plans.

A rolling is a budget (usually annual) kept continuously up to date by adding another accounting period (e.g. month or quarter) when the earliest accounting period has expired. Rolling budgets are suitable if accurate forecasts cannot be made (for example, in a fast moving environment) or for any area of business that needs tight control.

Illustration – Rolling budgets

A typical rolling budget might be prepared as follows:

(1) A budget is prepared for the coming year (say January – December) broken down into suitable, say quarterly, control periods.

(2) At the end of the first control period (31 March) a comparison is made of that period's results against the budget. The conclusions drawn from this analysis are used to update the budgets for the remaining control periods and to add a budget for a further three months, so that the company once again has budgets available for the coming year (this time April – March).

(3) The planning process is repeated at the end of each three-month control period.

7 Summary

Time series analysis helps with the isolation of trends, although these still may not be easy to extrapolate into the future. Remember that you are using historic data which will not reflect future economic and environmental changes.

Also, you must be able to calculate the seasonal variations and be able to de-seasonalise data if required.

In this chapter we also look briefly at sampling techniques and you should be aware of the definitions of the main sampling methods. Finally, we studied index numbers, a simple technique frequent in examinations.

Test your understanding answers

Test your understanding 1

2015	Q1	Q2	Q3	Q4
Actual price per tonne	£40	£44	£64	£76
Seasonal variation	– £4	– £8	+ £4	+ £8
Trend	£44	£52	£60	£68
2016				
Trend (increase of £8 per quarter)	£76	£84	£92	£100
Seasonal variation	– £4	– £8	+ £4	+ £8
Forecast price per tonne	£72	£76	£96	£108

Test your understanding 2

Regression line

(a) In the formula y represents total cost (the dependent variable), x represents the units of activity (the independent variable), 192 represents the fixed cost element (£), 2.40 represents the variable cost per unit (£).

The formula is estimating a linear relationship between activity level and total cost.

(b) (i)   x   =   500

y   =   192 + 2.40 (500)

=   £1,392

(ii) x   =   1,500

y   =   192 + 2.40 (1,500)

=   £3,792

Test your understanding 3

Income forecast

The forecast should be revised to **£5,800,000**.

Working:

Remove the 3% increase in selling price from forecast data:

£5,974,000 ÷ 1.03 = £5,800,000

 Test your understanding 4

Next year's sales = £1,325,000 × (1 + 2%)

Next year's sales = £1,351,500

Next year quarterly sales = £1,351,500 ÷ 4 = £337,875 per quarter

- Quarter 1   sales : £337,875 + £12,000 = £349,875
- Quarter 2   sales : £337,875 + £18,000 = £355,875
- Quarter 3   sales : £337,875 − £25,000 = £312,875
- Quarter 4   sales : £337,875 − £5,000 = £332,875

Quarter	£
1	£349,875
2	£355,875
3	£312,875
4	£332,875
Year	£1,351,500

Test your understanding 5

Price indices

$$\text{Simple price index} = \frac{P_1}{P_0} \times 100$$

$$= \frac{13.65}{12.50} \times 100$$

$$= 1.092 \times 100$$

$$= 109.2$$

This means that the price has increased by 9.2% of its base year price of £12.50.

Test your understanding 6

The 4% increase in energy consumption should be revised and reduced by 10% instead of increased by 4%.

(£2,970,000 ÷ 1.04) × (1 – 10%) = **£ 2,570,192**

Test your understanding 7

To calculate the sales revenue forecast for Year 2 at Year 1 prices, we take the sales revenue for Year 1 and divide it by its sales volume index of 130:

£250,000/130 = £1,923.07 (leave this number in your calculator)

We then multiply this by the Year 2 volume index of 131 so £1,923.07 × 131 = £251,923

To calculate the sales revenue forecast for Year 2 at expected prices, we take the sales revenue just calculated of £251,923, divide that by the Year 1 price index of 112 and multiply the result by the Year 2 sales price index of 115:

(£251,923/112) × 115 = £258,671

Sales revenue	Actual Year 1 £	Forecast Year 2 £	Forecast Year 3 £	Forecast Year 4 £	Forecast Year 5 £
At Year 1 prices	250,000	251,923	253,846	255,769	257,692
At expected prices		258,671	271,978	285,456	299,107

Dealing with fixed overheads

Introduction

Overhead is the general term used to describe costs which are not direct costs of production. They are also known as indirect costs and they may be indirect production costs or indirect non-production costs. When a management accountant is trying to ascertain the cost of a product or service, there are two possible approaches available for dealing with overheads.

Firstly, apportionment and allocation of all production overheads may be used to arrive at a 'full' cost per unit. This is known as absorption costing and is considered first. Remember that as well as the indirect production cost there are indirect non-production costs. These non-production costs are never included in the cost of the product, or inventory or cost of sales.

Alternatively, one can use only direct costs to arrive at the cost per unit and leave indirect costs as a general overhead not related to units of output. This approach is generally known as marginal costing and will be dealt with later in the chapter.

This chapter contains the essential understanding of accounting for overheads and overhead absorption which is necessary for your further studies.

ASSESSMENT CRITERIA	CONTENTS
<ul><li>Identify budgetary responsibilities and accountabilities (Element 2.1)</li><li>Calculate budgets for different types of cost (Element 2.4)</li></ul>	1 Allocation, apportionment and absorption of overheads 2 Activity-based costing (ABC)

1 Allocation, apportionment and absorption of overheads

1.1 Introduction

We have already identified two types of costs that make up the full production cost of a unit:

(a) Direct costs are those that can be uniquely identified with an individual cost unit (e.g. direct materials, direct labour, direct expenses).

(b) Indirect costs (overheads) are costs incurred in production but not easily 'traced' to individual units, e.g. machine power (variable), factory rent (fixed), heat and light (semi-variable).

The problem we are considering here is how to divide indirect production costs between cost units, in order to prepare a 'standard' total cost per unit for budgeting, inventory valuation and pricing purposes.

The method used to divide production overheads between production units is made up of three processes: allocation, apportionment and absorption.

Step 1 Identify the indirect cost with a cost centre

This can be done in two ways depending on the nature of the cost.

(a) **Allocation**

 Definition

Where the indirect cost is borne entirely by one cost centre, the entire cost is allocated to that cost centre.

(b) **Apportionment**

 Definition

Where the indirect cost is shared by more than one cost centre, the cost is apportioned between cost centres.

Step 2   Identify the indirect costs of the cost centre calculated in Step 1 with the cost units produced by that centre.

This is called *absorption*.

 Definition

Absorption is the technique of relating a cost centre's indirect costs to the units produced by the cost centre.

We shall now look at each of these in more detail.

1.2   Cost allocation

Certain cost items will be incurred entirely by one cost centre. Allocation deals with this type of cost and simply allots it to the cost centre which has incurred the cost.

Cost centre	Allocated cost
Canteen	Tea bags
	Spaghetti
	Chef's wages
Packing department	Cardboard
	String

1.3   Cost apportionment (primary)

More frequently, however, the benefit of an item of cost will be shared by a number of cost centres. The overhead will be split or apportioned between the relevant cost centres on an 'equitable' basis.

The rent of buildings, for example, can relate to the total floor space occupied by a number of different departments and it is usual to allot the rental charge to those departments in proportion to the floor space they occupy.

Nature of cost	Possible bases of apportionment
Rent and rates	Floor area occupied by various departments
Lighting and heating	Cubic capacity of locations or metered usage
Insurance of inventory	Value of inventory holdings in various locations

Example 1

A general cost in a manufacturing company is factory rental. Annual rental costs are £80,000. How should this cost be apportioned between production departments and service departments?

Rental costs are usually apportioned between departments on the basis of the floor space taken up by each department. For example, suppose that three departments have floor space of 10,000 square metres, 15,000 square metres and 25,000 square metres, and annual rental costs are £80,000. If we apportion rental costs between the departments on the basis of their floor space, the apportionment would be as follows.

Annual rental	£80,000
Total floor space (10,000 + 15,000 + 25,000)	50,000 square metres
Apportionment rate (£80,000/50,000)	£1.60/square metre

	£
Apportion to department with 10,000 square metres	16,000
Apportion to department with 15,000 square metres	24,000
Apportion to department with 25,000 square metres	40,000
	———
	80,000
	———

 Example 2

The costs of heating and lighting might also be apportioned on the basis of floor space. Alternatively, since heating relates to volume rather than floor space, it could be argued that the costs should be apportioned on the volume of space taken up by each department. Yet another view is that electricity costs relate more to the consumption of electrical power by machines, therefore the apportionment of these costs should be on the basis of the number and power of the machines in each department.

A reasonable argument could be made for any of these bases of apportionment.

1.4 Cost apportionment (secondary)

After completing the allocation and primary apportionment stages, you should have assigned all costs to cost centres.

Some cost centres, however, will not have production units passing through them; these cost centres are called service departments (e.g. quality control department, works canteen). Before the final stage of absorption into cost units can be carried out, it is necessary to perform a further type of apportionment whereby the total costs of the service cost centres are reassigned to production cost centres. This is known as secondary apportionment. This should be done on a fair basis to reflect the benefit derived from the service centre. The following example is an illustration of primary and secondary apportionment.

Example 3

Overhead analysis sheet			Period ending.....................		
	Total	**Production**		**Service**	
		Assembly	*Finishing*	*Stores*	*Canteen*
	£	£	£	£	£
Overheads allocated directly to cost centres	133,000	49,000	36,000	27,000	21,000
Overheads to be apportioned					
Rent (Apportionment basis: Floor area)	76,000	26,000	24,000	15,000	11,000
Equipment depreciation (Apportionment basis: Carrying value)	15,000	8,000	1,000	5,000	1,000
Total overhead	224,000	83,000	61,000	47,000	33,000
Apportioning of stores (Apportionment basis: Value of inventory)		31,000	16,000	(47,000)	
Apportioning of canteen (Apportionment basis: Number of employees)		14,000	19,000		(33,000)
		128,000	96,000	–	–

1.5 Absorption

Having collected all indirect costs in the production cost centres via overhead allocation and apportionment, the cost has to be spread over the output of the production cost centre.

The allotment of accumulated overhead costs to cost units is called overhead absorption. The absorption rate is normally calculated at the start of the period and therefore based on budgeted quantities. Various methods of absorption exist and the one most fitting should be chosen.

The following are the most common methods you will encounter.

(a) **Rate per unit**

The simple unit rate is obtained by dividing total budgeted overheads by the number of units budgeted to be produced. However, where more than one product is produced, this is an unsatisfactory basis for absorbing overheads as it will not reflect the relative demands of each product on the production departments through which they pass.

(b) **Alternative bases of absorption**

There are a number of bases commonly used as an alternative to the simple unit rate:

- rate per direct labour hour

- rate per machine hour

- percentage of material cost

- percentage of wage cost

- percentage of total direct cost (prime cost).

It is important to appreciate, however, that whichever method or combination of methods is used, the result will only be an approximate estimate of what that product actually costs.

In practice, many businesses use a 'direct labour hour rate' or 'machine hour rate' in preference to a rate based on a percentage of direct materials cost, direct wages or prime cost, as it may be possible to associate some overheads either with labour time or with machine time.

It may be possible to analyse the total overhead apportioned to each production department into fixed and variable elements. In this case a variable overhead rate per unit and a fixed overhead rate per unit can be calculated.

The absorption rates will normally be calculated at the beginning of a period and hence be based on budgeted costs and production levels. This can lead to problems when actual costs and volumes are not the same as budgeted leading to over- or under-absorption.

Example 4

For the year ended 31 December 20X4 the planned overhead for the Machining Cost Centre at Cuecraft Ltd was:

Overhead £132,000
Volume of activity 15,000 machine hours

In January 20X4 the cost centre incurred £12,000 of overhead and 1,350 machine hours were worked.

Task

Calculate the pre-determined overhead rate per machine hour and the overhead under or over-recovered in the month.

Solution

Absorption rate, based on the budget:

$$\frac{\text{Planned overhead}}{\text{Machine hours}} = \frac{£132,000}{15,000 \text{ machine hours}} = £8.80 \text{ per machine hour}$$

	£
Overhead absorbed	
1,350 machine hours at £8.80	11,880
Overhead incurred	12,000
Under-absorption	120

Here, the amount of overheads actually charged to production are £11,880, which is less than actual expenditure. We therefore have under-absorption of overhead.

Under-recovery of overheads is shown as a separate item in the Income statement. Since production has been charged with less overheads than the amount incurred, profit is adjusted downwards to take account of the under-absorption. In other words, under-absorption is a 'loss' item.

Test your understanding 1

Sandsend Engineers Ltd specialise in agricultural engineering. The business is divided into three cost centres: machining, fabrication and outside contract work.

The budgeted overhead for the quarter ended 31 March 2003 shows:

Cost centre	Machining	Fabrication	Outside contracts	Total
	£	£	£	£
Allocated overhead	21,000	25,500	19,500	66,000
Apportioned overhead	15,000	16,100	9,100	40,200
	———	———	———	———
	36,000	41,600	28,600	106,200
	———	———	———	———
Budgeted machine hours	4,000	5,200		
Budgeted labour hours			1,950	

In early January, the company receives an order for a replacement door on a grain silo for a local farmer. The specification of costs includes:

Direct material   £3,100

Direct labour rate per hour   £7.50

Machine hours and labour hours per cost centre:

Machining   12 hours

Fabrication   8 hours

Outside contracts   6 hours

The business has a pricing policy based on full absorption costing principles. It adds 10% to production costs to cover for administration, selling and distribution. It then plans for profit based on 25% of the selling price or contract price.

Complete the following:

Using absorption costing principles, the contract price of the replacement grain silo door will be £_____ (to the nearest '£'.)

Test your understanding 2

Roberts and Ranson are partners trading as licensed accounting technicians. They employ one other fully qualified technician and two trainees, together with a general administration assistant.

The budgeted salaries for the year comprise:

	£
Roberts	30,000
Ranson	30,000
Qualified senior	18,500
Trainee (1)	10,500
Trainee (2)	12,000
Administrator	14,500*
Total	**115,500**

*The administrator's salary is to be treated as overhead.

The budgeted overheads include:

	£
Building occupancy costs	9,100
Telephone, postage, stationery	4,700
Other overheads	11,200
Total	**25,000**

The total forecast labour hours for the year include:

	Hours
Partners	3,760
Qualified senior	1,880
Trainees (split equally)	3,760
Total	**9,400**

Clients' work is priced on full absorption costing principles. Overhead is recovered on labour hours. The labour charge-out rates for partners, the qualified senior and the trainees are based on their budgeted salaries divided by their labour hours.

The business accepts a new client, the White Rose Hotel, and the senior partner estimates, having met with the client, that the hours required on the work will be:

	Hours	
Partners	5	
Qualified senior	12	
Trainees	6	(3 hours each)
Total	**23**	

The pricing policy is based on adding an element for profit which will yield a 30% profit margin on the price charged to the client.

You are required to complete the OAR, charge-out rates and estimated fees calculation schedules below.

Overhead absorption rate £

Building occupancy

Telephone, postage and stationery

Other overheads

Administrator's salary

Total overheads

Number of labour hours

Overhead absorption rate per labour hour

£

Partner's labour charge-out rate = _____ per hour

Qualified senior = _____ per hour

Trainee (1) = _____ per hour

Trainee (2) = _____ per hour

White Rose Hotel estimated fee

£

Direct labour

Partners	=	
Qualified seniors	=	
Trainee (1)	=	
Trainee (2)		

Total direct labour

Overheads

Total overhead cost

Total cost

Thus charge to client

Test your understanding 3

Refer again to the scenario in Activity 1, Sandsend Engineers Ltd.

The actual overhead incurred during the quarter ended 31 March 20X3 was:

	£
Machining	37,800
Fabrication	42,000
Outside work	29,100
	108,900

Overhead is recovered on machine hours in machining and fabrication, and labour hours on outside work.

The actual level of activity in the quarter was:

Machining   4,250 machine hours

Fabrication   5,300 machine hours

Outside work   1,975 labour hours

Required:

(a)   Calculate the overhead recovered in each cost centre for the period.

(b)   Post both the actual overhead incurred and the overhead recovered to the overhead control ledger account for the period, showing the under or over recovery transferred to the Income statement.

 Test your understanding 4

Blidworth Loam Ltd manufacture a single product 'Cricketloam' and supply this product to cricket clubs for grounds at professional level through to village greens.

Its cost specification includes the following budgeted details per tonne of product, together with budgeted data for the current year:

Direct labour hours	4.5
Labour rate per hour	£8.50
Direct material	1.1 tonnes per tonne of good output
Material cost	£25 per tonne
Variable production overheads (total)	£378,000
Fixed production overheads (total)	£250,000
Selling price per tonne	£132
Production volume	12,000 tonnes
Sales volume	11,500 tonnes

Complete the following:

The budgeted marginal cost will be £_____per _____.

The contribution will be £_____per _____.

Test your understanding 5

MIF is a manufacturing company. Select an appropriate accounting treatment for each of the following costs:

- Re-design of the website
- Holiday pay for operatives on the production line
- Material wastage in the production process
- Cost of the IT department
- Administrative wages
- Maintenance services
- Production equipment cleaning
- Depreciation of machinery.

Options available are:

- Allocate to administrative overheads
- Direct costs
- Allocate to marketing overheads
- Charge to production in a machine hour overhead rate
- Charge to production in a labour overhead rate
- Activity based charge to production cost centres.

2 Activity-based costing (ABC)

2.1 Criticisms of absorption costs

Historically a direct labour rate for absorption of all fixed overheads was a very common method, as production tended to be highly labour-intensive. Such items as rent would be apportioned using the area involved, but the absorption rate would usually be labour hours. It was reasonable to assume that the more labour time spent on a product, the more production resources in general were being used. Thus the product should be charged with a higher share of the overheads.

However, nowadays, production is far more mechanised. This has two impacts as follows:

(a)   A higher proportion of the overheads is accounted for by machine-related costs (power, depreciation, maintenance, etc).

(b)   The amount of labour time spent upon a unit is far less representative of its final significance in the use of production resources.

To take a simple example, Product A may use 9 machine hours and 1 labour hour, whilst Product B requires 1 machine hour and 4 labour hours. The traditional approach would charge B with four times as much production overhead (including machine costs) as A, even though it takes half the time overall.

In this example, one solution would be to use machine hours as a basis. However, this still tries to relate all overhead costs, whatever their nature, to usage of machines. This would not necessarily be appropriate for, say, costs of receiving and checking materials going into the production process. This will be more likely to depend upon the number of times an order of material is received into stores for a particular product.

2.2   Activity-based costing (ABC) approach

Professors Robin Cooper and Robert Kaplan at the Harvard Business School have developed a costing system called activity-based costing (ABC) which avoids the problems experienced by traditional costing methods. If management are keen to control costs, then it is vital that they should know the activities that cause costs to arise.

(a)   **Cost drivers**

Those activities that are the significant determinants of cost are known as cost-drivers. For example, if production-scheduling cost is driven by the number of production set-ups, then that number is the cost-driver for the cost of production-scheduling. The cost-drivers represent the bases for charging costs in the ABC system, with a separate cost centre established for each cost-driver.

(b)   **Cost pools**

Where several costs are 'driven' by the same activity (e.g. engine oil, machine breakdown and repairs) then these costs are put into 'cost pools' and the total of the cost pool is absorbed by, say, machine hours.

KAPLAN PUBLISHING

2.3 Mechanics of ABC

The mechanics of operating an ABC system are similar to a traditional costing system.

The significant cost drivers need to be ascertained and a cost centre is established for each cost driver. Costs are allocated to products by dividing the cost centre costs by the number of transactions undertaken.

For example, in Plant Y a set up of a production run would be a cost driver. The cost of the engineers who do the set ups would be a cost centre. If the cost of the engineers is say £280,000 and the number of sets ups is 500, then the charging out rate is $\frac{280,000}{500}$ = £560. A product which has a number of small production runs will thus have a greater proportion of these costs relative to the quantity of the product produced, than a product with large production runs.

Other overheads will be allocated to products in a different way; which way depends upon the cost drivers which have been ascertained.

🔅 Example 5

Plant Y produces about one hundred products. Its largest selling product is Product A; its smallest is Product B. Relevant data is given below.

	Product A	Product B	Total products
Units produced pa	50,000	1,000	500,000
Material cost per unit	£1.00	£1.00	
Direct labour per unit	15 minutes	15 minutes	
Machine time per unit	1 hour	1 hour	
Number of set ups p.a.	24	2	500
Number of purchase orders for materials	36	6	2,800
Number of times material handled	200	15	12,000
Direct labour cost per hour			£5

Overhead costs

	£
Set up	280,000
Purchasing	145,000
Materials handling	130,000
Machines	660,000
	1,215,000

Total machine hours are 600,000 hours.

Traditional costing (absorbing overheads on machine hours):

Unit cost	A	B
	£	£
Material cost	1.00	1.00
Labour cost	1.25	1.25
Overhead per machine hour		

$$\frac{1,215,000}{600,000} = 2.025$$
| | 2.025 | 2.025 |
| | 4.275 | 4.275 |

The above costings imply that we are indifferent between producing Product A and Product B.

Using an ABC approach would show:

Step 1 Calculate the direct material and labour costs as for the traditional approach.

Unit cost	A	B
	£	£
Material cost	1.00	1.00
Labour cost	1.25	1.25
	2.25	2.25

Step 2   Calculate the overheads that will be charged to each product by:

(a)   Calculating the overhead cost per cost driver for each type of overhead (e.g. cost per set-up).

(b)   Charge cost to each unit by calculating the unit cost accordingly.

	A	B
Overheads:	£	£

Set up

$$\frac{280,000}{500} = £560 \text{ per set up}$$

	A	B
$\dfrac{560 \times 24}{50,000}$	0.27	
$\dfrac{560 \times 2}{1,000}$		1.12

Purchasing:

$$\frac{145,000}{2,800} = £51.786 \text{ per purchase order}$$

	A	B
$\dfrac{36 \times 51.786}{50,000}$	0.04	
$\dfrac{6 \times 51.786}{1,000}$		0.31

Materials handling:

$$\frac{130,000}{12,000} = 10.833 \text{ per time}$$

	A	B
$\dfrac{200 \times 10.833}{50,000}$	0.04	
$\dfrac{15 \times 10.833}{1,000}$		0.16

Machines:

$$\frac{660,000}{600,000} = £1.10 \text{ per machine hour} \qquad 1.10 \qquad 1.10$$

	1.45	2.69
Add: Direct material and labour costs	2.25	2.25
	£3.70	£4.94

Common sense would lead us to conclude that ABC is a more accurate representation of the relative real costs of the two products.

What must be considered, however, is whether the benefits of this approach outweigh the costs of implementing and applying the system.

The following example again contrasts a traditional product costing system with an ABC system and shows that an ABC system produces much more accurate product costs.

Example 6

Mayes plc has a single production centre and has provided the following budgeted information for the next period.

	Product A	Product B	Product C	Total
Production and sales (units)	40,000	25,000	10,000	75,000
Direct material cost	£25	£20	£18	£1,680,000
Direct labour hours	3	4	2	240,000
Machine hours	2	4	3	210,000
Number of production runs	5	10	25	40
Number of component receipts	15	25	120	160
Number of production orders	15	10	25	50

Direct labour is paid £8 per hour.

Overhead costs in the period are expected to be as follows:

	£
Set-up	140,000
Machine	900,000
Goods inwards	280,000
Packing	200,000
Engineering	180,000
	1,700,000

What are the unit costs of each product using:

(a)   the traditional approach?

(b)   the ABC method?

Solution

(a)   A traditional costing approach would cost each product as follows:

	Product A	Product B	Product C
	£	£	£
Direct materials	25.00	20.00	18.00
Direct labour (@ £8 per hour)	24.00	32.00	16.00
Overhead (@ £7.08 per hour – see below)	21.24	28.32	14.16
Total cost	70.24	80.32	48.16

Overhead recovery rate = $\dfrac{£1,700,000}{240,000}$

= £7.08 per direct labour hour

(b) An ABC system needs to investigate the cost determinants for the indirect overheads not driven by production volume. Assume that these are as follows.

Cost	Cost driver
Set-up	Number of production runs
Goods inwards	Number of receipts
Packing	Number of production orders
Engineering	Number of production orders

The machine overhead of £900,000 is likely to be related primarily to production volume, so it will be recovered on the basis of machine hours used = $\dfrac{£900,000}{210,000}$ = £4.29 per machine hour (after rounding).

The cost per activity for each of the other cost centres is as follows.

Set-up cost $\dfrac{£140,000}{40}$ = £3,500 per set-up

Goods inwards $\dfrac{£280,000}{160}$ = £,1750 per order

Packing $\dfrac{£200,000}{50}$ = £4,000 per production order

Engineering $\dfrac{£180,000}{50}$ = £3,600 per order

An ABC approach would allocate overheads to each of the product groups as follows:

	Product A	Product B	Product C
	£	£	£
Set-up costs			
5 × £3,500	17,500		
10 × £3,500		35,000	
25 × £3,500			87,500
Machine costs (rounded down)			
(2 × 40,000) × £4.29	343,000		
(4 × 25,000) × £4.29		429,000	
(3 × 10,000) × £4.29			128,000
Goods inwards costs			
15 × £1,750	26,250		
25 × £1,750		43,750	
120 × £1,750			210,000
Packing costs			
15 × £4,000	60,000		
10 × £4,000		40,000	
25 × £4,000			100,000
Engineering costs			
15 × £3,600	54,000		
10 × £3,600		36,000	
25 × £3,600			90,000
Total overhead	500,750	583,750	615,500
Average overhead per unit			
£500,750/40,000	£12.52		
£583,750/25,000		£23.35	
£615,500/10,000			£61.55
This compares to the traditional overhead absorption of:			
	£21.24	£28.32	£14.16

It can be seen that product C is significantly under-costed under the traditional system, while products A and B are over-costed. This situation arises because the large proportion of costs driven by product C is not picked up under the traditional costing system. Since it is the cost-drivers identified in the ABC system which generate the costs in the first place, the ABC system will produce a more accurate final analysis.

Test your understanding 6

Refer again to the scenario outlined in Blidworth Loam Ltd.

The accounting technician and the planning engineer have recently analysed the value adding processes and identified various activities, cost drivers within those activities and current volumes of production and decide to apply the ABC methodology.

Budgeted plans 2003

	Activity	Cost pool £	Cost driver volume
(1)	Process set up	260,000	200 set ups
(2)	Material procurement	74,000	50 purchase orders
(3)	Maintenance	64,000	12 maintenance plans
(4)	Material handling	120,000	2,500 material movements
(5)	Quality costs	80,000	200 inspections
(6)	Order processing	30,000	1,000 customers
Total		**£628,000**	

The company plan to produce 1,000 tonnes per month which will require the following approximate activity demand:

17 set ups	4 purchase orders	1 maintenance plan
210 material movements	16 inspections	80 customers.

Complete the following:

(a)

Process setup: The cost driver rate will be £_____ per _____.

Material procurement: The cost driver rate will be £_____ per _____.

Maintenance: The cost driver rate will be £_____ per _____.

Material handling: The cost driver rate will be £_____ per _____.

Quality costs: The cost driver rate will be £_____ per _____.

Order processing: The cost driver rate will be £_____ per _____.

(b)　Using ABC, complete the following to determine the amount of overhead to be recovered per tonne of product.

17	setups	x		=	
4	purchase orders	x		=	
1	maintenance plan	x		=	
210	material movements	x		=	
16	inspections	x		=	
80	customers	x		=	

Total cost

Thus, the overhead cost per tonne of product would be: £_____ per tonne.

3　Summary

This chapter has revised several fundamental cost accounting topics from your earlier studies, in particular the treatment of overheads including:

- allocation/apportionment/absorption
- service departments
- over-/under-absorption
- activity based costing approach.

Test your understanding answers

Test your understanding 1

Overhead recovery rates for each cost centre:

Machining $\dfrac{£36,000}{4,000 \text{ machine hours}}$ = £9.00 per machine hour

Fabrication $\dfrac{£41,600}{5,200 \text{ machine hours}}$ = £8.00 per machine hour

Outside contract work $\dfrac{£28,600}{1,950 \text{ labour hours}}$ = £14.67 per direct labour hr

Production cost of contract:		£
Direct material		3,100
Direct labour:		
Machining	12 hours	
Fabrication	8 hours	
Outside work	6 hours	
	26 hours × £7.50	195
Overheads:		
Machining	12 hours × £9.00	108
Fabrication	8 hours × £8.00	64
Outside work	6 hours × £14.67	88
Production cost		3,555
Add 10% for admin, selling and distribution		356
		£3,911

Selling price/contract price (£3,911/75) × 100 =	**£5,215**

Check:	£
Contract price/selling price	5,215
Cost	3,911
Profit	£1,304

Profit = 25% of selling price as required.

Test your understanding 2

Overhead absorption rate

	£
Building occupancy	9,100
Telephone, postage and stationery	4,700
Other overheads	11,200
Administrator's salary	14,500
Total overheads	39,500

Number of labour hours	9,400

£39,500/9,400

Overhead absorption rate per labour hour	4.20

		£	
Partner's labour charge-out rate £30,000/(3,760 /2)	=	15.96	per hour
Qualified senior £18,500/1,880	=	9.84	per hour
Trainee (1) £10,500/1,880	=	5.59	per hour
Trainee (2) £12,000/1,880	=	6.38	per hour

White Rose Hotel estimated fee

Direct labour

		£
Partners : 5 hours × £15.96	=	£79.80
Qualified seniors : 12 hrs × £9.84	=	£118.08
Trainee (1) : 3 hrs × £5.59	=	£16.77
Trainee (2) : 3 hrs × £6.38	=	£19.14
Total direct labour		233.79

Overheads

Total overhead cost 23 hrs × £4.20	£96.60
Total cost	**£330.39**
Thus charge to client (330.39/70 × 100)	**£471.99**

Test your understanding 3

Task

(a) **Sandsend Engineers Ltd overhead recovered:**

		£
Machining	4,250 machine hours × £9.00	38,250
Fabrication	5,300 machine hours × £8.00	42,400
Outside work	1,975 labour hours × £14.67	28,973
		£109,623

(b)

Overhead control account

	£		£
Actual:		*Recovered in work-in-progress*	
Machining	37,800	Machining	38,250
Fabrication	42,000	Fabrication	42,400
Outside work	29,100	Outside work	28,973
Over-recovered P/L			
account (bal)	723		
	109,623		109,623

Test your understanding 4

		£
Direct labour	4.5 hours × £8.50	38.25
Direct material	1.1 tonnes × £25	27.50
Variable overhead	£378,000/12,000 tonnes	31.50
Marginal cost = Total variable costs per tonne		£97.25

Contribution/tonne =   = Selling price − Variable cost
                     = £132 − £97.25
                     = £34.75

Test your understanding 5

Situation	Answer
Redesign of the website	Allocate to marketing overheads
Holiday pay for operatives on the production line	Charge to production in a labour hour overhead rate
Material wastage in the production process	Direct cost
Administrative wages	Allocate to administrative overheads
Machinery maintenance services	Charge to production in a machine hour overhead rate
Production equipment cleaning	Charge to production in a machine hour overhead rate
Depreciation of machinery	Charge to production in a machine hour overhead rate
Cost of IT Department	Activity based charge to production cost centres

Test your understanding 6

(a) **Cost driver rates:**

Activity	Cost pool £	Cost driver volume	Cost driver rate
Process set up	260,000	200 set ups	£1,300/set up
Material procurement	74,000	50 purchase orders	£1,480 per purchase order
Maintenance	64,000	12 maintenance plans	£5,333 per plan
Material handling	120,000	2,500 material movements	£48 per movement
Quality costs	80,000	200 inspections	£400 per inspection
Order processing	30,000	1,000 customers	£30 per customer

(b) Using the ABC method, the following overhead would be recovered for each 1,000 tonnes of output:

			£
17 set ups	×	£1,300	22,100
4 purchase orders	×	£1,480	5,920
1 maintenance plan	×	£5,333	5,333
210 material movements	×	£48	10,080
16 inspections	×	£400	6,400
80 customers	×	£30	2,400
			£52,233

Thus the overhead cost per tonne of product would be:

£52,233/1,000 = £52.23 per tonne.

Preparing budgets – the planning phase

5

Introduction

Having considered the ways in which cost, revenue and other business data may be collected, processed and analysed, we now turn to the task of putting this information to use in the future planning of the business.

The planning process starts with the identification of long term corporate objectives, based upon which a strategy is designed, resource utilisation and capital expenditure planned and ultimately short-term, quantified budgets are prepared. This chapter looks at this overall process.

In all 'Management Accounting: Budgeting' examinations you will be required to prepare budgets. You should also be prepared to discuss the budget preparation process and to suggest improvements to budget presentation.

ASSESSMENT CRITERIA

- Discuss the purpose of revenue and forecasts and their link to budget (Element 1.3)
- Identify budgetary responsibilities and accountabilities (Element 2.1)
- Identify and calculate the effect of production and sales constraints (Element 2.2)
- Prepare planning schedules for physical production resources (Element 2.3)
- Calculate budgets for different types of costs (Element 2.4)
- Prepare draft budgets from historical data, forecasts and planning assumptions (Element 2.5)
- Prepare cash flow forecasts (Element 2.6)
- Discuss the use of budgeting for planning, coordinating, authorising and cost control (Element 3.2)
- Break a budget down into control periods (Element 3.3)
- Discuss the basic methods of budgeting and make recommendations for their use (Element 4.1)
- Plan and agree draft budgets with all parties involved (Element 4.2)

CONTENTS

1 Functional budgets
2 Practical aspects of functional budgets
3 Problems in exam questions
4 The master budget
5 Basic methods of budgeting

1 Functional budgets

1.1 Budgets to be produced

The budgets that a business produces will generally be a standard set of budgets that starts with the sales budget and progresses through budgets for the costs associated with those sales.

You will typically be asked to produce the following budgets for a business that manufactures the goods that it sells. Note that generally you will produce the budgets for the number of units bought and sold before translating those into revenues and costs.

(a)   The sales budget.

(b)   The production budget of finished goods. This will follow from the sales budget. It will be the same as the sales budget unless there are changes in the inventories held of finished goods.

(c)   The raw materials purchases budget. This will follow from the production budget. **A business needs a production budget as a quantitative expression of its operational plan.**

The raw materials purchased will in general terms be the number of finished goods produced × the raw material per unit, (after adjustments for changes in inventories of materials and process losses).

(d)   The labour budget, and

(e)   The overheads budget.

1.2 Sales, production, materials, labour and overheads budgets

Preparing resource budgets for materials, labour and machine time in line with the projected operations of a business is a very important skill. You will be tested on this in the Budgeting assessment.

The most important aspect is to be sure of how to use the information given to you. In this chapter, we will learn to prepare those budgets.

We shall first of all look at a simple budget example.

Example 1

Toys Ltd budgets to sell 10,000 play cubes at £10 per cube in the month of July 20X8.

Inventory of finished cubes was 3,000 cubes at the start of the month and was budgeted to be 4,000 cubes at the end of the month.

Each cube requires 0.5 kg of material that costs £1 per kg. Opening inventory of material was 1,000 kg at the start of the month and is budgeted to be 750 kg at the end of the month.

Each cube requires 0.25 hours of direct labour. The labour rate is £12 per hour.

Production overheads are absorbed into production at the rate of £15 per hour.

Task

Produce the budgets for sales, production, materials, labour and overheads.

Solution

Step 1 – the sales budget

Number of cubes budgeted to be sold = 10,000 cubes

Budgeted sales revenue 10,000 × £10 = £100,000

Step 2 – the production budget

The standard layout for this is as follows – always work in units (cubes) first.

	Cubes
Sales budget	10,000
Closing inventory	4,000
	14,000
Opening inventory	3,000
Production of finished goods	11,000 cubes

(**Tutorial note.** There are no costs associated with the finished goods because the company manufactures them. The cost of the goods will be found when we deal with the budgets and costs of raw materials, labour and overheads. However we have to prepare the production budget in order to be able to prepare the raw materials budget.)

Step 3 – the raw materials budget

The standard layout for this is as follows – always work in units (kg) first. In this case remember that 1 cube requires 0.5 kg of raw material.

	Kg
For production budget 11,000 × 0.5 kg	5,500
Closing inventory	750
	6,250
Opening inventory	1,000
Purchases of raw material	5,250 kg

Budgeted purchases of raw materials = 5,250 × £1 = £5,250

Step 4 – the labour budget

To calculate the cost of labour we have to return to the production budget because the cost of labour is determined by the level of production.

Number of labour hours budgeted for month = 11,000 cubes × 0.25 hours = 2,750 hrs

Cost of direct labour = 2,750 hrs × £12 = £33,000

Step 5 – the overhead budget

To calculate the cost of overheads we have to return to the labour budget because the cost of the overhead is based on the number of hours worked.

Number of labour hours budgeted for month = 2,750 hrs

Cost of overhead = 2,750 hrs × £15 = £41,250

1.3 Calculating the sales budget and inventories of finished goods

Exam questions will frequently present information regarding sales and inventories as follows.

 Example 2

XYZ has 13 accounting periods of four weeks during the year. It had sales of £40,000 in accounting period 5 and budgets for sales to increase by 3% for each accounting period.

The company budgets to have closing inventory at the end of an accounting period equal to two weeks sales of the following period.

Produce the budget for sales and inventories for accounting periods 6, 7 and 8.

Solution

	Period 6	Period 7	Period 8	Period 9
	£	£	£	£
Sales 40,000 × 1.03	41,200			
41,200 × 1.03		42,436		
42,436 × 1.03			43,709	
43,709 × 1.03				45,020
Opening inventory	20,600 (W1)	21,218	21,854	
Closing inventory	21,218 (W2)	21,854 (W3)	22,510 (W4)	

Workings

1   £41,200 × 0.5 (i.e. two weeks sales of a 4 week period) = £20,600

2   £42,436 × 0.5 =   £21,218

3   £43,709 × 0.5 =   £21,854

4   £45,020 × 0.5 =   £22,510

The example below illustrates the preparation of the functional budgets, starting with projected sales information.

 Example 3

The following data will be used to explain the technique of budget preparation:

Hash Ltd makes two products – PS and TG. Sales for next year are budgeted at 5,000 units of PS and 1,000 units of TG. Planned selling prices are £100 and £140 respectively.

Hash Ltd has the following opening inventory and required closing inventory.

	PS units	TG units
Opening inventory	100	50
Projected closing inventory	1,100	50

You are also given the following data about the materials required to produce PS and TG and the machining and finishing processes involved in production.

	PS	TG
Finished products:		
Kg of raw material X, per unit of finished product	12	12
Kg of raw material Y, per unit of finished product	6	8
Direct labour hours per unit of finished product	8	12

Standard rates and prices:

Direct labour	£6.00 per hour
Raw material X	£0.72 per kg
Raw material Y	£1.56 per kg

Production overheads:

Variable	£1.54 per labour hour
Fixed	£0.54 per labour hour
	——
	£2.08 per labour hour
	——

You are required to prepare the functional budgets. Hash limited does not carry inventories of raw material.

Solution

(a) **The sales budget**

The sales budget represents the plan in terms of the quantity and value of sales, for sales management. In practice this is often the most difficult budget to calculate.

What is next year's sales budget?

The sales budget would be:

	Total	PS	TG
Sales units	6,000	5,000	1,000
Sales value	£640,000	£500,000	£140,000

In practice a business would market many more than two products. Moreover, the sales budget would probably be supported by subsidiary budgets to show analysis according to:

(i) responsibility e.g. Northern area, Western area, etc.

(ii) type of customer e.g. wholesale, retail, government, etc.

(b) **The production budget**

The production budget is usually expressed in quantity and represents the sales budget adjusted for opening/closing finished inventories and work in progress.

The production budget would be:

	PS units	TG units
Sales budget	5,000	1,000
Add projected closing inventory	1,100	50
	6,100	1,050
Less opening inventory	100	50
Production in units	6,000	1,000

The production budget needs to be translated into requirements for:

(i) raw materials

(ii) direct labour

(iii) factory overheads

(iv) closing inventory levels.

(c) The raw materials and purchases budget

(Remember that Hash Ltd is going to produce 6,000 units of PS and 1,000 units of TG.)

		PS kg		TG kg
Raw material usage				
X	6,000 × 12 kg	72,000	1,000 × 12 kg	12,000
Y	6,000 × 6 kg	36,000	1,000 × 8 kg	8,000

		PS £		TG £
Budgeted purchases:				
X	72,000 × £0.72	51,840	12,000 × £0.72	8,640
Y	36,000 × £1.56	56,160	8,000 × £1.56	12,480
		108,000		21,120

(d) The direct labour budget

		PS		TG
Usage	6,000 × 8 hrs	48,000 hrs	1,000 × 12 hrs	12,000 hrs
Cost	48,000 × £6	£288,000	12,000 × £6	£72,000

(e) Production overheads

		PS		TG
Variable costs	48,000 hours × £1.54	73,920	12,000 × £1.54	18,480
Fixed costs	48,000 hours × £0.54	25,920	12,000 × £0.54	6,480
		99,840		24,960

One of the most important points illustrated by this example is how the budgets are inter-related.

It is a simple example and you should be aware that in practice budgeting can be more than simply an arithmetical exercise. The practical problems are discussed later.

2 Practical aspects of functional budgets

2.1 Sales budgets

The sales income budget is uniquely difficult to prepare because it involves forecasting the actions of people outside the business (the potential customers).

The extent to which sales forecasting is necessary will depend on the period covered by the outstanding order book and on the consistency of the conversion rate from enquiries to orders. If there is a well-filled order book for some months ahead then less reliance will need to be placed on forecasting techniques.

Forecasts may be made in a variety of ways. The method used will depend on the nature of the business and the amount of information available, but a generalised formal procedure might be as follows:

- Review past years' sales for whatever period is appropriate to the company's business cycle.

- Analyse the time series to identify seasonal, cyclical and random fluctuations.

- Extrapolate from past years' figures, assuming no changes in products or prices. Adjust the extrapolation for proposed changes which are controllable by the company, such as price alterations, changes in marketing effort, the introduction of new products, and the discontinuance of existing products (depending on the products' life cycles).

- Adjust for market changes due to external factors, such as government controls, action of competitors or social changes affecting demand. In particular, appropriate adjustments should be made for changing price levels or seasonal trends.

- Check that the resultant quantities are compatible with the quantities that can be purchased or produced.

- Check acceptability of forecast to sectional sales managers. In addition, other personnel who might contribute towards making realistic forecasts of trends should be consulted.

- Check consistency of forecast with long-term corporate plans.

The forecasting method outlined above depends on the existence of a 'time series' of figures from which extrapolation can be made and is mainly applicable to items in continuous demand. For other types of business, the sales forecast will be based on some form of market survey or on subjective estimates by people familiar with the market concerned.

Whichever forecasting method is used, the forecast should take account of significant anticipated changes in circumstances which would affect the validity of any statistically derived calculations.

2.2 Cost budgets

Budgeting for costs, in the same way as budgeting for sales, begins with facts. What facts they are will depend on the nature of the business; but every business will employ people, and most businesses will use materials of some kind. A manufacturing business will use tools and probably machinery. Floor space will be needed, also office equipment and perhaps motor vehicles.

All these requirements will be related in some way to the output of the business – its sales and any changes in inventory or work in progress.

In practice there are a wide range of different ways to budget for costs, as follows:

- If standards for cost units are available, then there may be computer programs to identify the material and labour standards relative to a given output. It then remains for departmental managers to budget for material wastage or spoilage, labour efficiency and idle time.

Example 4

The quarterly production requirements for product Omega are shown below. 4 % of production fails the quality checks and must be scrapped. How many items of Omegas must be manufactured to allow for waste?

	Month 1	Month 2	Month 3
Required units	99,000 units	108,000 units	96,000 units
Manufactured units			

Solution

	Month 1	Month 2	Month 3
Required units	99,000 units	108,000 units	96,000 units
Manufactured units	$\dfrac{99,000}{96\%} =$ 103,125 units	$\dfrac{108,000}{96\%} =$ 112,500 units	$\dfrac{96,000}{96\%} =$ 100,000 units

---

- In a business carrying out long-term contracts, cost units (contracts) may be identical with cost centres (each contract having its own controller).

- In some businesses it may be sufficiently accurate for the budget for direct materials cost to be an extrapolation from past total figures, without any attempt at detailed justification or analysis.

2.3 Use of standards in budgeting

Budgeting will inevitably make use of standard costs, as in the worked example above, and you should ensure you are familiar with the techniques and principles involved in their determination.

However, budgeting will generally extend beyond the simple multiplication of planned production levels by the standard usages and costs for each product for the following reasons:

- Different ranges of output levels will often lead to changes in unit variable costs (e.g. materials discounts, learning effects, etc).

- Some variable costs will not vary neatly with production and will need to be estimated for each particular activity level (e.g. wastage, idle time, production set-up costs).

- Fixed costs are independent of production levels, although they may be stepped.

- A large proportion of a business's costs will not be directly involved in the production process (e.g. administration, marketing, capital expenditure, etc).

The following sections describe the common problems encountered in budgeting for the most common cost elements: labour, materials and overheads.

2.4 Budgeting for numbers and costs of employees

When budgeting for the number and costs of people to be employed, the starting point must be to assess the work to be done by people with various skills and this is equally necessary for manual, clerical and managerial activities.

Having defined what work is to be done, the establishment of budgets for the employment of people falls into two main stages:

- planning the number of people needed

- calculating the relevant costs.

KAPLAN PUBLISHING

In defining the productive workload for the budget year it will be necessary to balance the requirements of the sales budget against the productive capacity available. If there is excess capacity over the year as a whole then a decision will be needed whether to operate below full capacity or to use the excess capacity in making goods for inventory or getting ahead with work in progress for the following year.

If the sales budget does not provide a steady workload month by month, then in phasing the budgets it may be decided to keep productive output constant and to balance out the short-term differences by fluctuations in work-in-progress or finished inventory.

The degree of precision possible in budgeting for numbers of people employed will depend on the type of work involved and the extent to which work measurement is possible.

2.5 Budgeting for the cost of materials

Considerable effort can be involved in preparing detailed budgets of quantities and purchase prices of materials. Whether this effort is justified will depend on the significance of materials in relation to total costs, and the extent to which effective control can be exercised.

The starting point for materials budgeting is the quantity of material to be used during the budget year, whether in retail sales or in production or for indirect use.

The form of the materials usage budget will depend on the nature of the business. Where repetitive operations are carried out it will be possible, and worth the effort, to set standards for the usage of the various items of material, and these standards can be associated with the production forecast to build up the total material requirements.

The purchase prices to be applied to the usage of the various items may be obtained from inventory ledger records or recent purchase invoices, subject to adjustment for forecast price changes, using index numbers as necessary.

In budgeting for indirect materials (such as small tools, machine coolants and lubricants, fuel, cleaning materials and office stationery) the common practice is to budget merely for a total cost extrapolated from past experience. It will be important for control purposes, however, that the budget working papers contain as much detail as possible about anticipated usage, even though the individual items may not be evaluated separately.

Test your understanding 1

Wilmslow Ltd makes two products, the Alpha and the Beta. Both products use the same material and labour but in different amounts. The company divides its year into four quarters, each of 12 weeks. Each week consists of five days and each day comprises seven hours.

You are employed as the management accountant to Wilmslow Ltd and you originally prepared a budget for quarter 3, the 12 weeks to 17 September 2016. The basic data for that budget is reproduced below.

Original budgetary data: quarter 3
12 weeks to 17 September 2016

Product	Alpha	Beta
Estimated demand	1,800 units	2,100 units
Material per unit	8 kilograms	12 kilograms
Labour per unit	3 hours	6 hours

Since the budget was prepared, three developments have taken place:

1   The company has begun to use linear regression and seasonal variations to forecast sales demand. Because of this, the estimated demand for quarter 3 has been revised to 2,000 Alphas and 2,400 Betas.

2   As a result of the revised sales forecasting, you have developed more precise estimates of sales and closing inventory levels:

 • The sales volume of both the Alpha and Beta in quarter 4 (the 12 weeks ending 10 December 2016) will be 20% more than in the revised budget for quarter 3 as a result of seasonal variations.

 • The closing inventory of finished Alphas at the end of quarter 3 should represent five days' sales for quarter 4.

 • The closing inventory of finished Betas at the end of quarter 3 should represent 10 days' sales for quarter 4.

 • Production in quarter 4 of both Alpha and Beta is planned to be 20% more than in the revised budget for quarter 3. The closing inventory of materials at the end of quarter 3 should be sufficient for 20 days production in quarter 4.

3   New equipment has been installed. The workforce is not familiar with the equipment. Because of this, for quarter 3, they will only be working at 80% of the efficiency assumed in the original budgetary data.

Other data from your original budget which has not changed is reproduced below:

- 50 production employees work a 35-hour week and are each paid £210 per week.

- Overtime is paid for at £9 per hour.

- The cost of material is £10 per kilogram.

- Opening inventories at the beginning of quarter 3 are as follows:
  - – Finished Alphas   500 units
  - – Finished Betas   600 units
  - – Material   12,000 kilograms

- There will not be any work in progress at any time.

Required:

The production director of Wilmslow Ltd wants to schedule production for quarter 3 (the 12 weeks ending 17 September 2016) and asks you to use the revised information to prepare the following:

(a)   The revised production budget for Alphas and Betas.

(b)   The material purchases budget in kilograms.

(c)   A statement showing the cost of the material purchases.

(d)   The labour budget in hours.

(e)   A statement showing the cost of labour.

2.6   Budgeting for overheads

The nature of overheads will depend on the type of business, but common categories are as follows:

(a)   Premises charges

(b)   Costs of plant, motor vehicles and other non-current assets

(c)   Communication expenses

(d)   Travelling and entertaining

(e)   Insurances

(f)   Discretionary costs

(g)   Financial policy costs

(h)   Random costs.

2.7　Calculating budget and actual overheads

Earlier in the chapter we saw how budgeted overhead absorption rates (OARs) were calculated. The guidance notes to Budgeting state that examinations might require you to use overhead absorption rates to deduce budgeted and actual activity levels.

2.8　Budgeted activity level

If we know the overhead absorption rate and the budgeted fixed overhead then the budgeted activity level can be found.

$$OAR = \frac{\text{Budgeted fixed overhead}}{\text{Budgeted activity level}}$$

Therefore:

$$\text{Budgeted activity level} = \frac{\text{Budgeted fixed overhead}}{OAR}$$

 Example 5

A business has an overhead absorption rate of £2 per unit produced. The budgeted fixed overhead was £400,000. What was the budgeted activity level?

Solution

$$\text{Budgeted activity level} = \frac{\text{Budgeted fixed overhead}}{OAR}$$

$$= \frac{£400,000}{£2}$$

$$= 200,000 \text{ units}$$

2.9　Actual activity level

When overheads are absorbed, this is done on the basis of the actual production level using the budgeted overhead absorption rate. Any under or over absorption is due to the difference between the overhead absorbed and the overhead actually incurred.

Under/over absorption = Overhead absorbed – overhead incurred

Example 6

You are given the following information:

Budgeted fixed overhead	£250,000
Actual fixed overhead	£280,000
Budgeted activity level	100,000 units
Under absorption	£5,000

What was the actual activity level for the period?

Solution

$$\text{OAR} = \frac{£250,000}{100,000}$$

$$= £2.50 \text{ per unit}$$

$$\text{Overhead absorbed} = £280,000 - £5,000$$

$$= £275,000$$

$$\text{Actual activity level} = \frac{\text{Fixed overhead absorbed}}{\text{OAR}}$$

$$= \frac{£275,000}{£2.50}$$

$$= 110,000 \text{ units}$$

2.10 Permanent budget record

For every type of revenue or cost it is highly desirable that a permanent budget record be prepared, giving the detailed calculations from which the budgeted amount has been derived. In particular, the data relevant to projecting forecasts of income and expenditure must be identified. This will not only impose a discipline on the budget preparation but will also:

- facilitate the eventual explanation of any differences between budgeted and actual results

- provide a starting point for budget revisions or for the preparation of budgets in future years.

The important features of such a record are as follows:

- details of the budget calculation

- comparison with the actual figures for the previous year

- basis of variability, noting how the amount is related to such factors as levels of output or numbers of people employed.

2.11 Capital expenditure budget

All short-term operating budgets are in effect abstracts from a continuously developing long-term plan. This, however, is particularly true of the capital expenditure budget because the major items included in it will not be completed within the bounds of any one budget year.

The main purpose of the capital expenditure budget, therefore, is to provide a forecast of the amount of cash likely to be needed for investment projects during the year ahead. It also indicates what items of plant, equipment, vehicles and so on will be needed for the purpose of implementing the profit and loss (or operating) budget; and therefore it must be submitted for approval at an early stage in the budgeting timetable.

Any capital expenditure budget would include the following:

- a brief descriptive title for the project
- the total required expenditure
- an analysis of the costs over various time periods
- where appropriate, expenditure to date on the project
- estimates of future benefits from the project
- investment appraisal calculations including details of assumptions made
- intangible benefits from the expenditure.

3 Problems in exam questions

3.1 The raw materials budget with losses

A question may be set where the there is a percentage loss of raw materials in the production process. In practice this 'wastage' may be due to such things as evaporation, faulty materials supplied or materials damaged in the process.

Example 7

Each unit of a product called 'The Cube' requires 0.5 kg of material that costs £1 per kg. The business expects to produce 11,000 cubes in the month of March.

Opening inventory of material was 1,000 kg at the start of the month and is budgeted to be 750 kg at the end of the month. 5% of materials are lost during the manufacturing process.

The completed resource budget for materials looks as follows:

Resource budget – material for 'The Cube'		March	Note
Needed for production	kgs	5,500	(1)
Wastage	kg	289	(2)
Total requirement	kg	5,789	(3)
Closing inventory	kg	750	(4)
Opening inventory	kg	1,000	(5)
Purchases in month	kg	5,539	(6)
Cost per kg	£	1	(7)
Purchase cost of material	£	5,539	(8)

Notes:

(1) Multiply the production quantity of cubes for the month (11,000 units) by the amount of kilograms used for each unit (0.5 kgs) to get 11,000 × 0.5 = 5,500 kgs.

(2) You are told that 5% of material is wasted in the production process, so (100% – 5%) = 95% of it is **not** wasted. In this cell, we write 5,500 × (5/95) = 289 kgs.

(3) The total number of kilograms required, taking wastage into account, is therefore 5,500 kgs + 289 kgs = 5,789 kgs.

(4) You will be told in the exam how much closing inventory is needed.

(5) You will be told in the exam how much opening inventory of Material is at hand. Remember to deduct this figure when calculating purchases in the month. Opening inventory is available at the start of the month and used during the month, so purchases are reduced accordingly.

(6) Purchases in the month, in kgs, are calculated as follows:

Production + Wastage + Closing inventory – Opening inventory = 5,500 + 289 + 750 – 1,000 = 5,539 kgs.

(7) You will be told in the exam what the cost of material per kg is (£1 here).

(8) Purchases for the month, in £, is 5,539 × £1 = £5,539.

3.2 The production budget with losses

A question may be set where the there is a percentage loss of finished goods. In practice this may be due to such things as items rejected as inferior by quality control, items damaged in the warehouse or theft.

 Example 8

This month, the Production Manager has informed you that 4% of all units produced are faulty. You all agree that you must produce enough units in total each month, to cater for this.

Complete the budgeted spreadsheet, identifying good production required, faulty production and total production required for the months of June and July.

Production budget spreadsheet	June	July
Opening inventory at the start of the month	3,200	
Sub-total	9,500	8,100
Sales in month (unit)	7,000	5,400
Closing inventory at the end of the month	2,500	2,700
Good/fault-free production required		
Faulty production/wastage		
Total production		

Solution

Production budget spreadsheet	June	July
Opening inventory at the start of the month	3,200	2,500
Good/fault-free production in month	6,300	5,600
Sub-total	9,500	8,100
Sales in month (unit)	7,000	5,400
Closing inventory at the end of the month	2,500	2,700
Good/fault-free production required	6,300	5,600
Faulty production/wastage	263	233
Total production	6,563	5,833

3.3 Labour budgets and overtime requirements

Now we can look at the basic resource budget for labour and overtime requirements by looking at the following example:

Example 9

This month, the business expects to produce 1,200 units of its product called 'The Cube'. The month is a five-week month. Each cube requires 6 hours of labour but, due to renovation work, the workers can only operate at 95% capacity this month. 38 members of staff each work 38 basic hours per week, at £10 per hour.

Hours in excess of this are paid at a time and a half.

Resource budget – labour		Month A	Note
Needed for production	hours	7,200	(1)
Inefficiency	hours	379	(2)
Hours to be worked	hours	7,579	(3)
Basic hours available	hours	7220	(4)
Hours of overtime needed	hours	359	(5)
Cost of basic hours	£	£72,200	(6)
Cost of overtime hours	£	£5,385	(7)

The completed resource budget for labour would look as follows:

Notes

(1) To arrive at the hours needed for production, you multiply the production quantity of units for the month by the number of hours each one takes to produce: 1,200 units × 6 hours = 7,200 hours.

(2) You are told that the factory can only operate at 95% efficiency so is (100% – 95%) = 5% inefficient, so in this cell we put 7,200 × (5%/95%) = 379 hours.

(3) The total hours that will need to be worked are therefore the sum of the first two cells: 7,200 + 379 = 7,579. You can check this result by multiplying 7,579 by 95% = 7,200, the number of hours needed for production.

(4) You are told 38 staff each work 38 hours for each of the five weeks, so total hours available amount to 38 × 38 × 5 = 7,220 hours.

(5) As more hours are needed than are available as basic hours, overtime is required. This is calculated as required hours less basic hours: 7,579 – 7,220 hours = 359 hours.

(6) Basic hours are paid at the basic rate of £10 per hour, so the basic wage bill is £10 × 7,220 hours = £72,200.

(7) Overtime hours are paid at £10 × 1.5 × 359 hours = £5,385.

3.4 Machine time budgets

Extra machines may need to be hired to meet production requirements. Consider the following example:

Example 10

We are told that the business expects to produce 1,000 units of product A in a given month, and each unit of product A requires 5 hours of machine time.

In addition, the business will produce 1,200 units of product B (3 hours of machine time each) and 800 units of product C (5 hours of machine time each).

There are 45 machines in the factory, but more may be hired. Each machine (owned or hired) can be used for 250 hours in the month. The factory works at 100% efficiency with respect to machines.

The completed resource budget for **machine time** would look as follows:

Resource budget – machine time	Units	Hours per unit	Hours required
Product A	1,000	5	5,000
Product B	1,200	3	3,600
Product C	800	5	4,000
Total machine hours required			12,600
Factory machine hours available (45 × 250)			11,250
Additional machine hours required			1,350
Number of machines to hire (1,350/250)			6

4 The master budget

The master budget for approval by the board will take the form of a budgeted income statement, a forecast Statement of Financial Position as at the year-end and a cash budget. These will be supported by such summaries of the various functional budgets as may be required, and by calculations of the key ratios which indicate conformity with the objectives for the year.

Cash budgets will be assessed in Budgeting, so you should be aware of their existence.

4.1 The budgeted income statement

The budgeted income statement shows the net profit by deducting the budgeted costs from the budgeted sales revenue.

In the earlier example of Hash Ltd. which made the two products ('PS' and 'TG'), we had gathered and calculated the following budgetary information:

	PS	TG
Sales units	5.000	1,000
Sales value	£500,000	£140,000
Opening inventory	100 units	50 units
Closing inventory	1,100 units	50 units
Production	6,000 units	1,000 units
Purchases costs	£108,000	£21,120
Direct labour costs	£288,000	£72,000
Production overheads	£99,840	£24,960

Using this information, the budgeted profit and loss account would be as follows:

	£	£
Sales	500,000	140,000
Materials	108,000	21,120
Labour	288,000	72,000
Production overheads	99,840	24,960
Production cost	495,840	118,080
add opening inventory (working)	8,264	5,904
less closing inventory (working)	90,904	5,904
Cost of sales	413,200	118,080
Profit	86,800	21,920

Working

Inventory values = (production cost/units produced) × units of inventory.

1   Opening inventory of PS = (495,840/6,000) × 100 = £8,264

2   Closing inventory of PS = (495,840/6,000) × 1,100 = £90,904

3   Opening inventory of TG = (118,080/1,000) × 50 = £5,904

4   Closing inventory of TG = (118,080/1,000) × 50 = £5,904

4.2 The forecast Statement of Financial Position

In arriving at the forecast Statement of Financial Position, it will be necessary to take account of the following: ˙

- The capital expenditure budget.

- Changes in inventory levels and work in progress (as calculated in connection with the budgeting of material and labour costs). If work in progress and finished inventories are valued on a TAC basis, then it will be necessary to calculate overhead recovery rates.

- Changes in receivables balances. Subject to any special delays in collection, the closing receivables balances will be calculated by applying the company's normal credit terms to the phased budget of sales.

- Changes in payables balances. In theory, the closing payables will be calculated by applying a normal credit period to the phased budgets of material purchases, subcontracted work and any other relevant items. In practice, it may be necessary to review the budgeted cash flow before finalising a decision on the credit to be taken.

- Changes in the cash balance. Initially, the closing cash balance may be taken as the balancing figure on the Statement of Financial Position, but at some stage this should be validated by building up a cash budget itemised from the other budgets. This is discussed in the following paragraph.

5 Basic methods of budgeting

There are a few basic methods of budgeting students need to know for the exam.

5.1 Incremental budgeting

An incremental budget starts with the previous period's budget or actual results and adds (or subtracts) an incremental amount to cover inflation and other known changes.

It is suitable for stable businesses, where costs are not expected to change significantly. There should be good cost control and limited discretionary costs.

Advantages of incremental budgeting	Disadvantages of incremental budgets
(1) Quickest and easiest method.	(1) Builds in previous problems and inefficiencies.
(2) Suitable if the organisation is stable and historic figures are acceptable since only the increment needs to be justified.	(2) Uneconomic activities may be continued. For example, the company may continue to make a component in house, when it may be cheaper to outsource.
	(3) Managers may spend unnecessarily to use up their budgeted expenditure allowance this year, thus ensuring they get the same, or a larger) budget next year.

5.2   Zero-based budgeting (ZBB)

A method of budgeting that requires each cost element to be specifically justified, as though the activities to which the budget relates were being undertaken for the first time. Without approval, the budget allowance is zero'.

It is suitable for allocating resources in areas were spend is discretionary, i.e. non-essential. For example, research and development, advertising and training. ZBB is often practised in public sector organisations such as local authorities.

There are four distinct stages in the implementation of ZBB:

(1)   Managers should specify, for their responsibility centres, those activities that can be individually evaluated.

(2)   Each of the individual activities is then described in a decision package. The decision package should state the costs and revenues expected from the given activity. It should be drawn up in such a way that the package can be evaluated and ranked against other packages.

(3)   Each decision package is evaluated and ranked usually using cost/benefit analysis.

(4)   The resources are then allocated to the various packages.

Advantages of ZBB		Disadvantages of ZBB	
(1)	Inefficient or obsolete operations can be identified and discontinued.	(1)	It emphasises short-term benefits to the detriment of long-term goals.
(2)	ZBB leads to increased staff involvement at all levels since a lot more information and work is required to complete the budget .	(2)	The budgeting process may become too rigid and the organisation may not be able to react to unforeseen opportunities or threats.
(3)	It responds to changes in the business environment.	(3)	The management skills required may not be present.
(4)	Knowledge and understanding of the cost behaviour patterns of the organisation will be enhanced.	(4)	Managers may feel demotivated due to the large amount of time spent on the budgeting process.
(5)	Resources should be allocated efficiently and economically.	(5)	Ranking can be difficult for different types of activities or where the benefits are qualitative in nature.

Decision packages

A decision package was defined by Peter Pyhrr (who first formulated the ZBB approach at Texas Instruments) as:

A document that identifies and describes a specific activity in such a manner that senior management can:

(a)   evaluate and rank it against other activities competing for limited resources, and

(b)   decide whether to approve or disapprove it.

A decision package is a document that: analyses the cost of the activity (costs may be built up from a zero base, but costing information can be obtained from historical records or last year's budget); states the purpose of the activity; identifies alternative methods of achieving the same purpose; assesses the consequence of not doing the activity at all, or performing the activity at a different level; and finally, establishes measures of performance for the activity.

Pyhrr identifies two types of package.

(i) **Mutually exclusive packages**: these contain different methods of obtaining the same objective.

(ii) **Incremental packages**: these divide the activity into a number of different levels of activity. The base package describes the minimum effort and cost needed to carry out the activity. The other packages describe the incremental costs and benefits when added to the base.

For example, a company is conducting a ZBB exercise, and a decision package is being prepared for its materials handling operations.

The manager responsible has identified a base package for the minimum resources needed to perform the materials handling function. This is to have a team of five workers and a supervisor, operating without any labour-saving machinery. The estimated annual cost of wages and salaries, with overtime, would be $375,000.

In addition to the base package, the manager has identified an incremental package. The company could lease two fork lift trucks at a cost of $20,000 each year. This would provide a better system because materials could be stacked higher and moved more quickly. Health and safety risks for the workers would be reduced, and there would be savings of $5,000 each year in overtime payments.

Another incremental package has been prepared, in which the company introduces new computer software to plan materials handling schedules. The cost of buying and implementing the system would be $60,000, but the benefits are expected to be improvements in efficiency that reduce production downtime and result in savings of $10,000 each year in overtime payments.

The base package would be considered essential, and so given a high priority. The two incremental packages should be evaluated and ranked. Here, the fork lift trucks option might be ranked more highly than the computer software.

In the budget that is eventually decided by senior management, the fork lift truck package might be approved, but the computer software package rejected on the grounds that there are other demands for resources with a higher priority.

5.3 Priority-based budgeting

Priority-based budgeting is designed to produce a competitively ranked listing of high to low priority discrete bids for resources which are called "decision packages".

- It is a method of budgeting whereby all activities are re-evaluated each time a budget is set.

- Discrete levels of each activity are valued from a minimum level of service upwards and an optimum combination chosen to match the level of resources available and the level of service required.

- The concept of ranking bids for capital expenditure is well known; priority-based budgeting applies a similar process to more routine expenditure.

It is similar to zero-based budgeting but does not require a zero assumption.

5.4 Activity-based budgeting

ABB is defined as: 'a method of budgeting based on an activity framework and utilising cost driver data in the budget-setting and variance feedback processes'.

Or, put more simply, preparing budgets using overhead costs from activity based costing methodology.

Advantages of ABB	Disadvantages of ABB
(1) It draws attention to the costs of 'overhead activities' which can be a large proportion of total operating costs.	(1) A considerable amount of time and effort might be needed to establish the key activities and their cost drivers.
(2) It recognises that it is activities which drive costs. If we can control the causes (drivers) of costs, then costs should be better managed and understood.	(2) It may be difficult to identify clear individual responsibilities for activities.

(3)	ABB can provide useful information in a total quality management (TQM) environment, by relating the cost of an activity to the level of service provided.	(3)	It could be argued that in the short-term many overhead costs are not controllable and do not vary directly with changes in the volume of activity for the cost driver. The only cost variances to report would be fixed overhead expenditure variances for each activity.
		(4)	A considerable amount of time and effort might be needed to establish the key activities and their cost drivers.
		(5)	It may be difficult to identify clear individual responsibilities for activities.

6 Summary

The budget must be prepared in a logical and orderly manner, ensuring co-ordination and co-operation between departments and different levels of management. Final proposals must be fully understood and accepted by all involved via a clear set of instructions and detailed discussions where necessary.

You should be prepared to discuss the types of budgets that may be required for a particular business and how they might be prepared, probably with numerical illustrations.

Test your understanding answers

Test your understanding 1

(a) **Production budget – quarter ended 17 September 2016**

	Alphas (units)	Betas (units)
Budgeted sales	2,000	2,400
Add: Closing inventory (see Note 1)	200	480
Less: Opening inventory	(500)	(600)
Production (finished units)	1,700	2,280

	Alphas	Betas
Note 1		
Sales this quarter 3	2,000	2,400
Add 20% seasonal variation	400	480
Budgeted sales next quarter 4	2,400	2,880
Closing inventory (5/60 × 2,400 = 200)		
(10/60 × 2,880 = 480)	200	480

(b) **Material purchases budget – quarter ended 17 September 2016**

	Kilograms
Usage – Alpha production (8 kg × 1,700)	13,600
Usage – Beta production (12 kg × 2,280)	27,360
	40,960
Add Closing material stock (see Note 2)	16,384
Less Opening material stock	(12,000)
Purchases of material	45,344

Note 2
Closing inventory of materials:

Usage this period	40,960
Add 20%	8,192
Material required for production next period	49,152
Stock required (20/60 × 49,152)	16,384

(c) **Cost of purchases**

(45,344 kg × £10)   £453,440

(d) **Labour budget – quarter ended 17 September 2016**

	Hours
Labour hours required for Alpha production (3 hours × 1,700)	5,100
Labour hours required for Beta production (6 hours × 2,280)	13,680
Total hours required before efficiency adjustment	18,780
Efficiency adjustment (20%/80%)	4,695
Gross labour hours	23,475
Normal hours (50 employees × 35 hours × 12 weeks)	21,000
Overtime hours required	2,475

(e)	Normal hours (50 employees × 12 weeks × £210)	£126,000
	Overtime (2,475 hours × £9)	£22,275
	Direct labour cost	£148,275

Cash forecasts

Introduction

Initially, the closing cash balance may be taken as the balancing figure on the Statement of Financial Position, but at some stage this should be validated by building up a cash budget itemised from the other budgets.

In all 'Management Accounting: Budgeting' examinations you will be required to prepare a cash forecast. You will need to prepare cash flow forecasts from budget data to facilitate the achievement of organisational objectives, making due allowance for time lags or assumptions about changes in debtor, creditor and inventory balances.

You could also be asked to analyse a cash flow forecast into shorter control periods, allowing for time lags.

ASSESSMENT CRITERIA	CONTENTS
• Prepare cash flow forecasts (Element 2.6)	1 Cash budgeting: purpose 2 Cash budgeting: components

1 Cash budgeting: purposes

The purposes of the cash budget are as follows:

* To ensure that the various items of income and expenditure budgeted departmentally, and subject to the normal credit policy of the business, will result in cash flows which enable the company to pay its way at all times; in other words, to ensure that there is a practical plan.

* Where the cash flow over the year as a whole is satisfactory but there are intermediate periods of difficulty in financing operations, to give a basis from which the timing of particular items can be re-planned.

* Where cash proves inadequate to finance the plan as originally envisaged, to give the financial controller an opportunity to seek sources of additional capital. (If the budget cannot be financed as it stands, then a revised budget will have to be prepared.)

* Like any other budget, to provide a basis for control during the forth-coming year.

In the exam, you will have to prepare a cash flow forecast from the operating budget and Statement of Financial Position assumptions.

Example 1

Prepare the forecast from the operating budget and Statement of Financial Position assumptions. The SFP assumptions are as follows:

1   Receivables will increase by £4,000.

2   Materials payables will reduce by £4,500.

3   Labour costs are paid in the period in which they are incurred.

4   Other payables will increase by £3,000.

Operating budget	£	£
Sales revenue		172,000
Expenditure		
Materials	34,200	
Labour	38,500	
Other costs	16,400	89,100
Operating profit		82,900

Enter receipts and payments as positive figures:

Cash flow forecast	£	£
Sales receipts		
Payments		
Materials		
Labour		
Other costs		
Cash flow forecast		

Solution

Cash flow forecast	£	£
Sales receipts (172,000 – 4,000)		168,000
Payments		
Materials (34,200 + 4,500)	38,700	
Labour	38,500	
Other costs (16,400 – 3,000)	13,400	90,600
Cash flow forecast		77,400

2 Cash budgeting: components

2.1 Sales on credit and discounts

In some businesses a cash or settlement discount is offered to customers for payment within a certain time period. This means that although the cash is received sooner, a lower amount is received than was invoiced. This must be taken into account when preparing the cash budget.

Example 2

A business offers a 3% discount for payment received from credit customers in the month of sale. The business has found that 40% of customers take advantage of this by paying in the month of sale, 50% of customers pay in the month after the sale and 10% of customers pay two months after the month of sale.

Credit sales for the business are as follows:

	Actual			Budgeted	
	February	March	April	May	June
	£	£	£	£	£
Credit sales	20,000	22,000	24,000	18,000	21,000

What are the cash receipts from receivables for the three months ending 30 June?

Solution

Cash inflow

		April	May	June
		£	£	£
February sales	– 20,000 × 10%	2,000		
March sales	– 22,000 × 50%	11,000		
	22,000 × 10%		2,200	
April sales	– 24,000 × 40% × 97%	9,312		
	24,000 × 50%		12,000	
	24,000 × 10%			2,400
May sales	– 18,000 × 40% × 97%		6,984	
	18,000 × 50%			9,000
June sales	– 21,000 × 40% × 97%			8,148
Cash inflow		22,312	21,184	19,548

Note that the cash received in the month of sale is 97% of the amount invoiced as these customers have taken advantage of the settlement discount.

2.2 Sales quantities and prices

In the examples so far you have been given the monetary amount of the sales in each month in order to calculate the receipts from receivables. However, you may be given information about the sales quantity in units each month and the selling price per unit. From this, the total monetary amount of the sales for the month can be calculated.

2.3 Payments to payables

The determination of the cash payments that are to be made to payables each month can be a little more complicated than the calculation of the receipts from receivables as the information can be expressed in a variety of different ways. The simplest form in which you might come across payments to payables' information is similar to that for receipts from receivables – you will be told the amount of credit purchases and the payment pattern to payables.

Example 3

A business estimates that its credit purchases for February and March will be £14,000 but will increase by 10% each month thereafter. Its payment pattern to payables is that 60% are paid in the month following the purchases and the remaining 40% two months after the purchase.

What are the payments to payables for April, May and June?

Solution

	February £	March £	April £	May £	June £
Purchases (increasing by 10% each month)	14,000	14,000	15,400	16,940	18,634
Payments to payables					
– February purchases 14,000 × 40%			5,600		
– March purchases 14,000 × 60%			8,400		
14,000 × 40%				5,600	
– April purchases 15,400 × 60%				9,240	
15,400 × 40%					6,160
– May purchases 16,940 × 60%					10,164
Cash payments			14,000	14,840	16,324

Test your understanding 1

The following data and estimates are available for ABC Ltd for June, July and August:

	June	July	August
Sales	£45,000	£50,000	£60,000
Wages	£12,000	£13,000	£14,500
Overheads	£8,500	£9,500	£9,000

The following information is available regarding direct materials:

	June	July	August	September
Opening inventory	£5,000	£3,500	£6,000	£4,000
Material usage	£8,000	£9,000	£10,000	
Closing inventory	£3,500	£6,000	£4,000	

Notes:

(1) 10% of sales are for cash, the balance is received the following month.

   The amount to be received in June for May's sales is £29,500.

(2) Wages are paid in the month they are incurred.

(3) Overheads include £1,500 per month for depreciation. Overheads are settled the month following. £6,500 is to be paid in June for May's overheads.

(4) Purchases of direct materials are paid for in the month purchased.

(5) The opening cash balance in June is £11,750.

(6) A tax bill of £25,000 is to be paid in July.

Required:

(a) Calculate the amount of direct material purchases in EACH of the months of June, July and August.

(b) Prepare cash budgets for June, July and August.

Test your understanding 2

XYZ Ltd has the following forecast sales at list price for the nine months to 29 February 20X2:

June	£40,000	September	£48,000	December	£44,000
July	£44,000	October	£40,000	January	£42,000
August	£50,000	November	£45,000	February	£50,000

- 60% of the company's sales are on credit, payable in the month after sale. Cash sales attract a 5% discount off list price.

- Material costs amount to 40% of selling price, and purchases are paid for two months after delivery.

- Inventory is maintained at a level equal to 50% of the following month's sales, except that in November inventory is to be increased by £2,000 (at cost prices) to ensure that XYZ Ltd has a safety inventory during the period when its major supplier shuts down. This safety inventory will be released in March.

- Wages comprise a fixed sum of £2,000 per month plus a variable element equal to 10% of sales; these are payable in the month they are incurred.

- Fixed costs amount to £7,500 per month, payable one month in arrears, of which £1,500 is depreciation.

- XYZ Ltd has capital expenditure/receipts scheduled as follows:

Acquisitions:

	£
September	15,000
November	10,000
February	4,000

Disposal:

October	8,000

- Corporation tax, payable in November, amounts to £44,000.

- The bank balance on 1 September 20X1 is expected to be £5,000.

Task

Prepare a cash flow forecast for XYZ Ltd for EACH of the six months from September 20X1 to February 20X2, using a row and column format.

Test your understanding 3

Prepare a cash forecast for May from the following budget data

Budget data	March £	April £	May £	June £	Cash forecast	May £
Invoiced sales	2,500	3,000	2,800	4,000	Opening cash balance	(500)
Purchases	900	1,300	1,250	1,200	Customer receipts	
Wages	500	510	520	480		
Other overheads	600	660	620	630	**Payments**	
Capital expenditure	–	1,200	–	–	For purchases	
					For wages	
Average terms					For overheads	
					For capital expenditure	
Half of customers take 1 month to pay. Half take 2 months.					Total	
Purchases paid for after 2 months						
Wages paid in the current month					Closing cash balance	
Other overheads paid after one month						
Capital expenditure paid in the current month						

3 Summary

The budget must be prepared in a logical and orderly manner, ensuring co-ordination and co-operation between departments and different levels of management. You should be prepared to construct a cash budget for a particular business and how they might be prepared, probably with numerical illustrations.

Test your understanding answers

 Test your understanding 1

Tutorial note: Inventory is used up by material usage, and by closing inventory. This usage Is made up partly from opening inventory. The balance must be made up from purchases.

	June £	July £	August £
Material usage	8,000	9,000	10,000
Closing inventory	3,500	6,000	4,000
	11,500	15,000	14,000
Less: Opening inventory	5,000	3,500	6,000
Purchases	6,500	11,500	8,000

Tutorial note: The main points to watch out for are sales receipts and overheads. Tackle sales receipts by calculating separate figures for cash sales (10% of total sales, received in the month of sale) and credit sales (90% of last month's sales). For overheads, remember that depreciation is not a cash expense and must therefore be stripped out of the overheads cash cost.

Cash budgets, June – August

	June £	July £	August £
Receipts of cash			
Cash sales	4,500	5,000	6,000
Credit sales	29,500	40,500	45,000
	34,000	45,500	51,000

Cash payments			
Wages	12,000	13,000	14,500
Overheads	6,500	7,000	8,000
Direct materials	6,500	11,500	8,000
Taxation	–	25,000	–
	25,000	56,500	30,500
Surplus/(deficit) for month	9,000	(11,000)	20,500
Opening balance	11,750	20,750	9,750
Closing balance	20,750	9,750	30,250

Test your understanding 2

	Sept £	Oct £	Nov £	Dec £	Jan £	Feb £
Receipts						
Cash sales (W1)	18,240	15,200	17,100	16,720	15,960	19,000
Credit sales (W2)	30,000	28,800	24,000	27,000	26,400	25,200
Capital		8,000				
	48,240	52,000	41,100	43,720	42,360	44,200
Payments						
Materials (W3)	18,800	19,600	17,600	17,000	19,800	17,200
Wages (W4)	6,800	6,000	6,500	6,400	6,200	7,000
Fixed costs (W5)	6,000	6,000	6,000	6,000	6,000	6,000
Capital	15,000		10,000			4,000
Corporation tax			44,000			
	46,600	31,600	84,100	29,400	32,000	34,200
Surplus/(Deficit)	1,640	20,400	(43,000)	14,320	10,360	10,000
Balance b/f	5,000	6,640	27,040	(15,960)	(1,640)	8,720
Balance c/f	6,640	27,040	(15,960)	(1,640)	8,720	18,720

Workings

(W1) Since 60% of sales are credit sales, 40% are cash sales, e.g.

	£
September cash sales = £48,000 × 40% =	19,200
5% discount on £19,200	960
	18,240

(W2) August credit sales are paid in September, and so on.

Credit sales = 60% so the September receipt = 60% × £50,000 = £30,000

(W3)

	July	Aug	Sept	Oct	Nov	Dec
Sales:						
Stock used						
(40% of sales)	17,600	20,000	19,200	16,000	18,000	17,600
Opening inventory						
(50% of 40% of sales)	(8,800)	(10,000)	(9,600)	(8,000)	(9,000)	(8,800)
Closing inventory						
(50% of 40% of						
next month's sales)	10,000	9,600	8,000	9,000	8,800	8,400
Extra stock					2,000	
PURCHASES	18,800	19,600	17,600	17,000	19,800	17,200
Paid in	Sept	Oct	Nov	Dec	Jan	Feb

(W4) 10% of sales + £2,000

e.g., September:

(10% × £48,000) + £2,000 = £6,800

(W5) £7,500 − £1,500 Depreciation: £6,000

Test your understanding 3

Prepare a cash forecast for May from the following budget data.

Budget data	March £	April £	May £	June £
Invoiced sales	2,500	3,000	2,800	4,000
Purchases	900	1,300	1,250	1,200
Wages	500	510	520	480
Other overheads	600	660	620	630
Capital expenditure	–	1,200	–	–

Average terms

Half of customers take 1 month to pay. Half take 2 months.

Purchases paid for after 2 months

Wages paid in the current month

Other overheads paid after one month

Capital expenditure paid in the current month

Working 1

April   £3,000 × 0.5 = £1,500

March £2,000 × 0.5 = £1,250

Total = £1,500 + £1,250 = £2,750

Cash forecast	May £
Opening Cash balance	(500)
Customer receipts	2,750
Payments	
For purchases	900
For wages	520
For overheads	660
For capital expenditure	0
Total	2,080
Closing cash balance	170

Preparing budgets with limiting factors

7

Introduction

The final situation that we must be able to deal with arises when demand for an organisation's products is likely to outstrip its capacity to supply; this happens when it was originally planned to make a number of different products, but a shortage of some resource now makes the plan impossible. The resource that is preventing normal output is known as the **limiting factor.** The most common limiting factors are either materials or labour.

In all 'Management Accounting: Budgeting' examinations you will be required to prepare budgets when there are limits on resources and the most profitable products must be selected.

ASSESSMENT CRITERIA	CONTENTS
• Identify and calculate the effect of production and sales constraints (Element 2.2)	1 Preparing production budgets with limiting factors

1 Preparing production budgets with limiting factors

1.1 Limiting factors

The level of activity at which a business can operate will very seldom be unlimited. Limitations may be imposed, for example, by:

- market demand for its products or services
- the number of skilled employees available
- the availability of material supplies
- the space available either as a working area or for the storage of goods
- the amount of cash or credit facilities available to finance the business.

1.2 Production budget limited by sales

Most businesses gear their production to their expected sales, so this is the usual limiting factor – they would make more units if they could sell them.

1.3 Analysing limitations on production

When presented with an upper limit on production capacity, production adjustments may be necessary so that the maximum does no longer represent a problem.

 Example 1

Here is an extract from our basic production budget spreadsheet for months 1 and 2. The business can only produce a maximum of 2,500 units each month, but the production budget currently plans for production of 3,000 units in Month 2:

Production budget spreadsheet	Quantity in units	
	Month 1	Month 2
Good/fault-free production required	900	2,700
Faulty production/wastage	100	300
Total revised production in month	1,000	3,000

We need to adjust the production as follows:

Production budget spreadsheet	Quantity in units	
	Month 1	Month 2
Good/fault-free production required	900	2,700
Faulty production/wastage	100	300
Total production for the month	1,000	3,000
Capacity adjustment		**−500**
Total revised production in month		2,500

We have changed the production for Month 2 to the maximum possible, and made a reduction adjustment of 500 units.

This, in turn, increased the production in Month 1 by 500 units:

Production budget spreadsheet	Quantity in units	
	Month 1	Month 2
Good/fault-free production required	900	2,700
Faulty production/wastage	100	300
Total production for the month	1,000	3,000
Capacity adjustment	**+500**	**−500**
Total revised production in month	1,500	2,500

The total revised production for Month 1, taking into account the adjustment, is 1,000 + 500 = 1,500 units.

If a business has limited resources of materials, labour or machine time, but still wants to achieve its production/sales budget, it must work out how many items it can make using these limited resources, and how many will require extra resources to be found, – usually at greater than standard cost.

Example 2

In this example, the business expects to sell 1,200 units in the month and keeps no inventory of finished goods. You are also given data on the standard cost and current availability of materials, labour and machine time at this cost.

Production budget	Required to produce 1,200 units	Current availability	Units to be made from current availability	Extra resource needed
Materials: 0.75 kgs per unit	900 kgs	720 kgs	960 units	180 kgs
Labour: 1.25 hours per unit	1,500 hours	1,350 hours	1,080	150 hours
Machine time: 0.5 hours per unit	600 hours	667 hours	1,334 units	0 hours

1.4 Identifying the limiting factor

When a manager starts to prepare a budget he should review the elements in it and identify where limiting factors (or governing factors) exist.

They will not all be equally significant; but where one particular limitation is of major importance it may be necessary to budget for that item first and to construct the rest of the budget around it. This can happen not merely in one department but for the company as a whole, when the item concerned may be referred to as the principal budget factor or key factor.

Quite commonly, the rate of growth in sales is the principal budget factor and this would have to be forecast before any other budget plans were made.

It is essential to identify the principal budget factor and any other limiting factors at an early stage in the budgeting process so that management may consider whether:

- it is possible to overcome the limitation which they impose (e.g. by finding new markets for sales or by obtaining alternative supplies or substitute raw materials)

- the limitations imposed must be accepted and the business's budgets must be produced within those limitations.

Example 3

In this example, the business expects to sell 500 units in the month and has identified the availability of its resources as given in this table.

Resource	Usage		Maximum availability
Materials	2	litres per unit	890 litres
Labour	1	hours per unit	600 hours
Machine time	0.1	hours per unit	50 hours

No more resources are available.

Which resource is the limiting factor for production in the month, and how many units can be produced and sold?

Solution

Materials is the limiting factor, and only 445 units can be made and sold.

890 litres of material will produce 890/2 = 445 units, so production is limited to this quantity. The maximum labour will produce 600 units, and so does not limit production. The maximum machine time will be enough to produce 500 units if and when more material becomes available.

1.5 Changing the production mix because of a limiting factor

If a business makes more than one product and does not have enough resources to make all it can sell of all products, it must decide which one(s) to produce and in what quantity. This is done based on the contribution per unit of the limiting factor.

 Example 4

Barbecue Limited manufactures two products for which the following details are available.

	Product X		Product Y
Selling price	£38		£38
Direct materials 8 units @ £1	£8	4 units @ £1	£4
Labour 4 hours @ £2	£8	6 hours @ £2	£12
Variable overhead 4 machine hours @ £3	£12	3 machine hours @ £3	£9
Fixed overheads	£5		£7

Maximum demand for X is 2,500 units.

Maximum demand for Y is 2,000 units.

Calculate the optimum production plan for Barbecue in each of the following two situations:

(a) Labour in the next period is limited to *16,000* hours, with no limit on machine hours.

(b) Machine hours in the next period are limited to *12,000* hours, with no limit on labour hours.

Solution

We would like to produce Xs and Ys up to the point where maximum demand is reached. (There is no point producing beyond this, because customers do not want any more.) So ideally we would like to produce 2,500 X and 2,000 Y. To do this we would require the following resources.

	Labour hours	Machine hours
2,500 X	10,000	10,000
2,000 Y	12,000	6,000
	22,000	16,000

If labour is limited to 16,000 hours we will not have enough labour hours to achieve this. Similarly, if machine hours are limited to 12,000 our production will be restricted.

To tackle this problem we begin by calculating the contribution earned per unit of each product.

Contribution for each unit of X = £ (38 – 8 – 8 – 12) = £10 per unit
Contribution for each unit of Y = £ (38 – 4 – 12 – 9) = £13 per unit

(a) Labour is limited so we calculate the contribution earned per labour hour for each product.

X = £10/4 = £2.50 per labour hour

Y = £13/6 = £2.17 per labour hour

You get more contribution per labour hour for X than for Y so make as many Xs as possible.

Available hours = 16,000, and 2,500 Xs require 10,000 hrs

The remaining hours are all used to make as many Ys as possible.

Remaining Ys will take six hours each to make so produce 6,000/6 = 1,000 Ys.

Contribution = (2,500 × £10) + (1,000 × £13) = £38,000

(b) In this case, machine hours are the scarce resource so we calculate contribution per machine hour.

X = £10/4 = £2.50 per machine hour

Y = £13/3 = £4.33 per machine hour

Now it is better to make Ys. Making 2,000 Ys requires 2,000 × 3 = 6,000 machine hours. That leaves us a further 6,000 machine hours for making Xs.

6,000 remaining hours for X means making 6,000/4 = 1,500 Xs

Contribution = (1,500 × £10) + (2,000 × £13) = £41,000

Note that in the examination, if you are told the maximum demand for a product it is a big hint that this method should be used.

 Test your understanding 1

Your organisation is about to commence work on the preparation of the forthcoming year's annual budget.

As assistant management accountant, you have been asked to assist budget-holders and to respond to any queries which they may raise in the course of submitting their budget proposals.

The following notes are extracts taken from your organisation's budget manual.

'The key or principal budget factor in our organisation's budgetary process is sales volume ... The need for co-ordination in the budgetary process is paramount ...'.

The marketing manager is a budget holder and she has approached you with a number of queries concerning the above extract.

Required:

Prepare a memo for the marketing manager which provides brief answers to the following queries:

(a) What is meant by the term *key factor* and why is the determination of this factor so important in the budgetary process?

(b) How can co-ordination be achieved?

Test your understanding 2

You are a management accountant employed by Aspen Ltd and you report to Adrian Jones, the managing director. One of your responsibilities is the production of budgets. Aspen Ltd only has one customer, Advanced Industries plc, for whom it makes the Omega, a specialist product. Advanced Industries demands that Aspen keeps a minimum closing inventory of Omegas in case there is an error in the forecast requirements. There is no work-in-progress at any time.

- Both companies divide the year into four-week periods. Each week consists of five days and each day comprises eight hours.

- Advanced Industries plc has recently informed Aspen Ltd of its Omega requirements for the five periods ending Friday 25 May 2001. The details are reproduced below.

Forecast demand for Omegas					
Four weeks ending:	2 February Period 1	2 March Period 2	30 March Period 3	27 April Period 4	25 May Period 5
Number of Omegas required	5,700	5,700	6,840	6,460	6,080
Closing inventory of Omegas					
Closing inventories are to equal 3 days of the next period's demand for Omegas.					

The production director gives you the following information:

- The actual opening inventories for period 1, the four weeks ending 2 February, will be 1,330 Omegas.

- Each Omega requires 6 litres of material.

- The material is currently supplied under a long-term contract at a cost of £8.00 per litre and is made exclusively for Aspen by Contrax plc.

- Contrax only has sufficient production capacity to make a maximum of 34,000 litres in any four-week period. Aspen normally purchases the material in the same four-week period it is used.

- Should Aspen require more than 34,000 litres in a four-week period, Contrax would be willing to supply additional material in the preceding period, providing it had spare capacity.

- There is a readily available alternative source for the material but the cost is £12.00 per litre.

- Before buying from the alternative source, any shortage of material in a period should be overcome, where possible, by first purchasing extra material from Contrax in the immediately preceding period.

- There are 78 production employees who are paid a guaranteed basic wage of £160 per 40-hour week.

- Each Omega should take 2 labour hours to make but, due to temporary technical difficulties, the workforce is only able to operate at 95% efficiency in periods 1 to 4.

- Any overtime incurred is payable at a rate of £6.00 per hour.

Required:

Adrian Jones asks you to prepare the following budgets for each of the periods 1 to 4:

(a) The production budget in Omegas using the inventory levels given in the data.

(b) The material purchases budget in litres.

(c) The cost of the material purchases.

(d) The labour budget in hours including any overtime hours.

(e) The cost of the labour budget including the cost of any overtime.

Data

On receiving your budgets, Adrian Jones, the managing director, tells you that:

- He is concerned about the cost of the planned overtime and the extra cost of purchasing materials from the alternative supplier.

- The minimum demand in any four week period is forecast to be 5,700 Omegas.

- It is not possible to reduce costs by Advanced Industries plc improving its current method of forecasting.

However, he believes that some immediate and longer-term cost savings are possible.

Required:

Write a memo to Adrian Jones. In your memo you should:

(a) Use the budget information prepared above to identify ONE immediate possible cost saving proposal other than renegotiating the conditions imposed by Advanced Industries plc.

(b) Calculate the value of the cost savings in the proposal identified in part (a).

(c) Use the forecast minimum demand for Omegas to show whether or not:

    (i) the need to obtain material supplies from the alternative source is a short-term problem, and

    (ii) the need for overtime payments is also a short-term problem.

(d) Suggest TWO cost savings which may be possible in the longer term.

 Test your understanding 3

You have recently been promoted to the post of management accountant with Northern Products Ltd, a company formed four years ago. The company has always used budgets to help plan its production of two products, the Exe and the Wye. Both products use the same material and labour but in different proportions.

You have been asked to prepare the budget for quarter 1, the 12 weeks ending 24 March 2000. In previous budgets the closing inventories of both raw materials and finished products were the same as opening inventories. You questioned whether or not this was the most efficient policy for the company.

As a result, you have carried out an investigation into the inventory levels required to meet the maximum likely sales demand for finished goods and production demand for raw materials. You conclude that closing inventories of finished goods should be expressed in terms of days sales for the next quarter and closing inventories of raw materials in terms of days production for the next quarter.

Your findings are included in the data below which also shows data provided by the sales and production directors of Northern Products Ltd.

Product data

	Exe	Wye
• Budgeted sales in units, quarter 1	930 units	1,320 units
• Budgeted sales in units, quarter 2	930 units	1,320 units
• Budgeted material per unit (litres)	6 litres	9 litres
• Budgeted labour hours per unit	12 hours	7 hours
• Opening units of finished inventory	172 units	257 units
• Closing units of finished inventories (days sales next quarter)	8 days	9 days
• Failure rate of finished production*	2%	3%
• Finance and other costs of keeping a unit in inventory per quarter	£4.00	£5.00

* Failed products are only discovered on completion of production and have no residual value.

Other accounting data

• Weeks in accounting period	12 weeks
• Days per week for production and sales	5 days
• Hours per week	35 hours
• Number of employees	46 employees
• Budgeted labour rate per hour	£6.00
• Overtime premium for hours worked in excess of 35 hours per week	30%
• Budgeted cost of material per litre	£15.00
• Opening raw material inventories (litres)	1,878 litres
• Closing raw material inventories (days production current quarter)	5 days
• Financing and other costs of keeping a litre of raw material in inventory per quarter	£1.00

Required:

(a) Calculate the following information for *quarter 1,* the 12 weeks ending 24 March 2000:

    (i)   The number of production days.

    (ii)   The closing finished inventory for Exe and Wye in units.

    (iii) The labour hours available before overtime has to be paid.

(b) Prepare the following budgets for quarter 1, the 12 weeks ending 24 March 2000:

    (i)   The production budget in units for Exe and Wye including any faulty production.

    (ii)   The material purchases budget in litres and value.

    (iii) The production labour budget in hours and value including any overtime payments.

(c) Calculate the savings arising from the change in the required inventory levels for the 12 weeks ending 24 March 2000.

Test your understanding 4

Tipton Ltd makes two types of container for the chemical industry, the Exe and the Wye. Both containers use the same type of material and labour but in different amounts. You are the Management Accountant and you are responsible for preparing the production and resource budgets for both products. The company operates a five-day week for both production and sales and prepares production and resource budgets every 20 working days.

You are given the following information relating to period 1, the 20 working days ending 30 January 20X4.

Forecast sales volumes	Exe	Wye
Period 1: 20 days to 30 January 20X4	8,820 units	5,800 units
Period 2: percentage increase over period 1	20%	30%

Finished inventories

- At the beginning of period 1, there will be 4,410 Exes and 2,320 Wyes in finished inventory.

- The finished inventory of Exes at the end of period 1 must be equal to ten working days sales of Exes in period 2.

- The finished inventory of Wyes at the end of period 1 must be equal to eight working days sales of Wyes in period 2.

Materials

- Each Exe requires 5 square metres and each Wye requires 7 square metres of materials.

- The cost of material is £2.00 per square metre. There has been no change in the price of materials for several months. 2% of material issued to production is lost through wastage.

- At the beginning of period 1, the opening material inventory will be 16,950 square metres.

- At the end of period 1, the closing material inventory will be 18,000 square metres.

Labour

- Tipton produces six Exes per labour hour and four Wyes per labour hour.

- The company employs 22 production employees who work a 35-hour, five-day week.

- The labour rate per hour is £8.00 and any overtime is at a premium of 50% per hour.

- Any overtime premium is charged to the production overhead account and not directly to production.

Production overheads

- Overheads are charged to production at the rate of £12.00 per labour hour.

Required:

Prepare the following information for period 1, the 20 working days ending 30 January 20X4:

(a)   production budgets in units for the Exe and the Wye

(b)   material purchase budget in square metres

(c)   cost of materials purchases budget

(d)   budgeted labour hours to be worked, including any overtime

(e)   cost of labour budget

(f)   cost of production budgets for the Exe and the Wye.

Data

Susan Fellows is the Production Director of Tipton Ltd. She tells you that there will not be sufficient factory capacity in period 2 to meet the likely demand for the Exe and the Wye. One way of overcoming the capacity constraint in period 2 is to increase production of Exe in period 1 as Exe requires less material and labour than Wye. She tells you that:

- the surplus capacity of the factory in period 1 is equivalent to 88 labour hours and the production employees would be willing to work these extra hours

- Tipton can obtain up to 2,000 square metres of extra material for period 1.

Required:

Write a memo to Susan Fellows. In your memo you should:

(a)   identify whether it is the material or labour constraints that limit extra Exe production

(b)   prepare a revised production budget in units after allowing for the increased production of Exes

(c)   briefly identify TWO other short-term ways of overcoming the capacity constraint in period 2.

Test your understanding answers

Test your understanding 1

Your organisation

MEMORANDUM

To: Marketing Manager

From: Assistant Management Accountant

Date: 12 July 2016

Subject: Budgetary planning process

As requested, I provide below answers to your queries about the budgetary planning process.

(a) **The key factor**

Otherwise known as the principal budget factor or limiting factor, the key factor is the factor which limits the activity of an organisation. In our organisation it is sales volume, since there is a limit to how much we can sell. However, it is possible for other factors to be key factors, especially in the short term. Examples could be cash, machine capacity or skilled labour.

The determination of the key factor is important in the budgetary process because this is the budget which must be prepared first. Then all other budgets can be co-ordinated with this budget.

For example, once the sales budget has been determined, this will provide the basis for the production budget and for other budgets such as the materials purchasing budget and the cash budget.

(b) A number of steps can be taken to achieve co-ordination in the budgetary planning process, including the following:

(i) Set up a budget committee which consists of representatives from all parts of the organisation. Regular meetings of this committee should ensure that each part of the organisation is aware of what all other parts are doing.

(ii) Give one person the overall responsibility for ensuring that budgets are prepared on time and that they take into account all relevant factors. This person is often called the budget officer and will usually chair the budget committee.

(iii) Provide a timetable to all those involved in the budgetary process, detailing who is responsible for preparing each budget and when it must be prepared. This should reduce the risk of bottlenecks in the budgetary process and will co-ordinate the order of budget preparation.

(iv) Ensure that all those involved in the budgetary process have access to the budget manual which include the budget timetable mentioned above, instructions on completing the budget planning forms and proforma budgets, details on key assumptions to be made in the planning process (such as the inflation rate and exchange rate), links to the other budgets being drawn up and so on.

(v) Provide regular feedback on the progress of budget preparation.

The key to co-ordinated budget preparation is communication.

Test your understanding 2

(a) **Production budget in units**

	Period 1	Period 2	Period 3	Period 4	Period 5
Demand	5,700	5,700	6,840	6,460	6,080
Less Opening inventory	(1,330)	(855)	(1,026)	(969)	(912)
Add Closing inventory	855	1,026	969	912	
Production	5,225	5,871	6,783	6,403	

(b) **Material purchases budget (litres)**

		Period 1	Period 2	Period 3	Period 4
Production (units)		5,225	5,871	6,783	6,403
Material required (production × 6 litres)	(i)	31,350	35,226	40,698	38,418
Maximum material available	(ii)		34,000	34,000	34,000
Shortfall of material available (i – ii)			1,226	6,698	4,418
Reschedule purchases		1,226	−1,226		
Material purchases from Contrax plc	(iii)	32,576	34,000	34,000	34,000
Material purchases from outside supplier	(iv)			6,698	4,418

(c) **Material purchases budget (£)**

	Period 1 £	Period 2 £	Period 3 £	Period 4 £
Material purchases from Contrax plc (c) × £8	260,608	272,000	272,000	272,000
Material purchases from outside supplier (d) × £12			80,376	53,016
	260,608	272,000	352,376	325,016

(d) **Labour hours budget**

	Period 1	Period 2	Period 3	Period 4
Production (units of Omega)	5,225	5,871	6,783	6,403
Standard hours required (units × 2 hours)	10,450	11,742	13,566	12,806
Inefficiency (5/95 × standard hours)	550	618	714	674
Total labour hours required	11,000	12,360	14,280	13,480
Basic hours (78 employees × 4 weeks × 40 hours)	12,480	12,480	12,480	12,480
Overtime	Nil	Nil	1,800	1,000

(e) **Labour budget (£)**

	Period 1	Period 2	Period 3	Period 4
Basic wage (£160 × 78 employees × 4 weeks)	49,920	49,920	49,920	49,920
Overtime (Overtime hours × £6)			10,800	6,000
	49,920	49,920	60,720	55,920

MEMO

To: Adrian Jones

From: Management Accountant

Date: X-X-XX

Subject: Cost savings

Following our recent discussions and your observations regarding the level of overtime and the material supplier, I list my comments below.

(a) **Immediate cost savings**

The material available in period 1 is 34,000 litres, whereas our requirement is 32,576 litres. A further 1,424 litres is available from Contrax and could result in a saving in one of two ways.

(b) By bringing production forward to period 1, there would be a saving of £5,696 because of the reduction in purchases, at a later date, from the alternative supplier – 1,424 litres × £4 = £5,696.

The same saving is possible by simply buying the 1,424 litres in advance to be used in a later period.

(c) **Continuing difficulties**

If minimum demand for the product continues at 5,700 per four-week period, the material requirements will be 34,200 litres per period, which suggests that the material constraint is a longer term problem.

The planned labour hours for minimum demand would be 12,000 per period, even if the inefficiency problem continues. However, with 12,480 hours available each period, this constraint is considered short-term.

(d) **Possible long-term cost savings**

In the longer term it may be possible to renegotiate the stock requirements with Advanced Industries. This would allow a lower investment in finished stocks.

However, we would need to satisfy them that we could supply them on time if their forecast requirement were inaccurate. One way of dealing with this would be flexible working, whereby excess demand was met by working unpaid overtime and allowing time off, paid in lieu, when demand was low.

Test your understanding 3

(a) (i) Number of production days in quarter 1:

  12 weeks × 5 days   = 60 days

(ii) Units of closing finished stock:

  Exe 930 × $\dfrac{8}{60}$ = 124 units

  Wye 1,320 × $\dfrac{9}{60}$ = 198 units

(iii) Labour hours in the period before overtime:

  12 weeks × 35 hours × 46 employees = 19,320 hours

(b) (i) **Production budget for the 12 weeks ending 24 March 20X0**

	Exe	Wye
Budgeted sales (units)	930	1,320
Add Closing inventories	124	198
Less Opening inventories	(172)	(257)
Production of good units	882	1,261
Faulty production (Exe = 2/98 × 882, Wye = 3/97 × 1,261)	18	39
Gross production before faults	900	1,300

(ii) **Material purchases budget for the 12 weeks ending 24 March 20X0**

	Litres
Material requirement for Exe production (6 litres × 900 Exe)	5,400
Material requirement for Wye production (9 litres × 1,300 Wye)	11,700
Total material required for production	17,100
Add Closing raw material stock (5 days/60 days × 17,100 litres)	1,425
Less Opening raw material stock	(1,878)
Material purchases (litres)	16,647
Total material cost (16,647 × £15)	£249,705

(iii) Production labour budget for the 12 weeks ending 24 March 20X0

	Hours
Budgeted hours required for Exe production (12 hours × 900)	10,800
Budgeted hours required for Wye production (7 hours × 1,300)	9,100
Total planned labour hours	19,900
Hours available before overtime	19,320
Overtime hours	580
Cost of normal hours (19,320 × £6)	£115,920
Cost of overtime (580 × £6 × 130%)	£4,524
Total labour cost	£120,444

(c)	Finance and other savings per quarter		£192
	Exe	([172 – 124] × £4)	
	Wye	([257 – 198] × £5)	£295
	Raw material	([1,878 – 1,425] × £1)	£453
			£940

Test your understanding 4

(a) Production budget (units)

	Exe	Wye
Sales volume	8,820	5,800
Add closing finished stocks (W1)	5,292	3,016
Less opening finished stocks	(4,410)	(2,320)
Planned production	9,702	6,496

Working 1

Closing inventories

	Exe	Wye
Sales in period 1	8,820	5,800
Sales in period 2 (20%/30% higher)	8,820 × 1.20	5,800 ×1.30
Closing inventory = 10/8 days sales	$8,820 \times 1.2 \times \dfrac{10}{20}$	$5,800 \times 1.3 \times \dfrac{8}{20}$

(b) **Materials purchase budget**

	(square metres)
Production – Exe: 9,702 × 5 sq m	48,510
Production – Wye: 6,496 × 7 sq m	45,472
	93,982
Wastage (W2)	1,918
	————
Gross material issued to production	95,900
Add closing material stock	18,000
Less opening material stock	(16,950)
	————
Purchase (square metres)	96,950
	————

Working 2

Good production	98	93,982
Waste	2	?
	———	———
Input material	100	?
	———	———

Therefore waste = $\dfrac{93,982}{98} \times 2 = 1,918$

(c) **Cost of purchases budget**

96,950 × £2.00	£193,900

(d) **Labour hours worked budget**

Exe: 9,702/6	1,617
Wye: 6,496/4	1,624
	————
	3,241
Basic hours available: 22 × 35 × 4	3,080
	————
Overtime	161
	————

(e) **Cost of labour budget**

Basic hours: 3,080 × £8.00	£24,640
Overtime: 161 × £12.00	£1,932
	£26,572

(f) **Cost of production budget by product**

	Exe £	Wye £
Materials issued to production (W1)	99,000	92,800
Labour (W2)	12,936	12,992
Production overhead (W3)	19,404	19,488
	131,340	125,280

Workings

(W1) **Materials**

Exe: 48,510 × 100/98 × £2.00 = £99,000

Wye: 45,472 × 100/98 × £2.00 = £92,800

(W2) **Labour**

Exe: 1,617 × £8.00 = £12,936

Wye: 1,624 × £8.00 = £12,992

(W3) **Production overhead**

Exe: 1,617 × £12.00 = £19,404

Wye: 1,624 × £12.00 = £19,488

Note that it is a coincidence that the production overhead rate of £12 per hour equals the overtime rate. 161 hours of overtime at £4 per hour (£644) is charged to the production overhead account, along with the other (unspecified) overheads. These are all then charged to production at £12 per hour.

MEMO

To: Susan Fellows

From: Management Accountant

Date: 4 December 20X3

Subject: Production constraints period 2

(a) **Extra possible production of Exe**

The calculations to determine whether materials or labour are the constraint are as follows:

	Material	Labour
Available resource	2,000 sq m	88 hours
Waste (2,000 × 2%) =	40 sq m	–
	1,960 sq m	88 hours
Possible production	1,960 ÷ 5 = 392	88 × 6 = 528

Material is, therefore, the effective constraint in period 1 if extra production is required, and 392 extra units of Exe can be produced.

(b) **Revised production budget for period 1**

With no extra production of Wye, the revised production budget will be as follows:

	Exe	Wye
Original production budget	9,702	6,496
Add additional production	392	
Revised production budget	10,094	6,496

(c) **Other ways of overcoming the constraint in period 2**

There are several possible short-term solutions. The company should consider:

- holding less raw material stock: this will reduce the material constraint identified above

- holding less finished stock, which would release Exes and Wyes for sale

- sub-contracting out extra production.

Preparing budgets – the control phase

8

Introduction

This chapter is, first of all, concerned with the classification of costs by behaviour. Much of the information here has been met in previous units so should be considered to be revision of relevant areas.

Some costs change when activity levels change, whilst others do not. The ability to isolate cost elements by behaviour is essential to management who are concerned with predicting future costs as part of the planning and decision making processes. It will also be necessary to enable a marginal costing approach to be taken, as covered in the next chapter.

In order to be able to compare actual figures with budgeted figures to give a meaningful analysis, a *flexible* or *flexed* budget must be prepared. This will lead to budget variances and the broad principles are similar to those already studied in the chapters on variance analysis.

A further important aspect of budgeting that appears in examinations is the effect of the budgeting process and the final budget on the motivation of managers and employees.

ASSESSMENT CRITERIA

- Identify budgetary responsibilities and accountabilities (Element 2.1)
- Discuss how budgeting can promote effective, ethical and focused management (Element 3.1)
- Integrate standard costing into budgetary control (Element 3.5)
- Prepare and explain a flexed budget (Element 3.6)
- Calculate variances between budget and actual income and expenditure (Element 3.7)

CONTENTS

1 Cost centres

Definition

A cost centre is a location, function or item(s) of equipment in respect of which costs may be accumulated and related to cost units for control purposes.

A cost centre therefore is used as an initial collection point for costs; once the total cost of operating the cost centre for a period has been ascertained, it can be related to the cost units that have passed through the cost centre.

The location, function or item of equipment referred to in the definition can be directly related to production, to a service department or to a business.

1.1 Examples of cost centres

Production	Assembly line Packing machine
Service department	Stores Canteen Quality control
Service	Tax department (accountants) Ward (hospital) Faculty (college)

1.2 Responsibility for cost centres

Control can only be exercised by people, and for every cost somebody must be responsible; so whether a cost centre is impersonal or personal there must always be a manager in whose sphere of responsibility that cost centre is included.

1.3 Profit centres

> ### 🔍 Definition
>
> A profit centre is a location, function or item(s) of equipment in respect of which costs and revenues may be ascertained for the purposes of controlling the resulting profit.

Thus, while the paint shop in a factory might be treated as a cost centre (to monitor the costs incurred there), a large company might treat its French operations as a profit centre (since they generate both costs and revenues).

2 Cost classification

2.1 Types of cost classification

Costs can be classified (collected into logical groups) in many ways. The particular classification selected will depend upon the purpose for which the resulting analysed data will be used.

Purpose	Classification
Cost control	By nature – materials, labour, overheads, etc.
Cost accounts	By relationship to cost units – direct/ indirect costs, etc.
Budgeting, contribution analysis	By behaviour – fixed/variable costs.
Decision-making	Relevant and non-relevant costs.
Responsibility accounting	Controllable and uncontrollable costs.

You will come across these classifications in more detail as you work through this study text. At this stage, we will revise the basic classification terms used in cost accounting.

2.2 Direct and indirect costs

For cost accounting purposes, the costs of the business will be classified in quite a different way from the analysis required by a financial accountant for the income statement in published accounts.

The basic classification of costs in cost accounting may be illustrated as follows.

Example 1

	£	£
Direct costs		
Direct materials		250,000
Direct labour		120,000
Direct expenses		10,000
		———
Prime cost (= total of direct costs)		380,000
Indirect production costs		25,000
		———
Production cost		405,000
Indirect non-production costs		
Administration overhead	20,000	
Selling and distribution overhead	25,000	
	———	
		45,000
		———
Total cost		450,000
		———

2.3 Direct costs

Definition

Direct costs are costs which can be related directly to one cost unit. Direct costs comprise direct materials, direct labour and direct expenses.

For example, considering a cost unit of a chair, direct costs will include the cost of wood and screws used (direct material cost) and the cost of manufacturing labour hours per chair (direct labour cost).

In a service context, the direct costs relating to, say, a student enrolled at a college would include the costs of books provided, individual tuition and marking costs.

2.4 Indirect costs

 Definition

Indirect costs cannot be identified directly with a cost unit and are often referred to as *overheads*.

For inventory valuation purposes a distinction needs to be made between overheads incurred in the production process (factory costs, e.g. factory rent and rates, power etc) and non-production costs.

Non-production costs are indirect costs involved in converting finished goods into revenue, comprising:

(a) administrative overhead costs (e.g. executive salaries and office costs) and

(b) marketing, selling and distribution overhead costs.

Non-production costs are not included in inventory valuation since they are not costs of making a product, but costs of selling it. Inventory on hand at the end of a period is valued at total production cost only, including production overheads (in a total absorption costing system).We shall return to this point in the next chapter.

Considering the cost unit of a chair, the salaries of the sales representatives who promote and sell the chairs to retail outlets would be a selling overhead.

Indirect costs associated with a college would include premises running costs, lecturers' salaries and administrative staff costs.

Overhead costs can always be identified with cost centres. Because cost centres are the responsibility of particular functional managers one will usually find overheads classified according to the main functional divisions of the business.

3 Cost behaviour

3.1 The nature of costs

We mentioned earlier the need for cost classification by behaviour for budgeting purposes. In order to make predictions of future cost levels, we must determine the basis of the charge.

As an example, consider the cost of direct materials expected next month. The charge would depend on the amount used and the cost per unit. The amount used would depend, in turn, on the production anticipated for the period.

In order to derive this cost therefore we must make an estimate such as the following:

(a)	Production levels	10,000 units

(b) Usage of materials per unit:

Material A	2 kg
Material B	1 kg
Material C	0.2 kg

(c) Costs of materials:

Material A	30 pence per kg
Material B	25 pence per kg
Material C	50 pence per kg

Estimate of next month's material cost

		£
Material A	20,000 kg @ 30p/kg	6,000
Material B	10,000 kg @ 25p/kg	2,500
Material C	2,000 kg @ 50p/kg	1,000
Total estimated material cost		9,500

3.2 Variable costs

Once we can identify the factors affecting material cost we can set up a simple mathematical model which will, for any level of production, usage and cost of materials, enable the total level of cost in a future period to be predicted. In practice, we may wish to build in other variables which affect the cost such as wastage rates thus producing a slightly more complex model.

Direct labour costs may tend to vary due to changes in productivity and other factors in addition to the more obvious variables such as grade and rate of payment. A certain amount of estimation will be required; if payment is on a production related basis we would expect a cost which, like materials, will vary in line with the volume of production.

As a rule-of-thumb guide, therefore direct material, labour and expenses will vary roughly in line with anticipated production levels or the level of activity. We call such costs **variable** costs.

3.3 Fixed costs

This will not be the case with all costs. If we take the cost of rent and rates, for example, the charge is not determined on the basis of the intensity of usage of the premises but rather on the basis of time. Costs that are unaffected by the volume of production are called **fixed costs**. Rent and rates are an example. Labour paid on a time basis (for example, a monthly salary) would also fall under this heading. How then can we predict the cost of such expenses for next month? Well, there is no difficulty in doing this as all we have to do is consult our rental agreement and the rates notice and we can forecast with complete certainty what these costs will be for the month.

3.4 Classification of costs by behaviour

The above example illustrates the need for cost behaviour classification. For cost prediction purposes, we must make a distinction between costs which vary with production or activity levels (variable costs) and those which do not (fixed costs). There also exists a type of cost which moves in sympathy with production levels but contains an element which does not, such as an electricity charge which contains a minimum standing charge plus an element which relates to the usage of the period. Such a cost would be described as semi-variable or mixed.

🔍 Definition

Variable costs are those that vary (usually assumed in direct proportion) with changes in level of activity of the cost centre to which they relate (e.g. output volume). An example would be the raw material used in a product. It should be noted that the variable cost per unit may not remain constant over a wide range. It may be possible, for example, to obtain discounts for large purchases of material, reducing the cost per unit.

Fixed costs are those that accrue with the passage of time and are not affected by changes in activity level; they are therefore also known as period costs, for example rent of premises.

Stepped costs are fixed over a range of output and then suddenly increase in one big jump, for example a staffing level of up to 20 people may only require one supervisor but, if the staff level is more than 20, an extra supervisor will be needed.

Semi-variable (mixed) costs contain both a fixed and a variable element. When output is nil, the fixed element is incurred, but costs also increase, like variable costs, as output increases. An example is telephone charges where there is a fixed rental to which is added the charge for calls made. These are also sometimes known as semi-fixed costs.

3.5   Graphical illustrations

Various cost behaviour patterns are illustrated in the graphs below.

(a)   **Variable cost:** direct materials, the purchase price per unit being constant

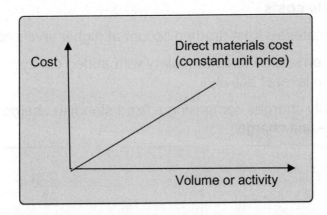

(b)   **Fixed cost:** rent of factory payable under a long-term lease

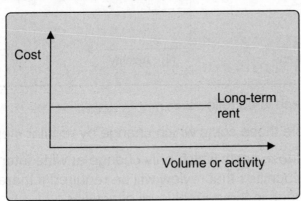

(c) **Stepped costs**

(i)   Canteen cost where additional assistants are required as increases in activity result in larger numbers of factory personnel.

(ii)   Rent of premises, additional accommodation eventually being required.

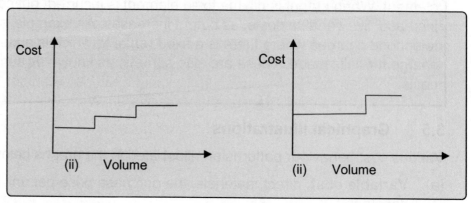

(d) **Semi-variable costs**

(i)   Direct materials cost (trade discount at higher levels of activity).

(ii)   Salesmen's remuneration (salary with added commission from a certain level of activity).

(iii)   Electricity charges comprising a fixed standing charge and variable unit charge.

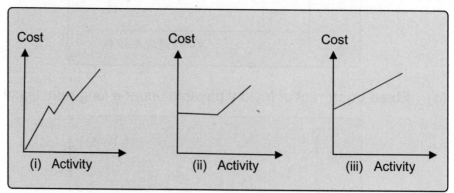

The common approach is as follows:

(a)   Treat as variable those costs which change by regular steps.

(b)   Treat as fixed those costs which only change at wide intervals of activity; this recognises that review will be required if there is a permanent change in the normal level of activity.

4 Cost estimation

4.1 Introduction

As we have seen, some costs may have both fixed and variable elements. These will need to be identified for budgeting purposes.

If it is not easy to do this directly (as it is in the case of the telephone cost, where the bill clearly shows the fixed charge and rate per unit), then an analysis of past cost and volume data will need to be carried out. For simplicity, it is assumed that there is a linear relationship, i.e.:

Total cost = Fixed cost + (Variable cost per unit × Units produced)

and that the total fixed cost and the variable cost per unit are constant at all levels of production unless told otherwise.

Possible techniques include the high/low method and linear regression. Linear regression (which we referred to in Chapter 1) is a statistical technique which estimates a line of best fit for the observed costs at various activity levels and derives a total cost equation to identify variable and fixed costs at any activity level within the normal range. You will not be expected to apply this method in the exam. A simpler method is the high/low method.

5 The high/low method

5.1 Introduction

This is a simple method of estimating future costs from past results. It takes the costs for the highest and lowest activity levels, and assumes that a linear relationship covers the range in between.

Example 2

Widgets are produced by a process that incurs both fixed and variable costs.

Total costs have been recorded for the process for each of the last six months as follows.

Month	Output (units)	Total cost £
1	4,500	33,750
2	3,500	30,500
3	5,100	34,130
4	6,200	38,600
5	5,700	38,000
6	4,100	31,900

(a)   What is the estimated fixed cost element and estimated variable cost per unit?

(b)   What would be the estimated total cost at the budgeted activity level for month 7 of 6,000 units?

Solution

Select the months with the highest and lowest output levels as follows.

	Output (units)	Total cost £
Lowest output	3,500	30,500
Highest output	6,200	38,600
Increase	2,700	8,100

For an increase of 2,700 units, cost has increased by £8,100. If we assume that the fixed cost element remains constant, this cost increase must represent a change in variable costs only.

Assuming a straight-line relationship, then the variable cost per unit =

$$\frac{£8,100}{2,700} = £3 \text{ per unit}$$

Note that the factor determining which values to choose is the total cost at the highest output level and the total cost at the lowest output level. These are not necessarily the highest and lowest costs. The high/low observations are always based on the independent variable (in this case, output).

We can now substitute back into either of the two output levels to obtain the fixed cost.

At the 3,500 units level:

	£
Total cost	30,500
Variable cost (3,500 × £3)	(10,500)
Fixed costs	20,000

As a check on the accuracy of the calculations, at the 6,200 units level:

	£
Total costs	38,600
Variable cost (6,200 × £3)	(18,600)
Fixed costs	20,000

(a) Therefore the estimated fixed cost element is £20,000 and the estimated variable cost is £3 per unit.

(b) At an output level of 6,000 units the total estimated cost would be:

	£
Variable cost (6,000 × £3)	18,000
Fixed cost	20,000
Total cost	38,000

5.2 Advantages of high-low method

- Simple to operate.
- Easy to understand.

5.3 Disadvantages of high-low method

The problem with the high-low method is that it could give a completely inaccurate result. This is because we are only considering two sets of data, and ignoring all of the others.

It is possible that the points we have chosen are completely unrepresentative of the rest of the data. This is a distinct possibility since we have chosen the two points at the extreme ends of the activity range.

At these levels it is more likely that operating conditions will be atypical compared with more normal output. One way around this problem is to choose the 'next to highest' and 'next to lowest' figures, but this destroys some of the simplicity of the model.

6 Flexing budgets

6.1 Variable and fixed costs

In connection with expense budgeting, the budget working sheets should include some indication of the 'basis of variability' of each item of cost.

The most common general bases of variability of costs are in line with sales or the volume of productive output. In some systems of budgetary control, therefore, costs are divided between those which tend to vary with the output or sales achieved, and those which tend to remain fixed regardless of sales or the volume of output over an expected range of volumes.

6.2 Flexed budgets

This distinction having been established then, for variable costs, it is possible to establish in any period an allowable level of cost appropriate to the output actually achieved. This new level is known as the budget allowance for that volume of output. This is also known as a flexed budget. The total variance from the original budget figure will then be divided into two parts:

* The difference between the original budget and the budget allowance, assumed to arise from the nature of the business. This is sometimes referred to as an 'activity variance' and may be excluded from sectional control reports.

* The difference between the budget allowance and the actual cost incurred. This, by definition, should not have occurred and might be thought of as the 'controllable variance' of the manager concerned.

Example 3

	Budget	Actual
Sales volume	100 units	90 units
Sales value	£1,000	£990
Variable costs	£500	£495
Fixed costs	£200	£210
Profit	£300	£285

The Finance Director wishes to blame someone for the fact that profit is down by £15: "It is obvious who is to blame. Sales are below target and fixed costs have not been controlled."

In the example above, it is futile to compare the actual variable costs with the budget. To do so suggests that the manager is doing better than budget, but actual volume is below budget, so costs should be lower. It is vital to produce a revised budget to use for comparison.

This does not mean that the original budget is useless. It merely means that in order to analyse the £15 difference, it is important to **start by removing the impact of volume changes** on the various headings which are affected by it.

	Budget	Revised budget	Actual
Sales volume	100 units	90 units	90 units
Sales value	£1,000	£900	£990
Variable costs	£500	£450	£495
Fixed costs	£200	£200	£210
Profit	£300	£250	£285

This recalculates the budget using **actual volume, but budget prices** and shows that the expected profit for 90 units is £250. Thus the impact on profit of the fall in sales is a reduction of £50 and this can be identified as sales volume variance £(50). Now, the other variances can be calculated.

7 Flexible budgets

A system incorporating budget allowances is referred to as flexible budgetary control.

This idea has been seized on by writers of textbooks and setters of examination questions and converted into the concept of 'flexible budgets'. in other words, at the beginning of the year there should be a schedule showing what the various cost allowances would be at various levels of output. The use of spreadsheets makes this very simple.

Example 4

You are the budget officer of Majestic Limited, which produces a single product. The following forecasts have been prepared from the best information available for the production costs to be incurred at the highest and lowest production levels likely to be encountered in any particular period.

	Production level	
	10,000 *units*	20,000 *units*
	£	£
Direct materials	2,000	4,000
Direct labour	15,000	30,000
Warehouse rental	8,000	13,000
Machine maintenance	2,400	3,000
Factory rent, rates, etc	4,000	4,000
Factory power	4,500	6,300

Machine maintenance is under contract with the machine supplier. The period cost is based upon the production level and is charged at £15 per 100 units, with a minimum charge payable of £2,400 per period.

Warehouse rent is fixed per warehouse per period. One warehouse is sufficient to cope with the storage demands up to 12,500 units. Should production exceed this level, a further warehouse will need to be rented for the period, at an additional cost of £5,000. This will give sufficient space to cover the highest production level.

All other variable costs and the variable part of semi-variable costs follow constant linear patterns.

Required:

Prepare a set of flexible budgets which show the budget allowance for the period for the following activity levels: 10,000 units; 12,500 units; 15,000 units; 17,500 units; 20,000 units.

Solution

The following steps illustrate a good approach to such a question. You may like to try preparing your own answer as we go through before looking at our solution at the end.

1   **Draw up a proforma statement**

This will have the cost headings listed down the left-hand side and columns headed up with each production level; in this case, five columns will be needed. It is also a good idea to have an additional column next to the cost headings in which to insert references to workings (e.g. 'Note 2' etc).

The statement should also have a heading.

2   **Insert known figures**

You have already been given the costs for the lowest and highest production levels, so put these in.

3   **Deal with the particular costs you have further information about (in this case, machine maintenance and warehouse rental)**

Machine maintenance

This cost will be fixed up to a certain production level (to cover the minimum charge) and will then rise linearly (at £15 per 100 units or £0.15 per unit).

The level up to which the minimum charge is applicable is £2,400/£0.15 = 16,000 units. So the charge for the 12,500 and 15,000 unit levels will also be £2,400.

For 17,500 units the charge will be 17,500 × £0.15 = £2,625 and for 20,000 units it will reach 20,000 × £0.15 = £3,000 (as given).

These can now be inserted in your statement.

Warehouse rental

This is an example of a 'stepped' fixed cost. It will remain at £8,000 for all levels up to (and including) 12,500 units, and will rise to £13,000 for all levels above this.

These can now be inserted in your statement.

4 Deal with remaining costs

These will be strictly fixed, strictly variable or semi-variable.

Strictly fixed costs

These will be obvious – here, factory rent and rates must be fixed within the range, as the costs for the lowest and highest production levels are the same.

Insert this fixed cost across all levels on your statement.

Strictly variable costs

Usually direct materials and direct labour costs will be strictly variable. You can see here that, as the production level doubles, so does the cost. Use either level to determine the cost per unit.

Direct materials: £2,000/10,000   =   £0.20 per unit

Direct labour: £15,000/10,000   =   £1.50 per unit

Use these to calculate the appropriate cost for the other levels and insert them on the statement.

Semi-variable costs

These costs will not be the same for the two extreme levels, but they will not increase proportionately from one to the other either. If you are not sure, calculate a cost per unit at the two levels; these will not be the same, as they would be if the cost were strictly variable.

In this example, the power cost is semi-variable. It can be split between the fixed and variable elements by the 'high-low' method which we saw in a previous chapter.

	Production level (units)	Cost £
Highest	20,000	6,300
Lowest	10,000	4,500
Change	+10,000	+1,800

Variable cost = £1,800/10,000 = £0.18 per unit

Using the lowest level to determine the fixed cost element:

	£
Total cost	4,500
Less: Variable element (10,000 × £0.18)	(1,800)
Fixed element	2,700

So for each level, the total power cost can be calculated as follows.

$£2,700 + (£0.18 × Production level)$

For example, the cost for 15,000 units will be as follows.

$£2,700 + (£0.18 × 15,000) = £5,400$

The remaining costs can be calculated in this way and the statement completed, as below.

Budget allowance for activity levels between 10,000 and 20,000

	Production level				
	10,000 units	12,500 units	15,000 units	17,500 units	20,000 units
	£	£	£	£	£
Direct materials	2,000	2,500	3,000	3,500	4,000
Direct labour	15,000	18,750	22,500	26,250	30,000
Warehouse rental	8,000	8,000	13,000	13,000	13,000
Machine maintenance	2,400	2,400	2,400	2,625	3,000
Factory rent, rates	4,000	4,000	4,000	4,000	4,000
Factory power	4,500	4,950	5,400	5,850	6,300
Total	35,900	40,600	50,300	55,225	60,300

7.1 Budgetary control statement

A typical continuation to the above example would be the requirement to produce a budgetary control statement (or budget report) given some actual data for the period.

 Example 5

In period 3 Majestic Limited produced 17,500 units and incurred the following costs.

	£
Direct materials	3,200
Direct labour	29,750
Warehouse rental	13,000
Machine maintenance	3,150
Factory rent, rates, etc	3,800
Factory power	4,720

Produce a budgetary control statement to compare these actual costs with the flexed costs that would be budgeted for.

Solution

The budgetary control statement will compare the actual costs with the relevant budget allowances from the flexible budget to highlight variances.

In this case, the relevant flexed budget is that for 17,500 units.

We have also included the original budget (for 20,000 units). This is good practice, as it is probable that a lot of managers who see the budgetary control statement will have had access to the original budget. If they don't see those figures on the statement, they will think they were given the wrong information before, or else they will think they are being given the wrong information now!

	20,000 units original budget (£)	17,500 units flexed budget (£)	17,500 units actual (£)	Flexed to actual variance (£)
Direct materials	4,000	3,500	3,200	300 F
Direct labour	30,000	26,250	29,750	3,500 A
Warehouse rental	13,000	13,000	13,000	–
Machine maintenance	3,000	2,625	3,150	525 A
Factory rent, rates, etc	4,000	4,000	3,800	200 F
Factory power	6,300	5,850	4,720	1,130 F
	60,300	55,225	57,620	2,395 A

You may then be asked to comment on the variances, suggesting any further investigations or action that might be required.

Note that if the actual costs for output of 17,500 units were compared to the original budget of 20,000 units of output, the resulting variances would be meaningless.

 Test your understanding 1

Visiguard Ltd is a division of Alton Products plc. It makes a single product, the Raider. Just over a year ago, the chief executive of Alton Products, Mike Green, was concerned to find that Visiguard was budgeting to make only £20,000 profit in the year to 31 May 20X0. As a result, he imposed his own budget on the division. His revised budget assumed:

- increased sales volume of the Raider

- increased selling prices and

- that suppliers would agree to reduce the cost of the material used in the Raider by 10%.

The only other changes to the original budget arose solely as a result of the increased volume in the revised budget.

The original budget and the revised budget imposed by Mike Green are reproduced below, together with the actual results for the year to 31 May 2000.

Visiguard Limited
Budgeted and actual operating statements for one year ended 31 May 20X0

	Original budget £	Revised budget £	Actual results £
Sales and production volume	10,000	11,000	11,600
	£	£	£
Revenue	1,400,000	1,760,000	1,844,400
Variable materials	400,000	396,000	440,800
Production and administrative labour	580,000	630,000	677,600
Light, heat and power	160,000	164,000	136,400
Fixed overheads	240,000	240,000	259,600
Budgeted profit	20,000	330,000	330,000

Required:

Using the information provided in the two budgets, calculate the following:

(a) The unit selling price of the Raider in the revised budget.

(b) The material cost per Raider in the revised budget.

(c) The variable cost of production and administrative labour per Raider.

(d) The fixed cost of production and administrative labour.

(e) The variable cost of light, heat and power per Raider.

(f) The fixed cost of light, heat and power.

Data

On receiving the actual results for the year, Mike Green states that they prove that his revised budget motivated managers to produce better results.

Required:

Write a memo to Mike Green. Your memo should:

(a) Use the information calculated before to prepare a flexed budget statement for Visiguard including any variances.

(b) Identify TWO situations where an imposed budget might be preferable to one prepared with the participation of managers.

(c) Briefly discuss whether or not his requirement that material costs be reduced would have motivated the managers of Visiguard.

(d) Identify TWO ways in which profit could have increased without additional effort by the managers of Visiguard.

8 Investigating and reporting variances

8.1 Reconciling budgeted and actual performance

We have seen that standard costs are developed in advance of the period under review. During the course of that period, actual costs are compared with standard costs. Any variances are isolated for investigation as to their cause, enabling corrective action to be taken as soon as possible.

Management will wish to see a clear and succinct summary of the results for the period and in particular will want any unusual or unexpected items to be brought to their attention (exception reporting). In general, this will take the form of a reconciliation between budgeted and actual profits which highlights the variances between them. To be useful as a management tool, the reconciliation should be part of an overall report to management.

Example 6

The calculation of basic cost variances is covered in previous AAT units.

The following budgeted and actual data for TJB Limited for 20X1 will be used to revise the principles and computations, and lead on to reporting these variances.

TJB Limited – Budgeted profit for the year ending 31 December 20X1

Produce and sell   10,000 units

		Produce and sell 10,000 units	
		£	£
Budgeted sales units	10,000		100,000
Production cost	£/unit		
Direct materials – 10,000 tons @ £1 per ton (1 ton per unit)	1.00	10,000	
Direct labour – 20,000 hours @ 50p per hour (2 hours per unit)	1.00	10,000	
Fixed production overhead – 20,000 hours @ 75p per hour	1.50	15,000	
Total budgeted production cost	3.50		35,000
Budgeted profit for the period			65,000

During the year to 31 December 20X1, the following actual results were obtained.

TJB Limited – Actual profit for the year ending 31 December 20X1

Production and sales 8,000 units

	£	£
Sales		96,000
Production cost		
Direct materials – 7,750 tons purchased and used (£1.0968 per ton)	8,500	
Direct labour – 16,500 hours paid (£0.4545 per hour)	7,500	
Fixed production overhead incurred	15,500	
Total actual production cost		31,500
Total profit		64,500

The purpose of a cost analysis is to reconcile the budgeted costs of £35,000 to the actual costs of £31,500.

This reconciliation is the budgetary control statement or budgetary control report.

Solution

Cost variances

	Flexed budget cost of producing 8,000 units * £	Actual cost of producing 8,000 units £	Difference (variance) £	
Direct materials	8,000	8,500	500	A
Direct labour	8,000	7,500	500	F
Fixed production overhead	12,000	15,500	3,500	A
Total	28,000	31,500	3,500	A

*In a total absorption costing system such as the one used here by TJB Ltd., the initial flexed budget will flex every line of the costs recorded by the actual activity level. This leads to a fixed cost figure of £1.50 × 8,000 = £12,000 and it is this figure the company will have absorbed. We will see below how this is dealt with in the control statement.

All these total variances can be analysed into at least two further types of variance:

(a) a price variance

(b) a usage or utilisation variance, which in some cases can be broken down further.

Total direct material cost variance

		£	
(a)	The actual amount of material used at the actual price	8,500	
(b)	The standard amount of material that should have been used for the actual production at the standard price – 8,000 tons × £1	8,000	
	Total variance	500	A

To analyse this further we need first to calculate the actual amount of material used at the standard price: the direct materials price variance.

Direct materials price variance

	Tons	£
Actual materials purchased, at actual price	7,750	8,500
Actual materials purchased, at standard price per ton (£1)	7,750	7,750
Materials price variance	–	750 A

TJB Ltd. has paid more than they had hoped for the materials they bought, reducing profits by £750.

We next need to compare this with the standard materials that should have been used for that level of production: the direct materials usage variance.

Direct materials usage variance

	Tons	£
Actual materials used at standard price	7,750	7,750
Standard materials allowed for production achieved at standard price	8,000	8,000
Materials usage variance (@ £1 per ton)	250	250 F

TJB Ltd. have used less material to make the goods than expected, improving profits by £250.

Total direct material cost variance = £750 A + £250 F
                                                              = £500 A

The reduced material usage, combined with the higher cost of the purchases has produced a £500 drop in profit overall.

Total direct labour cost variance

	£
(a) The actual hours paid at the actual rate per hour	7,500
(b) The standard time allowed to produce the output, priced at the standard rate per hour (16,000 × £0.50)	8,000
Total variance	500 F

The total variance can be analysed into rate and efficiency variances as with materials.

Labour rate variance

	Hours	£	
Actual hours paid at actual rate per hour	16,500	7,500	
Actual hours paid at standard rate per hour (50p/hour)	16,500	8,250	
Direct labour rate variance	–	750	F

TJB Ltd. has paid less than they expected for the labour they used, increasing profits by £750.

Total labour efficiency variance

	Hours	£	
Actual hours paid at standard rate per hour	16,500	8,250	
Standard hours allowed for production achieved at standard rate per hour (50p)	16,000	8,000	
Direct labour usage variance		250	A

TJB Ltd. have used more labour hours to make the goods than expected, reducing profits by £250.

Total direct labour cost variance = £750 F + £250 A
= £500 F

The cheaper cost of labour, combined with longer time taken to produce the goods has produced a £250 drop in profit overall.

Total fixed overhead cost variance

	£	
Actual fixed overhead cost	15,500	
Standard cost absorbed into actual production (8,000 × £1.50 per unit)	12,000	
Total fixed overhead cost variance	3,500	A

This is then analysed into price (expenditure) and volume variances. The volume variance is then sub-analysed into usage (efficiency) and capacity variances.

Fixed overhead price variance

	£
Actual fixed overhead cost	15,500
Budgeted fixed overhead cost	15,000
Fixed overhead price variance	500 A

This variance is also known as the fixed overhead expenditure variance.

Fixed overhead volume variance

This is the under-absorption (at standard rates) due to the lower actual production level than that budgeted.

	Units	£
Actual production	8,000	
Budgeted production	10,000	
Fixed overhead volume variance (in units)	2,000	
Valued at standard absorption rate (£1.50 per unit)		3,000 A

The variance is adverse because we have under-absorbed fixed overhead by 2,000 units' worth. We thus require an extra charge to the cost account to compensate for this under-absorption.

The £3,000 adverse volume variance can be analysed further.

Fixed overhead efficiency variance

	Hours	
Actual hours worked for actual production	16,500	
Standard hours allowed for actual production achieved	16,000	
Efficiency variance @ £0.75 per hour	500	= £375 A

Fixed overhead capacity variance

	Hours	
Actual hours worked	16,500	
Budgeted hours for the period	20,000	
Capacity variance @ £0.75 per hour	3,500	= £2,625 A

The two variances add up to the volume variance (£375 + £2,625 = £3,000 adverse), and shows that the principal reason for our under-production was a failure to devote sufficient hours to production (3,500 hours short).

Having computed all the variances, we can now reconcile budgeted costs with actual costs.

		Adverse £	Favourable £	£
Total budgeted cost				28,000
Cost variances				
Materials	Price	750		
	Usage		250	
Labour	Rate		750	
	Efficiency	250		
Fixed overheads	Expenditure	500		
	Usage	375		
	Capacity	2,625		
Total/net cost variances		4,500	1,000	3,500
Total actual cost				31,500

8.2 Marginal costing

The previous example of TJB Limited was based upon total absorption costing as the fixed production overhead was absorbed into the standard cost of the product. Under marginal costing the fixed overhead is charged to the income statement as a period cost and is not absorbed into the cost of the product.

For the purpose of variances this means that the only fixed overhead variance that exists is the fixed overhead price or expenditure variance. There is no volume variance.

8.3 Materials price variance and price changes

In some examination tasks you may be given information about specific price indices that have affected the materials prices during the period. In these circumstances it is then possible to split the materials price variance into that element that relates to the price increase and any other cause of the variance.

Example 7

The standard material cost for a business' single product is 4 kg at a price of £12.00 per kg. The standard price was set when the index for this material price stood at 120. During August, 10,000 units of the product were made using 42,000 kgs at a total cost of £525,000. The August price index for this material is 122.

What is the total materials price variance, the element relating to the price increase and the element relating to other causes?

Solution

Total materials price variance

		£
Standard cost of actual materials	42,000 × £12.00	504,000
Actual cost		525,000
		———
		21,000 Adverse
		———

This adverse variance of £21,000 can then be split into the element relating to the price increase and the element relating to other factors:

Variance relating to price increase

		£
Standard cost of actual materials	42,000 × £12.00	504,000
Adjusted price for actual materials	42,000 × (£12.00 × 122/120)	512,400
		———
		8,400 Adverse
		———

Variance relating to other factors

		£
Adjusted price for actual materials	42,000 × (£12.00 × 122/120)	512,400
Actual cost		525,000
		———
		12,600 Adverse
		———

9 Measuring the significance of variances

9.1 Introduction

As we have seen, the key tool for management control within a standard costing system is some form of variance analysis report or budgetary control statement. The aim is to prepare a report to management on a routine basis in which variances are clearly identified and can be acted upon as appropriate.

In exercising control, it is generally impracticable to review every variance in detail at each accounting period and attention will usually be concentrated on those variances which have the greatest impact on the achievement of the budget plan.

9.2 Identifying significant variances

One method of identifying significant variances is to express each variance as a percentage of the related budget allowance or standard value. Those showing the highest percentage deviation would then be given the most urgent attention.

This method, however, could result in lack of attention to variances which, although representing a small percentage of the standard value, nevertheless involve significant sums of money. Both percentages and absolute values should be looked at in deciding where the priorities for control actually lie.

In practice, management will review the variance report presented to them and decide which variances should be investigated on the basis of whether the costs of investigation are outweighed by the benefits.

Management may request that a more detailed analysis and explanation of specific variances is produced.

9.3 Fluctuating variances – looking at trends

The variances in a particular period may not be representative of a general trend. Items like stationery costs can fluctuate widely from month to month, depending on the invoices received.

Sometimes, the accountant will make estimated adjustments to either the budget or the actual figures in an attempt to give a better picture of the underlying trend but this is not a completely satisfactory way of dealing with the matter.

The simplest way of getting the month's figures into context is to show also the accumulated cost for the year to date. High cost and low cost periods will then be revealed but will balance out in the cumulative figures.

A development of the above idea is also to report, each period, the manager's latest forecast compared with the annual budget. It will then be possible to see whether variances from budget currently being reported are likely to continue to accumulate during the remainder of the year, or whether they will be offset by later opposite variances.

Although this technique is dependent on managers' subjective assessments, it ensures that the correct control actions are taken based on the current figures.

 Example 8

You might like to spend a few minutes considering what the report below tells you about the business.

Income statement – Seven periods cumulative to … 20…

	Current period		Var.	Seven months cumulative		Var.	Annual budget	Latest annual forecast
	Budget	Actual	Fav / (Adv)	Budget	Act.	Fav / (Adv)		
	£000	£000	£000	£000	£000	£000	£000	£000
Sales	500	600	100	3,500	3,420	(80)	6,000	6,200
Direct cost of sales	280	322	(42)	1,960	1,951	9	3,500	3,850
Factory overhead	58	69	(11)	420	400	20	700	750
Administration and selling costs	122	123	(1)	840	800	40	1,320	1,147
Total costs	460	514	(54)	3,220	3,151	69	5,520	5,747
Operating profit	40	86	46	280	269	(11)	480	453
Profit: sales %	8.0%	14.3%		8.0%	7.9%		8.0%	7.3%

Solution

(a) Sales, which had obviously been below budget for the first six periods of the year, are significantly in excess of budget for period 7 (reducing the cumulative shortfall to £80,000), and are now expected to exceed the budget for the year as a whole.

(b) Direct costs are naturally higher when sales are higher. The percentage of direct costs to sales value is not consistent, however, as the following calculations show:

	Budget	Actual
Period 7		
(280/500 322/600)	56.0%	53.7%
Cumulative to date		
(1,960/3,500 1,951/3,420)	56.0%	57.0%
Forecast for whole year		
(3,500/6,000 3,850/6,200)	58.3%	62.1%

For the seven periods as a whole, direct costs have been in excess of the budgeted percentage and even though the budget for the twelve months provides for an increase in that percentage the forecast actual increase is still higher. Period 7 in isolation shows an anomalous result, perhaps due to some peculiarity in sales mix.

(c) The variance on factory overhead, which is favourable over the seven periods as a whole, has become adverse in period 7 and is forecast as adverse for the year as a whole (though not at the rate experienced in period 7).Failure to budget adequately for inflationary increases is one possibility.

(d) Administration and selling costs have a cumulative favourable variance to date of £40,000 against a budget of £840,000, i.e. 4.8%. By the end of the year a favourable variance of £173,000 (13.1% on budget) is expected. It would appear that considerable economies are planned, and have already commenced. The fact that period 7 above shows a small adverse variance is not significant. Such results can emerge in administration costs, which can be influenced by random occurrences like a large purchase of stationery or a major visit overseas by the managing director.

9.4 Comparing against forecasts

Some large organisations in the UK have taken the idea of comparing against forecasts a step further. Many companies employ the following comparisons.

	Comparison	Information
1	Budget v actual	What progress have we made towards achieving objectives?
2	Budget v forecast	Will we continue to progress towards achievement of objectives?
3	Budget v revised forecast	Will suggested corrective actions lead us back to achievement of objectives?
4	Latest forecast v previous	Why are the forecasts different and are circumstances getting better or worse?
5	Actual v past forecast	Why were forecasts incorrect and can they be improved?

It may not be necessary to perform each of these control comparisons every month or quarter. The actual versus past forecast may only be necessary annually or less frequently.

It must be remembered that managers will need to be motivated to produce these forecasts and use them. They must be educated to recognise why and how they can use them to enable them to do a better job and not feel that they are just another means for higher level management to check on them and apply pressure.

Finally, this year's results are sometimes compared with those for the corresponding period last year. In some cases this may be helpful in establishing a trend, but it must never be forgotten that the budget is this year's plan, and it is against that plan that performance must be controlled.

Test your understanding 2

You have recently been appointed as the management accountant of Parkside Manufacturing Ltd. Parkside Manufacturing makes a single product, the Delta. The previous management accountant has already prepared an analysis of budgeted and actual results for the year to 30 November 2000. These are reproduced below.

Parkside Manufacturing Ltd
Operating statement for year ended 30 November 2000

Volume (number of Deltas)	Budget		Actual		Variance
	100,000		125,000		
	£000	£000	£000	£000	£000
Revenue		2,000		2,250	250 (F)
Material	600		800		200 (A)
Light, heat and power	200		265		65 (A)
Production labour	120		156		36 (A)
Rent, rates and depreciation	140		175		35 (A)
Administrative expenses	110		110		Nil
		1,170		1,506	
Profit		830		744	86 (A)

Key: (F) = favourable
(A) = adverse

Judith Green, the production director, tells you that the following assumptions were made when the budget was originally prepared:

- Material is entirely a variable cost.

- Light, heat and power is a semi-variable cost. The fixed element included in the budgeted figure was £40,000.

- Production labour is a stepped cost. Each production employee can make up to 10,000 Deltas. Each production employee was budgeted to receive a basic wage of £12,000 per year with no overtime and no bonuses.

- There are no part-time employees.

- Rent, rates and depreciation, and administrative expenses are fixed costs.

Required:

(a) In preparation for the next Board meeting of Parkside Manufacturing Ltd, calculate the:

    (i) budgeted cost of material per Delta

    (ii) budgeted variable cost per Delta of light, heat and power

    (iii) number of production employees assumed in the budget.

(b) Prepare a statement which compares the actual results of Parkside Manufacturing with the flexed budget and identify any variances.

Data

On receiving your flexible budget and variances, Judith Green tells you that:

- She does not understand why there is a need for the two types of budget, the one prepared by the previous management accountant and the flexed budget prepared by yourself.

- She does not know if it is necessary to investigate all variances.

- She is concerned that the original budgeted sales volume was so different from the actual sales volume and is considering the use of linear regression to improve sales forecasting of Deltas.

Required:

Judith Green asks you to write a brief report in preparation for the Board meeting. In your report you should:

(a) Briefly explain the different purposes of the two types of budget and explain which one should be used to compare with the actual results.

(b) Suggest THREE general factors that need to be taken into account in deciding whether or not to investigate variances.

(c) Briefly explain THREE limitations to the use of linear regression in sales forecasting.

10 Investigation of variances

10.1 Introduction

Variance analysis, if properly carried out, can be a useful cost-controlling and cost-saving tool. However, the traditional variance analysis seen so far is only a step towards the final goal of controlling and saving costs.

10.2 Generalised reasons for variances

The causes of variances can be classified under four headings:

- Planning errors
- Measurement errors
- Random factors
- Operational causes

Planning errors lead to the setting of inappropriate standards or budgets. This may be due to carelessness on the part of the standard setter (not taking account of known changes in the production process or expected price rises, for example) or due to unexpected external changes (a market shortage of a resource leading to increased price. These need to be isolated from hindsight information and a revision of the standard considered for future budgets.

Measurement errors include errors caused by inaccurate completion of timesheets or job cards, inaccurate measurement of quantities issued from stores, etc. The rectification of such errors or errors caused by random factors will probably not give rise to any cost savings (though this is a generalisation).

Random factors are by definition uncontrollable, although they need careful monitoring to ensure that they are not, in fact, one of the other types of variance.

10.3 Operational causes of variances

Examples of some specific reasons for individual variances are shown below.

Variance		Possible causes
Materials:	Price	Bulk discounts
		Different suppliers/Different materials
		Unexpected delivery costs
		Different buying procedures
	Usage	Different quality material
		Theft, obsolescence, deterioration
		Different quality of staff
		Different mix of material
		Different batch sizes and trim loss
Variance		*Possible causes*
Labour:	Rate	Different class of labour
		Excessive overtime
		Productivity bonuses
		National wage negotiations
		Union action
	Efficiency	Different levels of skill
		Different working conditions
		The learning effect
		Lack of supervision
		Works to rule
		Machine breakdowns
		Lack of material
		Lack of orders
		Strikes (if paid)
		Too long over coffee breaks
Overhead:	Price	Change in nature of overhead
		Unforeseen price changes
	Volume	Excessive idle time
		Increase in workforce

It will nearly always be useful to consult staff working in operational departments to resolve any queries in the data as they will have 'local' knowledge of the day-to-day operations.

Example 9

An adverse materials usage variance of £50,000 arose in a month as follows:

Standard cost per kg	£10
Actual cost per kg	£12
Units produced	2,000
Standard quantity per unit	25 kg
Actual quantity used	55,000 kg

	£
Standard cost of actual usage (55,000 kg × £10)	550,000
Standard cost of standard usage (2,000 × 25 kg × £10)	500,000
Adverse usage variance	50,000

On further investigation, the following is ascertained.

1   The actual quantity used was based on estimated inventory figures. A inventory count showed that 53,000 kg were in fact used.

2   3,000 kg is the best estimate for what might politely be called the monthly 'shrinkage' but, in less polite circles, theft.

3   2,000 kg of inventory was damaged by hoodlums who broke into the stores through some of the shaky panelling.

4   The supervisor feels that existing machinery is outmoded and more efficient machinery could save 1,000 kg a month.

Additional considerations

1   A security guard would cost £9,000 a year to employ and would stop 20% of all theft. Resultant dissatisfaction amongst works staff might cost £20,000 per annum.

2   Given the easy access to stores, vandals might be expected to break in every other month; £10,000 would make the stores vandal-proof.

3   New machinery would cost £720,000.

Analyse the usage variance in the light of this information and comment on your results.

Solution

The original £50,000 usage variance could be analysed as follows:

		Adverse/(favourable) variance £
(a)	Bad measurement (53,000 – 55,000) × £10	20,000
(b)	Theft (3,000 × £10)	30,000
(c)	Damage (2,000 × £10)	20,000
(d)	Obsolete machinery (1,000 × £10)	10,000
(e)	Other operational factors (balance)	(30,000)
		50,000

In each case, the variances should be studied and compared with the cost of rectification.

(a) **Bad measurement** – Assuming no costly decisions were made, or are likely to be made in the future, such as over-stocking, the component is of no future consequence.

(b) **Theft** – Annual cost due to theft is 12 × £30,000 or £360,000; 20% of this saved would amount to £72,000 at a cost of £9,000 + £20,000, thus the security guard is worth employing.

(c) **Damage** – Annual cost due to vandalism is 6 × £20,000 or £120,000; this would presumably be avoided by spending £10,000 now; again worthwhile.

(d) **Obsolete machinery** – Annual cost of using old machines is 12 × £10,000 or £120,000; the cost of making this saving (the saving would increase as purchase prices increased or if production increased) is £720,000; the decision over this investment would require further consideration such as discounted cash flow analysis.

(e) **Other factors** – We now see a favourable usage variance once all known factors above have been accounted for. This may need further investigation, particularly if it affects the quality of goods produced.

10.4 Fixed overhead variances

These are worth a special note, due to the particular nature of the fixed overhead volume variance.

We have seen that the volume variance is a product of the TAC system, and represents the adjustment for over-/under-absorption of fixed costs due to actual production being higher or lower than budgeted. Unlike the other variances, it does not actually represent a cost saving or overspend.

If this is the case, is it worth spending any time on the investigation of fixed overhead volume variances? Does it really matter if overheads are under-/over-absorbed, since it will all be adjusted for in the end?

The problem with having an inappropriate absorption rate is that decisions may have been taken on a unit cost that is too high or too low – for example, in setting the price of a product. If this is too high, sales may have been unnecessarily lost; if it is too low, profit margins may have been significantly eroded.

To minimise such effects of over-/under-absorption, regular reviews should be conducted of expenditure and activity levels arising throughout the period. The absorption rate can then be adjusted if it is felt necessary to reflect more recent estimates of expenditure and activity levels.

10.5 The cost of variance analysis

The provision of any information involves the costs of collecting the basic data, processing it, and reporting the results. Variance analysis is no exception and, as with other forms of management information, the benefits to which it gives rise must be commensurate with the costs incurred.

Benefits include:

(a) Variance analysis allows 'management by exception' and it is presumably for this purpose that a standard costing system has been introduced.

(b) When variances are known to exist, failure to make adequate investigations, even on a random basis, will weaken the control system and thus the motivation of managers.

(c) The amount of analysis required can sometimes be reduced by defining levels of significance below which detailed investigation is not required.

(d) The costs of clerical work can be over-estimated. In most working days there will be some spare capacity that can be utilised without extra cost.

What has to be considered, therefore, is the amount of detail that can be incorporated usefully in variance analysis. This will fall into two categories:

(a) **Including more detailed codings** in source documents indicating causes and responsibilities. Such coding is likely to involve people outside the accounts department, who may be unwilling to give time to the task. How useful the analysis will be, will depend on whether or not it is practicable to identify causes and responsibilities at the time the document is initiated.

(b) **Investigations and re-analysis of variances after the event**. This can involve the time of quite senior people, but the process of investigation may well be more useful from the point of view of the management of the business than any quantity of formal variance calculations.

Utilising variance information to improve budgeting practices means that budget planning and control has been used to create a cycle of **continuous improvement**. A continuous improvement culture will help ensure that the internal budget process is efficient and effective and remains relevant to the organisation's needs and priorities. Measuring budget accuracy (with variances) and timeliness on an ongoing basis and periodically conducting more formal reviews are two ways to identify areas for improvement.

11 Responsibility accounting and the interdependence of variances

11.1 Introduction

It is part of any system aimed at improving the performance of a business or any part of the business, that actions shall be traced to the person responsible. This may give the impression of 'laying the blame', but it is equally possible to award praise (and remunerate accordingly).

We have seen that responsibility accounting is a system which recognises various decision centres within a business and traces costs (and possibly revenues) to the individual managers who are primarily responsible for making decisions about the items in question.

Example 10

An opportunity arises for a buying department to obtain a consignment of a particular material at an exceptionally low price. The purchase is made; a favourable price variance is recorded and the buying department is duly praised.

Subsequently, when products are being manufactured using this type of material, significant adverse material usage variances and labour efficiency variances are recorded, and are initially regarded as the responsibility of the department where the work is done.

Is it fair to blame the adverse variances on the operational departments?

Solution

Investigations may reveal a number of relevant facts, for example:

- The 'cheap' material was of poor quality, and in consequence much of it was wasted in the process of machining. The resultant material usage and labour efficiency variances should presumably be regarded as the responsibility of the buying department, to offset the favourable price variance.

- Due to an employee leaving it had been necessary to use an operator who was not familiar with the job. At least part of the excess usage of materials could be attributed to this cause; but whether it should be regarded as the responsibility of the operating department or of the personnel department (for failing to recruit a replacement) is still open to question. If the employee who left had been highly paid, his removal might cause a favourable wage rate variance in the period under review – an offset to the adverse efficiency variance.

- The tools used had been badly worn, thus causing excessive time on the job. It would be necessary to consider whether this condition was attributable to the operating department (failing to sharpen tools or to requisition replacements) or to the tools store-keeper or to the buying department (for failing to buy on time or for buying poor quality items again).

The important points to bear in mind are as follows:

- Different types of variance can be inter-linked by a common cause.

- In many cases, the responsibility for variances cannot be identified merely by reference to the cost centre where the variance has been reported. Responsibility may be shared by several managers or may lie completely outside the cost centre in which the variance has arisen.

12 Exchange rates and price variances

12.1 Introduction

Material price variances are sometimes caused by movements of the exchange rate of a currency when the materials are imported from an overseas country.

The following table illustrates the effect on the Sterling price in the UK of good which is imported from the United States if the exchange rate of the pound and dollar changes:

Price of good in US	Exchange rate	Price of good in UK
$1	£1 = $1.50	$£\dfrac{1}{1.50} = £0.67$
$1	£1 = $2.00	$£\dfrac{1}{2.00} = £0.50$

The price of the good in the US does not change, but as the exchange rate changes, the UK price also changes.

Thus, when £1 = $1.50, the imported good costs £0.67. But when the pound strengthens against the dollar (so that you now buy $2 rather than $1.50 for every pound), the imported good becomes cheaper – it now only costs £0.50.

The dollar price of course remains the same. However, because £1 buys more dollars, UK importers get more for their money so that the UK price in pounds falls.

12.2 Price variances

How does this affect price variances?

The first thing to note is that it doesn't affect the total variance – that can still be calculated as before. However, a changing exchange rate does affect the way we can analyse and explain a price variance.

Consider the following example.

Example 11

D Ltd buys 2,000 kg of material for £2,000 in March 20X5. The standard cost of the material was set at £1.05 per kg when the standards were set in May 20X4. The material is imported from the US. The exchange rate has changed from £1 = $1.50 in May 20X4 to £1 = $1.65 in March 20X5.

(a) **Calculating the price variance using the traditional method.**

Amount that should have been paid for 2,000 kg = 2,000 × £1.05	=	£2,100
Amount actually paid	=	£2,000
		———
Price variance		£100 (F)
		———

(b) **Calculating the price variance taking account of the changed exchange rate.**

The person responsible for purchasing the materials may feel pleased if they are given credit for the £100 favourable variance.

However, things may not be as they seem.

Hence, we shall separate out the effect of the exchange rates. We do this by altering the standard cost in line with the exchange rate and calculating two price variances.

(i) a price variance caused by the exchange rate (sometimes referred to as a 'planning variance' because a factor outside the company control has caused the original standard to be wrong)

(ii) a price variance caused by the way the company actually bought the materials (sometimes called an 'operating variance' because it is caused by the normal operations of the company).

The relevant prices and variances can be set out as follows:

Original standard cost = 2,000 kg × £1.05 = £2,100 ⎫
⎬ £191 (F) (Planning)
Exchange rate adjusted = 2,000 kg × $\left[£1.05 \times \dfrac{1.50}{1.65} \right]$ = £1,909 ⎭⎫
⎬ £91 (A) (Operating)
Actual cost = 2,000 × £1.00 = £2,000 ⎭
Total variance £100 (F)

The total variance is still £100 (F) but this is due to a movement in the exchange rate. The company's operations have resulted in an unfavourable price variance of £91.

Test your understanding 3

Rivermede Ltd makes a single product called the Fasta. Last year, Steven Jones, the managing director of Rivermede Ltd, attended a course on budgetary control. As a result, he agreed to revise the way budgets were prepared in the company. Rather than imposing targets for managers, he encouraged participation by senior managers in the preparation of budgets.

An initial budget was prepared but Mike Fisher, the sales director, felt that the budgeted sales volume was set too high. He explained that setting too high a budgeted sales volume would mean his sales staff would be demotivated because they would not be able to achieve that sales volume. Steven Jones agreed to use the revised sales volume suggested by Mike Fisher.

Both the initial and revised budgets are reproduced below complete with the actual results for the year ended 31 May 20X3.

Rivermede Ltd – Budgeted and actual costs for the year ended 31 May 20X3

	Original budget	Revised budget	Actual results	Variances from revised budget
Fasta production and sales (units)	24,000	20,000	22,000	2,000 (F)
	£	£	£	£
Variable costs				
Material	216,000	180,000	206,800	26,800 (A)
Labour	288,000	240,000	255,200	15,200 (A)
Semi-variable costs				
Heat, light and power	31,000	27,000	33,400	6,400 (A)
Fixed costs				
Rent, rates and depreciation	40,000	40,000	38,000	2,000 (F)
	575,000	487,000	533,400	46,400 (A)

Assumptions in the two budgets

1   No change in input prices.

2   No change in the quantity of variable inputs per Fasta.

As the management accountant at Rivermede Ltd, one of your tasks is to check that invoices have been properly coded. On checking the actual invoices for heat, light and power for the year to 31 May 20X3, you find that one invoice for £7,520 had been incorrectly coded. The invoice should have been coded to materials.

Required:

(a)   Using the information in the original and revised budgets, identify:

- the variable cost of material and labour per Fasta

- the fixed and unit variable cost within heat, light and power.

(b)   Prepare a flexed budget, including variances, for Rivermede Ltd after correcting for the miscoding of the invoice.

Data

On receiving your flexed budget statement, Steven Jones states that the total adverse variance is much less than the £46,400 shown in the original statement. He also draws your attention to the actual sales volume being greater than in the revised budget. He believes these results show that a participative approach to budgeting is better for the company and wants to discuss this belief at the next board meeting. Before doing so, Steven Jones asks for your comments.

Required:

Write a memo to Steven Jones. Your memo should:

(a)   *Briefly* explain why the flexed budgeting variances differ from those in the original statement given.

(b)   Give TWO reasons why a favourable cost variance may have arisen other than through the introduction of participative budgeting.

(c)   Give TWO reasons why the actual sales volume compared with the revised budget's sales volume may not be a measure of improved motivation following the introduction of participative budgeting.

Test your understanding 4

You are an accounting technician employed by Telford plc. Telford has a subsidiary, Shifnal Ltd that makes one product, the Omega. Barry Jones, the Finance Director of Telford, has asked you to prepare a statement analysing the performance of Shifnal Ltd. He gives you a copy of the company's latest operating statement and tells you the assumptions made about costs when preparing the statement.

Shifnal Ltd: operating statement – 12 months ended 30 November 2003

	Budget	Actual
Number of Omegas produced and sold	120,000	95,000
	£000	£000
Revenue	4,800	3,990
Variable expenses		
Material A	480	456
Material B	840	665
Material C	360	266
Semi-variable expenses		
Light, heat and power	290	249
Water	212	182
Stepped expenses		
Labour	200	168
Maintenance	60	54
Fixed expenses		
Rent and rates	360	355
Distribution expenses	600	620
Administrative expenses	300	280
Operating profit	1,098	695

Assumptions made

- Budgeted semi-variable expenses

  - The variable cost of light, heat and power was £2.00 per Omega.

  - The fixed cost of water was £20,000 per year.

- Budgeted stepped expenses

  - For every £5,000 spent on labour, Shifnal could produce up to 3,000 Omegas.

  - For every £10,000 spent on maintenance, Shifnal could produce up to 20,000 Omegas.

- The budgeted selling price per Omega was the same throughout the year.

- There were no inventories of any kind.

Required:

(a) Calculate the budgeted selling price per Omega.

(b) Calculate the budgeted variable cost per Omega of:

(c) (i) material A

    (ii) material B

    (iii) material C.

(c) Calculate the:

    (i) budgeted fixed cost of light, heat and power

    (ii) budgeted variable cost of water per Omega.

(d) Prepare a statement showing Shifnal's actual results, the flexible budget and any variances.

Test your understanding 5

Excelsior Manufacturing Company

Excelsior Manufacturing Company produces a single product on an assembly line. As budget officer you have prepared the following production budgets from the best information available, to represent the extremes of high and low volume of production likely to be encountered by the company over a three month period.

	Production of 4,000 units £	Production of 8,000 units £
Direct materials	80,000	160,000
Indirect materials	12,000	20,000
Direct labour	50,000	100,000
Power	18,000	24,000
Repairs	20,000	30,000
Supervision	20,000	36,000
Rent, insurance and rates	9,000	9,000

Supervision is a 'step function'. One supervisor is employed for all production levels up to and including 5,000 units. For higher levels of production, an assistant supervisor (£16,000) is also required. For power, a minimum charge is payable on all production up to and including 6,000 units. For production above this level, there is an additional variable charge based on the power consumed.

Other variable and semi-variable costs are incurred evenly over the production range.

Required:

(a) Prepare a set of flexible budgets for presentation to the production manager to cover the following levels of production over a period of three months:

    (i)   4,000 units

    (ii)   5,000 units

    (iii) 6,000 units

    (iv) 7,000 units

    (v)   8,000 units

(b) During the three months July to September (covering most of the summer holiday period) 5,000 units were produced. Costs incurred during the three-month period were as follows:

	£
Direct materials	110,000
Indirect materials	14,000
Direct labour	70,000
Power	18,000
Repairs	30,000
Supervision	20,000
Rent, insurance and rates	8,000

Note that **price variances** have been eliminated from the figures for direct and indirect materials and **rate variances** have been eliminated from the labour and supervision costs.

Required:

You are preparing a budget report for presentation to the production manager. For each variance suggest any further investigations which might be required and any action which might be taken by the production manager.

 Test your understanding 6

WH Limited (AAT CA D94)

WH Limited uses a standard costing system which produces monthly control statements to manufacture product M, a perishable, high quality raw material which is carefully weighed by direct employees. Some wastage and quality control rejects occur at this stage. The employees then compress the material to change its shape and create product M.

All direct employees are paid a basic hourly rate appropriate to their individual skill level and a bonus scheme is in operation. Bonuses are paid according to the daily rate of output achieved by each individual.

A standard allowance for all of the above operational factors is included in the standard cost of product M. Standard cost data for one unit of product M is as follows:

		Standard cost £ per unit
Direct material X:	4.5 kg × £4.90 per kg	22.05
Direct labour:	10.3 hours × £3.50 per hour	36.05
		———
Standard direct cost		58.10
		———

During November, the following costs were incurred producing 400 units of product M.

		Actual costs £
Direct material X	2,100 kg	9,660
Direct labour	4,000 hours	16,000
Actual direct cost		25,660

Required:

(a) Calculate the following direct cost variances for product M for November:

   (i)   Direct material price

   (ii) Direct material usage

   (iii) Direct labour rate

   (iv) Direct labour efficiency

(b) Present the variances in a statement which reconciles the total standard direct cost of production with the actual direct cost for product M in November.

Task

As assistant accountant for WH Limited, you are asked to write a memo to the production manager which explains the following:

(a) the meaning of each of the direct cost variances calculated for product M

(b) two possible causes of each of the variances which you have calculated for product M for November

(c) two examples of interdependence which may be present in the variances which you have calculated for product M for November. Explain clearly why the variances may be interdependent, so that the manager can better understand the meaning of the finance director's statement.

Test your understanding 7

Revamp Furniture Limited

Revamp Furniture Limited manufacture a lounge chair by subjecting plasticised metal to a moulding process, thereby producing the chair in one piece.

(a) From the information provided below, you are required to analyse the cost variances and prepare a reconciliation of budgeted with actual cost incorporating the result of your analysis.

Standard/budget data

Unit variable costs:	
Direct material	6 kgs at 50p per kg
Direct labour	2 hours at 160p per hour
Budgeted fixed overhead for the year (240 working days)	£30,000
Budgeted production/sales for the year	60,000 chairs
Actual data for period 1	
Number of working days	20
Production/sales	5,200 chairs

Fixed overhead is absorbed on the basis of direct labour hours.

Direct material received and used:

Delivery No 1	12,000 kgs	Cost	£5,880
Delivery No 2	14,000 kgs	Cost	£6,790
Delivery No 3	6,000 kgs	Cost	£3,060
Direct labour hours worked	10,080	Cost	£17,540
Fixed overhead			£2,550

(b) 'Cost variances are often found, upon investigation of causes, to be interdependent.'

Briefly explain this statement using as illustrations:

(i) material price and usage variances

(ii) labour rate and efficiency variances

taken from your answer to (a) above and comment briefly on any possible interdependence between material cost variances and labour cost variances.

13 Using variances backwards

13.1 Introduction

So far, variance calculations have started with standard and actual costs given in the question and you have been required to calculate the variances.

The assessor may also set questions where the question will, for example, give the standard and the variance and ask you to calculate the actual.

Example 12

A Ltd purchases 1,000 kg of material at a cost of £550.

The adverse material price variance is £50. What was the standard cost of 1 kg of material?

Solution

	£
Actual cost of 1,000 kg	550
Adverse variance	(50) (A)
Therefore, standard cost of 1,000 kg	500
Therefore, standard cost of 1 kg	0.50

Example 13

Alternatively, you could be given data on the standard cost and variance and be asked to calculate the actual cost paid.

For example, B Ltd purchases 200 litres of oil which should have cost £1 per litre at standard. The adverse material price variance is £0.10 per litre. Calculate the actual cost of the 200 litres purchased.

Solution

	£
200 litres should have cost 200 × £1	200
Price variance = 200 × £0.10	20 (A)
Therefore, 200 litres did cost	£220

Example 14

An added complication could involve a change in inventory, for example.

C Ltd produces 600 widgets in March.

The standard cost card for a widget shows the following:

	Standard cost per unit £
Material – 3 kg at £2 per kg	6.00

There was no materials usage variance.

There was no opening inventory but closing inventory of material was 200 kg.

There was a £200 adverse price variance.

Calculate the actual amount paid for materials purchased in March.

Solution

	Kg
Standard amount of material used (600 × 3 kg)	1,800
No usage variance, therefore actual amount used	1,800
Closing inventory	200
Total purchased	2,000

	£
Standard cost of purchases 2,000 × £2	4,000
Price variance	200 (A)
Actual cost	4,200

14 Summary

Much of cost accounting is about gathering information about current costs and making predictions about future costs. Some costs, direct costs, can be allocated directly to a cost unit whereas other costs, indirect costs or overheads, are allocated initially to a cost centre.

Costs can also be usefully classified according to their behaviour. This is particularly useful when budgeting costs for future periods or for making decisions about activity levels. Costs can be classified as variable, fixed, stepped or semi-variable.

For semi-variable costs the fixed element and the variable element will need to be identified for forecasting purposes. This can be done using the high/low method.

In this chapter we have examined ways of measuring the significance of variances and the way in which management might introduce controls based on the variance reports provided to them. The investigation of variances is a part of this process and it is important that you understand the causes of variances and their typical remedies.

We then considered briefly responsibility accounting and the possible interaction of variances. This is a very important area in the context of management appraisal. As we have seen, purchasing of cheap materials may cause a knock-on effect into the working of those materials thereby giving the impression that the workforce (and by implication the managers of the workforce) are inefficient. This will not be the case as the problems are caused by poor purchasing of materials rather than inefficient labour.

Test your understanding answers

Test your understanding 1

(a) Revised budgeted selling price:
(£1,760,000/11,000) **£160**

(b) Material cost per unit in revised budget:
(£396,000/11,000) **£36**

(c) Variable cost of production and administrative labour – high/low method:

Increase in budgeted labour cost (£630,000 – £580,000)	£50,000
Increase in budgeted volume (11,000 – 10,000)	1,000
Variable cost of labour per unit (£50,000/1,000)	£50

(d) Fixed cost of production and administrative labour:

Total budgeted cost of labour for 11,000 units	£630,000
Variable cost of labour (11,000 × £50)	£550,000
	———————
Budgeted fixed cost of labour	£80,000
	———————

(e) Variable cost of light, heat and power – high/low method:

Increase in budgeted light, heat and power (£164,000 – £160,000)	£4,000
Increase in budgeted volume	1,000
Budgeted variable cost of light, heat and power per unit (£4,000/1,000)	£4

(f) Fixed cost of light, heat and power:

Total budgeted cost of light, heat and power for 11,000 units	£164,000
Variable cost of light, heat and power (11,000 × £4)	£44,000
	———————
Budgeted fixed cost of light, heat and power	£120,000
	———————

MEMO

To: Mike Green

From: Management Accountant

Date: 22 June 20X0

Subject: Motivation and performance

I attach a budgetary control statement for Visiguard based on the flexible budget technique and wish to make the following observations.

(a) **Visiguard Ltd – Flexible budgetary control statement for the year ended 31 May 20X0**

	Flexed budget	Actual results	Variances
Sales and production volume (units)	11,600	11,600	Nil
	£	£	£
Revenue (£160 × 11,600)	1,856,000	1,844,400	11,600 (A)
Variable materials (£36 × 11,600)	417,600	440,800	23,200 (A)
Production and administrative labour (£80,000 + [£50 × 11,600])	660,000	677,600	17,600 (A)
Light, heat and power 120,000 + [4 × 11,600]	166,400	136,400	30,000 (F)
Fixed overheads	240,000	259,600	19,600 (A)
Profit	372,000	330,000	42,000 (A)

(b) There is an assumption that a participative approach to budgets and budgetary control will improve management motivation and results. However, there are a number of situations where imposed budgets may be more effective than participative budgets. These include:

- Managers' objectives may not be those of the organisation as a whole.

- Managers do not have the training, skill or technical knowledge to set budgets.

- Managers would prefer not to set their own targets.

- Time constraint whereby full participation is not practicable.

(c) Setting of budgetary targets that are not achievable can be demotivating. If managers recognise this they are likely not even to attempt to achieve the target. Impossible targets can also bring into disrepute the whole planning process; and managers may question the validity and usefulness of the budgetary process.

This might have been the case in terms of the request to reduce material costs. If Visiguard do not have an alternative supplier, the managers may have little control over material prices.

(d) It does not always follow that improved performance compared to the original budget is because managers were motivated by the budget revision.

- Actual activity was greater than the agreed revision. This may have been due to the increased energy and motivation of managers. However, there may have been, outside the control of managers, a general increase in demand for the product.

- The only cost less than planned in the budget is light, heat and power. This may have been an inaccurate forecast or because weather conditions have been milder, thus reducing heating costs. It is unlikely that the power supplier has reduced costs.

Test your understanding 2

(a) **Budgeted data**

(i) Budgeted cost of material per unit of Delta:

£600,000/100,000 Deltas   =   £6.00

(ii) Budgeted variable cost of light, heat and power per Delta:

(£200,000 – £40,000)/100,000   =   £1.60

(iii) Number of budgeted production employees:

£120,000/£12,000   =   10 employees

(b) **Flexible budgetary control statement for the year ended 30 November 20X0**

	Flexible budget	Actual results	Variance
Volume (number of Deltas)	125,000	125,000	Nil
	£000	£000	£000
Revenue (@ £20)	2,500	2,250	250 (A)
Material (W1)	750	800	50 (A)
Light, heat and power (W2)	240	265	25 (A)
Production labour (W3)	156	156	0
Rent, rates and depreciation	140	175	35 (A)
Administrative expenses	110	110	0
Profit	1,104	744	360 (A)

Key:
A = Adverse
F = Favourable

Workings for flexed budget

(W1) Material   125,000 units × £6.00 = £750,000

(W2) Light, heat and power   £40,000 + (125,000 × £1.60) = £240,000

(W3) Labour   13 employees × £12,000 = £156,000

REPORT
THE ROLE OF BUDGETS, FORECASTING AND VARIANCES AT PARKSIDE MANUFACTURING LTD

To: Judith Green
Prepared by: Management Accountant
Date: X-X-XX Introduction

The purpose of this report is to provide a background and prior briefing on planning to be discussed at the Board meeting.

(a) **Budgets used at Parkside**

There are two types of budget used in the company. A fixed budget is one which is essentially a planning device and sets a target to which management are in the short-run committed. A flexible budget, however, is a control device. It is principally a revision of the original plan, whereby allowances are given for both cost and revenue, to match the level of activity actually achieved.

This enables a 'like with like' comparison to be made – the flexed budget v the actual results.

From this comparison meaningful variances can be reported, on which a measure of control can focus.

(b) Factors to take into account before investigating variances

It is not practicable to investigate all variances. Because of this, exception techniques are used by applying both a minimum absolute value and a minimum percentage variance before investigation is recommended.

A variance may be investigated if it is an element of a continuing trend.

Variances would not be investigated if the cause is a factor, of which management are aware. It is also not worth investigating variances if they are not controllable, e.g. insurances.

It is essential that the benefits of investigation, at all times, outweigh the cost.

(c) Limitations of linear regression techniques

- Assumption of linearity whereas sales volume might not follow that pattern.

- Use of historical data; past performance is not always a good guide to the future.

- Does not account for the effects of a product life cycle.

Test your understanding 3

(a) Calculation of unit variable costs – high/low method

	High original budget	Low revised budget	Range	Variable unit cost
Fasta units	24,000	20,000	4,000	
Variable costs	£	£	£	
Material	216,000	180,000	36,000	£9
Labour	288,000	240,000	48,000	£12
Semi-variable costs				
Heat, light and power	31,000	27,000	£4,000	£1

Analysis of heat, light and power

Variable cost (£1/unit)	£24,000	£20,000
Total cost	£31,000	£27,000
Fixed cost	£7,000	£7,000

(b)   **Rivermede Ltd**

Flexible budgetary control statement for the year ended 31 May 20X3

	Flexed budget	Actual results	Adjustment	Revised actual	Variance
Production and sales (units)	22,000	22,000		22,000	
	£	£	£	£	£
Variable costs					
Material (W1)	198,000	206,800	7,520	214,320	16,320 (A)
Labour (W2)	264,000	255,200		255,200	8,800 (F)
Semi-variable costs					
Heat, light and power (W3)	29,000	33,400	(7,520)	25,880	3,120 (F)
Fixed costs					
Rent, rates and depreciation	40,000	38,000		38,000	2,000 (F)
	531,000	533,400		533,400	2,400 (A)

Workings for flexed budget:

(W1) Material	22,000 × £9
(W2) Labour	22,000 × £12
(W3) Heat, light and power	(22,000 × £1) + £7,000

MEMO

To: Steven Jones

From: Management Accountant

Date: 16 June 20X3

Subject: Flexible budgetary control

(a)   The original operating statement compares an actual level of activity of 22,000 units with a revised forecast of 20,000 units. This is not a 'like with like' comparison and is of little use for management control purposes.

The flexible budget, however, informs on a 'like with like' comparison by giving an allowance for costs and revenue in relation to the actual level of activity achieved. The variances reported are therefore smaller and also are more meaningful. The reduction in these variances is not attributable to participative budgeting.

(b) There are a number of reasons why favourable cost variances may arise other than with the introduction of participative budgeting.

- A favourable variance may arise for a reason outside management's span of control.

  The variance on fixed expenditure relates to rent, rates and depreciation which are costs that are not controllable.

  A further example is that the fixed charge for heat, light and power may be different from planned.

- Managers may have deliberately inflated costs in the budget to improve their reported performance and potentially increase any performance related rewards payable.

(c) Similar reasons could be argued for the increase in sales volume.

- There could have been a general increase in demand without extra sales effort.

- The revision to the budget may have been too low. This may have been a genuine concern that the original target was not achievable. However, it may have been intentional, since by understating forecast demand, the actual performance looks better.

We should continue with participative budgeting but based on the flexible budgetary control technique.

📝 Test your understanding 4

(a)	**Budgeted unit selling price:** £4,800,000/120,000		£40.00
(b)	**Budgeted variable cost of material**		
	(i)	**A:** £480,000/120,000	£4.00
	(ii)	**B:** £840,000/120,000	£7.00
	(iii)	**C:** £360,000/120,000	£3.00
(c)	(i)	**Budgeted fixed cost of light, heat and power**	
		Total budgeted cost	£290,000
		Variable cost: £2 × 120,000	£240,000
			£50,000

(ii) Budgeted variable cost of water

Budgeted total cost	£212,000
Budgeted fixed cost	£20,000
Total variable cost	£192,000
Unit variable cost (£192,000/120,000)	£1.60

(d) **Shifnal Ltd: Flexible budget statement year ended 30 November 20X3**

Omegas produced and sold	Flexed budget 95,000	Actual 95,000	Variance	
	£000	£000	£000	
Revenue (95,000 × £40)	3,800	3,990	190	(F)
Material A (95,000 × £4)	380	456	76	(A)
Material B (95,000 × £7)	665	665	–	(A)
Material C (95,000 × £3)	285	266	19	(F)
Light, heat and power (W1)	240	249	9	(A)
Water (W2)	172	182	10	(A)
Labour (W3)	160	168	8	(A)
Maintenance (W4)	50	54	4	(A)
Rent and rates	360	355	5	(F)
Distribution expenses	600	620	20	(A)
Administrative expenses	300	280	20	(F)
Operating profit	588	695	107	(F)

Workings

(W1) £50,000 + (£2.00 × 95,000) = £240,000

(W2) £20,000 + (£1.60 × 95,000) = £172,000

(W3) Up to 3,000 units cost £5,000 of labour

95,000 units require $\frac{95,000}{3,000}$ = 31.67 'groups' of labour 3,000

This is rounded to 32 as it is a stepped cost and you cannot employ part of a 'group'. Cost of labour = 32 × £5,000 = £160,000

(W4) 95,000/20,000 = 4.75. Round up, therefore cost is 5 × £10,000 = £50,000

Test your understanding 5

Excelsior Manufacturing Company

(a)

	Production level (units)				
	4,000	5,000	6,000	7,000	8,000
	£	£	£	£	£
Direct materials (W1)	80,000	100,000	120,000	140,000	160,000
Indirect materials (W2)	12,000	14,000	16,000	18,000	20,000
Direct labour (W3)	50,000	62,500	75,000	87,500	100,000
Power (W4)	18,000	18,000	18,000	21,000	24,000
Repairs (W5)	20,000	22,500	25,000	27,500	30,000
Supervision (W6)	20,000	20,000	36,000	36,000	36,000
Rent, insurance and rates	9,000	9,000	9,000	9,000	9,000
Total cost	209,000	246,000	299,000	339,000	379,000

Workings:

(W1) **Direct materials**

£80,000/4,000 units = £20 per unit

So at 5,000 units for example £20 × 5,000 = £100,000

(W2) **Indirect materials**

At 4,000 units the cost is £12,000 or £3 per unit but at 8,000 units the cost is £20,000 or £2.5 per unit. Since the costs are not rising linearly, the cost must be semi-variable.

For semi-variable costs use the high low method

Increase in cost (£20,000 – £12,000) = £8,000

Increase in volume (8,000 – 4,000) = 4,000

Cost per unit – £8,000/4,000 = £2

Fixed element at 4000 units = £12,000 – (4,000 × £2) = £4,000

So at 5,000 units for example £4,000 + (5,000 × £2) = £14,000

(W3) **Direct labour**

£50,000/4,000 units = £12.50 per unit

So at 5,000 units for example £12.50 × 5,000 = £62,500

(W4) Power

Minimum charge payable up to 6,000 units, therefore minimum charge is £18,000

At 8,000 units cost is £24,000, an increase of £6,000 for 2,000 units over minimum level or £6,000/2,000 = £3 per unit

So at 7,000 units for example £18,000 + £3 × (7,000 – 6,000) = £21,000

(W5) Repairs

At 4,000 units the cost is £20,000 or £5 per unit but at 8,000 units the cost is £30,000 or £3.75 per unit. Since the costs are not rising linearly, the cost must be semi-variable.

For semi-variable costs use the high low method

Increase in cost (£30,000 – £20,000) = £10,000

Increase in volume (8,000 – 4,000) = 4,000

Cost per unit – £10,000/4,000 = £2.50

Fixed element at 4000 units = £20,000 – (4,000 × £2.5) = £10,000

So at 5,000 units for example £10,000 + (5,000 × £2.5) = £22,500

(W6) Supervision

A stepped fixed cost, for 6,000 units and above cost is £20,000 = £16,000 = £36,000

(b)

	Budget £	Actual £	Variance £
Direct materials	100,000	110,000	10,000 (A)
Indirect materials	14,000	14,000	–
Direct labour	62,500	70,000	7,500 (A)
Power	18,000	18,000	–
Repairs	22,500	30,000	7,500 (A)
Supervision	20,000	20,000	–
Rent, insurance and rates	9,000	8,000	1,000 (F)
Total cost	246,000	270,000	24,000 (A)

Comments on variances

- Direct materials: more was used than expected. Possibly waste in production, poor quality materials, operatives need more training. Is a particular department or machine at fault?

- Direct labour: again more was used than expected. Investigate reasons. Excessive overtime (should not be needed at a low level of production)?

- Repairs: needs investigation. Possible exceptional item. Do some pieces of capital equipment need replacing?

- Rent, insurance and rates: this is probably a price variance. Is this a one-off item or does the budget need to be altered in future?

Test your understanding 6

WH Limited

(a) **Calculation of direct cost variances**

Direct materials price variance

	kg	£	
Actual materials purchased, at actual price	2,100	9,660	
Actual materials purchased, at standard price per kg (£4.90)	2,100	10,290	
Materials price variance		630	F

Direct materials usage variance

	kg	£	
Actual materials used, at standard price	2,100	10,290	
Standard materials allowed for production achieved at standard price (400 × 4.5 kg)	1,800	8,820	
Materials usage variance		1,470	A

Direct labour rate variance

	hr	£	
Actual hours paid, at actual rate per hour	4,000	16,000	
Actual hours paid, at standard rate per hour (£3.50)	4,000	14,000	
Direct labour rate variance		2,000	A

Direct labour efficiency variance

	hr	£	
Actual hours paid, at standard rate	4,000	14,000	
Standard hours allowed for production achieved at standard rate (400 × 10.3 hr)	4,120	14,420	
Direct labour efficiency variance		420	F

(b) **Reconciliation statement**

		Adverse £	Favourable £	£
Total budgeted cost (400 × £58.10)				23,240
Cost variances				
Materials	Price		630	
	Usage	1,470		
Labour	Rate	2,000		
	Efficiency		420	
Total net variances		3,470	1,050	2,420
Total actual cost				25,660

Task (a) – (c)

WH Limited

MEMORANDUM

To: Production Manager

From: Assistant Accountant

Date: 12 December 20X4

Subject: Direct cost variances for November

As requested I detail below explanations of the direct cost variances and possible suggestions as to their cause in November. Page 1 of 3

(a) **The meaning of the variances**

Direct material price variance

This variance shows the saving or overspending which resulted from paying a lower or higher price than standard for the direct material used in the period. The favourable variance indicates that a lower than standard price was paid.

Direct material usage variance

This variance shows the saving or overspending, at standard prices, which resulted from using less or more material than standard to manufacture the production for the period. The adverse variance indicates that more material was used than standard.

Direct labour rate variance

This variance shows the saving or overspending which resulted from paying a lower or higher hourly rate than standard for the hours worked in the period. The adverse variance indicates that a higher than standard hourly rate was paid.

Direct labour efficiency variance

This variance shows the saving or overspending, at standard rates, which resulted from working less or more hours than standard to manufacture the production for the period. The favourable variance indicates that less hours were worked than standard.

(b) **Possible causes of the variances**

Favourable direct material price variance

Bulk discounts were received which were not allowed for in the standard. The standard price of material was set too high. A lower quality material was purchased, at a lower price than standard. Effective negotiations by the buyer secured a price lower than the standard.

Adverse direct material usage variance

Material wastage was higher than allowed in the standard. The standard usage was set too low. There was a higher than standard level of rejects. Theft of material.

Adverse direct labour rate variance

High levels of overtime were paid for compared with the standard allowance. The standard wage rate was set too low.

A higher grade of labour was used.

Bonus payments were higher than standard.

Favourable direct labour efficiency variance

Employees were working faster than standard. More skilled employees were used.

There were savings through the learning effect.

The standard labour time was set too high.

The material was easy to process, leading to savings against the standard time.

(c)   Two examples of interdependence, where one variance can be related to others, could include the following.

The savings made on material price (favourable material price variance) may indicate that poor quality material was purchased, leading to high wastage, rejects and an adverse usage variance.

Bulk discounts may have resulted in the saving on material price. However, the consequent excessive stocks may have led to deterioration and write-offs, hence the adverse usage variance.

Direct workers may have been of a higher grade than standard, resulting in higher hourly rates and the adverse rate variance. However, the higher skill level may have led to time savings and the favourable efficiency variance.

Higher than standard bonus payments may have caused the adverse labour rate variance, but the bonuses may have resulted from faster working and hence the favourable efficiency variance.

Faster working resulted in the favourable efficiency variance, but less care may have been taken over weighing and handling the material, hence the adverse material usage variance.

Test your understanding 7

Revamp Furniture Limited

(a) **Reconciliation for Period 1 (see workings)**

	£	£	£
Flexed budgeted cost (W1)			34,840
Cost variances			
Materials (W2)			
Price	270		
Usage		400	
Labour (W3)			
Rate of pay		1,412	
Efficiency	512		
Fixed overhead (W4)			
Expenditure		50	
Efficiency	80		
Capacity	20		
	882	1,862	980
Actual cost (W5)			35,820

(b) (i) Although standard costing has, as one of its purposes, the allocation of responsibility for cost variances, it is often found in practice that the analysis of variances is merely the beginning of a further task of investigation before ultimate responsibility can be fairly assigned.

On the operating statement submitted for part (a) of this question there is disclosed a favourable material price variance and an adverse usage variance. Theoretically this should indicate that the buyer is operating efficiently and the production manager inefficiently. This need not necessarily be true, however. The buyer could have taken advantage of a special offer of material at less than standard price, not appreciating that the material was slightly below standard quality. It is very likely that the inferior material would give rise to production problems of machining, handling and possibly others which could well result in excess usage; hence the adverse usage variance.

(ii)   As regards labour, the payment of higher than standard rates (suggested by the adverse rate of pay variance in the operating statement) may well have had the effect of providing greater motivation, and hence speedier work, which is reflected in the favourable efficiency variance.

There may well be interdependence between the material and labour cost variances; for instance, the speedier work suggested by the favourable labour efficiency variance may have been accomplished by disregarding material usage standards.

From the foregoing it will be seen that not only is there possible interdependence between the variances of each element of cost, but also cross-interdependence between the elements of cost.

Workings

(W1) Standard cost per unit

	£
Materials (6 × 50p)	3.00
Labour (2 × £1.60)	3.20
Fixed overhead $\dfrac{£30,000}{120,000\,(*)}$ = 25p per hour × 2 hours	0.50
	6.70

Flexed budgeted cost 5,200 × £6.70   £34,840

(*) Fixed overhead is budgeted to be absorbed over (60,000 × 2 hours) = 120,000 hours

(W2) Materials

(i)   **Direct materials price variance**

	kg	£
Actual materials purchased, at actual price (5,880 + 6,790 + 3,060)	32,000	15,730
Actual materials purchased, at standard price per kg (50p)	32,000	16,000
Materials price variance		270 F

(ii) Direct materials usage variance

	kg	£
Actual materials used, at standard price	32,000	16,000
Standard materials allowed for production achieved at standard price (5,200 × 6 kg)	31,200	15,600
Materials usage variance		400 A

(W3) Labour

(i) Direct labour rate variance

	hr	£
Actual hours paid, at actual rate per hour	10,080	17,540
Actual hours paid, at standard rate per hour (£1.6)	10,080	16,128
Direct labour rate variance		1,412 A

(ii) Direct labour efficiency variance

	hr	£
Actual hours paid, at standard rate	10,080	16,128
Standard hours allowed for production achieved at standard rate (5,200 × 2 hr)	10,400	16,640
Direct labour efficiency variance		512 F

(W4) Fixed overhead

(i) Fixed overhead expenditure (price) variance

	£
Actual fixed overhead cost	2,550
Budgeted fixed overhead cost	2,500
Fixed overhead expenditure variance	50 A

(ii) **Fixed overhead efficiency variance**

	hr	£	
Standard hours allowed for actual production achieved	10,400		
Actual hours worked for actual production	10,080		
Efficiency variance @ 25p per hour	320	80	F

(iii) **Fixed overhead capacity variance**

	hr	£	
Actual hours worked	10,080		
Budgeted hours for the period (60,000 chairs/240 days × 20 days × 2 hours)	10,000		
Capacity variance @ 25p per hour	80	20	F

(W5) **Actual cost statement**

	£
Materials (5,880 + 6,790 + 3,060)	15,730
Labour	17,540
Fixed overhead	2,550
	35,820

Preparing budgets – the decision making phase

Introduction

Cost variances, covered earlier, give one type of performance indicator – how individual operational managers perform against pre-set budget and standard cost targets. Here we continue this theme, but look at measures for productivity, efficiency, ratios that assist in assessment of resource utilisation, and overall profitability measures that may be applied to operating divisions and the business as a whole. We also look at the particular performance evaluation aspects of service industries, in particular the measurement of quality of service. The objective will always be to highlight activities, processes, products and business units that need some attention in order to enhance their value to the business.

ASSESSMENT CRITERIA

- Recommend appropriate measures to support budgetary control (Element 3.4)
- Effectively present budgetary issues to management (Element 4.4)

CONTENTS

1 Types of performance indicator

1.1 Introduction

Performance indicators may be categorised as financial or physical measures.

1.2 Financial performance indicators

Financial measures are expressed in numerical terms which include the following:

(a) average selling price

(b) profit percentage of sales revenue

(c) material cost per unit of purchase

(d) labour rate per hour

(e) cost per unit of production

(f) sales and cost variances.

1.3 Physical performance indicators

Physical performance indicators usually relate to production outcomes, productivity and production efficiency. Examples relevant to business and managerial performance would include the following:

(a) **Quality** indicators, such as reject rates.

(b) **Efficiency** indicators such as the number of products made per labour hour or idle time ratios.

(c) **Capacity** measures such as machine utilisation (or asset utilisation) ratios.

1.4 Efficiency and effectiveness

Performance indicators can be used to measure the efficiency and effectiveness of organisations.

 Definition

Efficiency can be defined as the relationship between inputs and outputs achieved. The fewer the inputs used by an organisation to achieve any given output, the more efficient is that organisation. In commercial organisations, efficiency is usually measured in terms of profitability, often in relation to assets employed.

Effectiveness is the degree to which an objective or target is met.

2 Ratio analysis

2.1 Introduction

Ratio analysis is one of the main tools utilised in appraising the performance of a company, the main advantage being that the magnitude of the individual figures is eliminated, allowing the appraiser to concentrate on relative movements.

Ratio analysis is generally utilised in two ways as follows:

(a) comparison of performance year to year

(b) comparison with other companies.

The techniques covered here occur in many branches of accountancy and it is important that you can calculate and interpret appropriate ratios.

2.2 Types of ratios

The main types of ratio used are:

(a) profitability ratios

(b) liquidity ratios

(c) gearing ratios

(d) investment ratios.

Of these, profitability and liquidity ratios are of the greatest significance to the management accountant and it is those we shall examine in more detail.

Example 1

In order to illustrate the most common ratios, let's look at some calculations based on the summarised accounts of Knotty plc. The information from Knotty plc's financial statements will be used in the following sections.

Income statement for the year ended 31 July 20X9

	Notes	20X9	20X9	20X8	20X8
		£000	£000	£000	£000
Revenue			37,589		30,209
Cost of sales			(28,380)		(22,808)
Gross profit			9,209		7,401
Distribution costs		(3,755)		(3,098)	
Administrative expenses		(2,291)		(2,030)	
			(6,046)		(5,128)
			3,163		2,273
Other operating income			108		0,279
Operating profit			3,271		2,552
Interest receivable			7		28
			3,278		2,580
Finance costs			(442)		(471)
Profit on ordinary activities before taxation			2,836		2,109
Tax on profit on ordinary activities			(1,038)		(650)
Profit on ordinary activities after taxation			1,798		1,459
Preference dividend			(6)		(6)
			1,792		1,453
Ordinary dividends			(606)		(441)
Retained profit for the year			1,186		1,012

Balance sheet as at 31 July 20X9

	Notes	20X9		20X8	
		£000	£000	£000	£000
Non-current assets					
Tangible assets			8,687		5,669
Investments			15		15
			8,702		5,684
Current assets					
Inventories		8,486		6,519	
Receivables	1	8,836		6,261	
Cash at bank and in hand		479		250	
		17,801		13,030	
Current liabilities					
Bank loans and overdrafts		(929)		(511)	
Other amounts falling due within one year		(9,178)		(6,645)	
		(10,107)		(7,156)	
Net current assets			7,694		5,874
Total assets less current liabilities			16,396		11,558
Non-current liabilities					
Debentures			(2,840)		(2,853)
Net assets			13,556		8,705

Capital and reserves			
Called up share capital			
Ordinary shares of 20p each	2	2,003	1,762
4.2% cumulative preference shares of £1 each		150	150
		2,153	1,912
Share premium account		123	123
Other reserves		2,576	–
Income statement		8,704	6,670
		13,556	8,705

Notes

1   Receivables at 31 July 20X9 include trade receivables of £8,233,000 (20X8 £5,735,000).

2   The number of ordinary shares in issue at 31 July 20X9 was 10,014,514 (20X8 8,808,214).

3 Profitability

3.1 Return on capital employed (ROCE)

Return on capital employed (ROCE) expresses profit as a percentage of the assets in use (the capital employed in the business) and can be further subdivided into profit margin and asset turnover (use of assets):

Profit margin   × Asset turnover   = Return on capital employed (ROCE)

$$\frac{\text{Profit}}{\text{Turnover}} \times \frac{\text{Turnover}}{\text{Assets}} = \frac{\text{Profit}}{\text{Assets}}$$

The equation helps to demonstrate how management can influence the rate of return on capital employed:

(a)   By increasing profit margins:

(i)   increase sales prices

(ii)   reduce costs.

(b)   By increasing asset turnover (use of assets):

(i)   increase sales

(ii)   reduce assets (capital employed).

3.2 Year-end or average capital employed

Ideally, the profits for the year ended 31 July 20X9 should be related to the assets in use throughout the year (the average capital employed). In practice, the ratio is usually computed using the assets at the year-end (the year-end capital employed). Using year-end figures of capital employed can distort trends and inter-company comparison; if new investment has been undertaken near to the year-end and financed (for example) by the issue of new shares, the capital employed will have risen by the total finance raised, whereas the profits will only have a month or two of the new investment's contribution.

A range of different acceptable measures of the assets in use is available; the matter of principle should be that the profit figure which is related to the capital employed should include all types of return on those assets.

Solution

For Knotty plc, a suitable calculation would be as follows.

	20X9	20X8
	£000	£000
Capital and reserves	13,556	8,705
Add: Debentures	2,840	2,853
Year-end capital employed	16,396	11,558

	20X9	20X8
	£000	£000
Operating profit	3,271	2,552
Interest receivable	7	28
Profit before finance costs and tax	3,278	2,580

So the return on capital employed is calculated as:

$$\frac{\text{Profit before interest and tax}}{\text{Capital and reserves and long-term debt}} \times 100\%$$

20X9 $\quad \dfrac{3,278}{16,396} \times 100 = 20.0\%$

20X8 $\quad \dfrac{2,580}{11,558} \times 100 = 22.3\%$

The capital employed figure includes the long-term debt, the debentures. Therefore, the profit used must be that available to these providers of capital, the profit before finance costs.

The rate of return on year-end capital employed has fallen in 20X9 compared with 20X8 and might indicate less effective management. To comment further, we need to sub-analyse the ratio into profit margin and asset turnover.

3.3 Profit margin

If the profitability ratios are to interlock perfectly, the profit margin will be calculated expressing the same profit before finance costs and tax as a percentage of revenue:

$$\frac{\text{Profit before interest and tax}}{\text{Turnover}} \times 100\%$$

A small problem with the approach in this example is that the profit includes interest receivable which is not represented in revenue; however, as the amount is small, this can be ignored.

In order that the profit can be related more fairly to revenue, profit margin is sometimes calculated using operating profit.

Solution

For Knotty plc: 20X9 $\dfrac{3,278}{37,589} \times 100 = 8.7\%$

20X8 $\dfrac{2,580}{30,209} \times 100 = 8.5\%$

Profit margins have improved slightly over the last year, possibly due to better cost control.

Sectors which have traditionally generated relatively high margins include publishing, electronics manufacturing, distillers and brewers, whereas food retailing and motor vehicle distribution are examples of low margin businesses.

Low margins within a sector may arise from a policy designed to increase market share by cutting selling prices, or may be due to high development costs associated with new products, both of which may be positive factors for the future. However, low margins are often associated with inefficiency and poor quality management.

Conversely, high margins relative to competitors, or improving margins, are usually taken as indicators of efficiency and good management. High margins achieved by dominating a particular market may, however, attract competitors into that market and imply lower margins in the longer term.

3.4 Asset turnover

Another aspect of efficient management is to 'make the assets work'. This may involve disposing of those 'underperforming' assets which cannot be made to generate sales, as well as developing and marketing the company's products or services.

> **Solution**
>
> Once again, the simplest method of computing the ratio is to relate revenue to the same figure of year-end capital employed used in calculating return on capital employed:
>
> $$\text{Asset turnover} = \frac{\text{Turnover}}{\text{Capital employed}}$$
>
> 20X9 $\dfrac{37,589}{16,396}$ = 2.3 times   20X8 $\dfrac{30,209}{11,558}$ = 2.6 times

However, as with profit margins, certain assets represented by capital employed have no revenue implications. One method of avoiding this illogicality is to exclude long and short-term investments from capital employed. For companies with substantial investments this will make a considerable difference.

Asset turnover will tend to be lower in capital-intensive manufacturing industries, which carry substantial tangible non-current assets, inventories and trade receivables, than in service industries where the principal resource is people rather than plant and machinery, and where inventories are low.

There are often trade-offs between asset turnover and profit margins in different sectors. For example, food retailers have relatively low profit margins compared to electronic equipment manufacturers, but asset turnover is higher. Typical numbers might be:

	Profit margin %	×	Asset turnover	=	ROCE %
Food retailer	3.7	×	6.7	=	24.8
Electronic equipment manufacturer	10.3	×	2.3	=	23.7

3.5 Gross profit margin

The profit margin given above used a profit figure that included non-productive overheads and sundry items of income. The gross profit margin looks at the profitability of the pure trading activities of the business:

$$\frac{\text{Gross profit}}{\text{Turnover}} \times 100\%$$

Solution

For Knotty plc: 20X9 $\frac{9,209}{37,589} \times 100 = 24.5\%$

20X8 $\frac{7,401}{30,209} \times 100 = 24.5\%$

The company has maintained its gross profit margin; thus the slight rise in net profit margin must be due to overhead costs being better controlled.

4 Liquidity

4.1 Current ratio and quick ratio

When analysing a company's balance sheet without access to management information, it is customary to calculate two ratios as indicators of the company's ability to pay its way:

Current ratio $= \dfrac{\text{Current assets}}{\text{Current liabilities}}$

Quick ratio (or acid test ratio) $= \dfrac{\text{Current assets less stocks}}{\text{Current liabilities}}$

> **Solution**
>
> For Knotty plc:
>
> | | *20X9* | *20X8* |
> |---|---|---|
> | Current ratio | $\dfrac{17,801}{10,107} = 1.76$ | $\dfrac{13,030}{7,156} = 1.82$ |
> | Quick ratio | $\dfrac{9,315}{10,107} = 0.92$ | $\dfrac{6,511}{7,156} = 0.91$ |

4.2 Cash and funds flow analysis

Although current and quick ratios are used to measure liquidity, they are limited insofar as they concentrate on only one area of the balance sheet. If the company needs adequate cash to meet its obligations, there are sources other than the sale of inventories and the collection of amounts owed by receivables.

Analysis of cash flows is a more comprehensive method of assessing liquidity, although significant variations in the liquidity ratios may indicate important changes.

4.3 Other working capital ratios

A more detailed analysis of the movement in the elements of working capital can be made with the help of the following ratios.

4.4 Inventory holding period (Inventory days)

Inventory holding periods can be compared if they relate costs of sales as a measure of activity to inventories which are usually included at cost:

$$\frac{\text{Inventories}}{\text{Cost of sales}} \times 365\%$$

> **Solution**
>
> 20X9 $\dfrac{8,486}{28,380} \times 365 = 109$ days   20X8 $\dfrac{6,519}{22,808} \times 365 = 104$ days
>
> There has been a slight increase in the holding period, indicating inventory is taking longer to sell. A review of inventories may be necessary to determine whether levels of obsolete or damaged inventories are increasing. There may be a deliberate policy to increase inventories.

4.5 Average receivables collection period (receivables days)

This calculation is always made using revenue since trade receivables includes the profit element:

$$\frac{\text{Trade receivable s}}{\text{Revenue}} \times 365 \text{ days}$$

Solution

20X9 $\dfrac{8,233}{37,589} \times 365 = 80$ days

20X8 $\dfrac{5,735}{30,209} \times 365 = 69.29$ days

The company is taking approximately 11 days longer, on average, to collect its debts.

As the year-end figures may be unrepresentative (due perhaps to seasonality of sales), an average receivables figure for the year might be used if this were available.

4.6 Average payables payment period (payables days)

A similar calculation can be made to determine the payables payment (settlement) period:

$$\frac{\text{Trade payables}}{\text{Purchases or cost of sales}} \times 365 \text{ days}$$

Purchases should normally be used for this ratio but if it is not available from the information then cost of sales can be used as a substitute.

Solution

Ideally we would have an exact figure for trade payables but here we have used 'Other amounts falling due within one year' as a substitute.

20X9 $\dfrac{9,178}{28,380} \times 365 = 118$ days   20X8 $\dfrac{6,645}{22,808} \times 365 = 106$ days

The company is taking approximately 12 days longer, on average, to pay its debts.

As the year-end figures may be unrepresentative (due perhaps to seasonality of purchases), an average payables figure for the year might be used if this were available.

Example 2

Work through the following example to ensure that you understand how to calculate and interpret basic ratios.

The outline balance sheets of the Nantred Trading Co Limited were as shown below.

Balance sheets as at 30 September

	20X6 £	20X6 £	20X5 £	20X5 £
Non-current assets (at written-down values)				
Premises	98,000		40,000	
Plant and equipment	162,000		65,000	
		260,000		105,000
Current assets				
Inventory	95,300		31,200	
Trade receivables	30,700		19,700	
Bank and cash	26,500		15,600	
	152,500		66,500	
Current liabilities				
Trade payables	55,800		23,900	
Corporation tax	13,100		11,400	
Proposed dividends	17,000		17,000	
	85,900		52,300	
Working capital		66,600		14,200
Net assets employed		326,600		119,200
Financed by				
Ordinary share capital	200,000		100,000	
Reserves	26,600		19,200	
Shareholders' funds		226,600		119,200
7% debentures		100,000		–
		326,600		119,200

The only other information available is that:

- revenue for the years ended 30 September 20X5 and 20X6 was £202,900 and £490,700 respectively

- profit before tax and interest (operating profit) for the years to 30 September 20X5 and 20X6 was £21,500 and £44,500 respectively.

(a) Calculate, for each of the two years, two suitable ratios to highlight the liquidity and two suitable ratios to highlight the profitability of the company.

(b) Comment on the situation revealed by the figures you have calculated in your answer to (a) above.

Solution

(a)

		20X6	20X5
(i)	$\dfrac{\text{Current assets}}{\text{Current liabilities}}$	$\dfrac{152,500}{85,900} = 1.78:1$	$\dfrac{66,500}{52,300} = 1.27:1$
(ii)	$\dfrac{\text{Quick assets}}{\text{Current liabilities}}$	$\dfrac{57,200}{85,900} = 0.67:1$	$\dfrac{35,300}{52,300} = 0.67:1$
(iii)	$\dfrac{\text{Profit before tax and interest}}{\text{Capital (net assets) employed}}$	$\dfrac{44,500}{326,600} \times 100 = 13.6\%$	$\dfrac{21,500}{119,200} \times 100 = 18.0\%$
(iv)	$\dfrac{\text{Profit before tax and interest}}{\text{Sales}}$	$\dfrac{44,500}{490,700} \times 100 = 9.1\%$	$\dfrac{21,500}{202,900} \times 100 = 10.6\%$

(b) The situation revealed by the ratios calculated in (a) above may be summarised as follows.

Liquidity ratios (i) and (ii)

The current ratio indicates a substantial surplus of current assets over current liabilities and this has improved over the year. The liquid assets (receivables and bank) to current liabilities ratio shows no change and based on past experience does not signify any liquidity difficulties.

Profitability ratios (iii) and (iv)

The overall return on capital employed has decreased by a substantial amount. This may be because full benefit has not yet been received from the additional investment of £100,000 from the debentures issued during the year. The level of net profit per £ of sales has also decreased and this may be for the same reasons. Fortunately the overall return is high enough to mean that the 7% paid to the debenture holders is still easily achieved and the surplus return will improve returns to the ordinary shareholders, compensating them for the risk they have undertaken in introducing gearing (the debentures) into the organisation.

4.7 Comparing entities using performance indicators

Comparing an entity with a similar one may come up as a very practical task in an assessment. The likely situation is where you have two firms in competition with each other, and one of them sets itself a performance indicator as a target to help it achieve a competitive advantage. The other firm must try to match or better that target.

4.8 What if? analysis

'What if? analysis' or 'scenario planning' is a technique used to test the effect on a set of figures of altering one of the variables that produced those figures. Flexible budgeting is a form of what if? analysis – what if we produce 20,000 units rather than 15,000, say?

Example 3

Theta division makes only one product, the Devon. In the year to 30 June 20X5, its results were as follows:

	£
Sales	500,000
Receivables at 30 June 20X5	105,000
Cash at 30 June 20X5	20,000

The main competitor in the Devon market is Gamma Co, which sells Devons at a 15% higher price than Theta. It has been estimated that Theta could also charge a higher price without reducing sales volume. Gamma's results for the same period as Theta are as follows:

	£
Sales	700,000
Receivables	72,500
Cash	10,000

What would be the effect on the cash balance of Theta achieving Gamma's success?

Solution

The requirement in this example can be read as – what if Theta raised its prices and implemented credit controls to achieve Gamma's levels of sales and receivables?

	Theta	Gamma
Receivable days	$\dfrac{£105,000}{£500,000} \times 365 = 77$	$\dfrac{£72,500}{£700,000} \times 365 = 38$

Theta's revised figures

	£	£
Existing cash		20,000
Sales increase (£500,000 × 1.15) – £500,000		75,000
Change in receivables:		
Revised receivables		
(£500,000 × 1.15) × $\dfrac{38}{365}$	59,863	
Existing receivables	105,000	
	———	
		45,137
		———
Revised cash balance		140,137
		———

Therefore Theta division would increase its cash balance by £120,137 by raising its prices and reducing its debt collection period.

5 Manufacturing industries

5.1 Introduction

The performance of a manufacturing business and its constituent activities will commonly be measured in quantitative terms, mainly monetary. However, we shall also consider relevant non-monetary and qualitative factors that can be useful.

5.2 Productivity

This is a measure of the efficiency of resource usage and expresses the rate of output in relation to resource used, often in non-financial terms.

Examples include the following:

(a) units produced per labour or machine hour

(b) productive hours to total hours paid

(c) actual output to full capacity output

(d) sales units per salesperson

(e) value added, in total or per employee.

Productivity is closely linked with both efficiency and resource utilisation (which is considered later).

5.3 Labour activity, capacity and efficiency ratios

Three control ratios are often used to measure productivity, as follows:

Activity ratio: $\dfrac{\text{Actual output measured in standard hours}}{\text{Budgeted production hours}}$

Capacity ratio: $\dfrac{\text{Actual hours worked}}{\text{Budgeted hours}}$

Efficiency ratio: $\dfrac{\text{Actual output measured in standard hours}}{\text{Actual production in hours}}$

🔆 Example 4

	Budget	Actual
Output (units)	10,000	9,000
Hours worked	200	190

Calculate:

(a) the activity ratio

(b) the capacity ratio

(c) the efficiency ratio.

Solution

(a) Output per standard hour $= \dfrac{10,000}{200} = 50 \text{ units}$

Actual output in standard hours $= \dfrac{9,000}{50} = 180$

Activity ratio: $\dfrac{180}{200} = 90\%$

In other words, the production level was only 90% of the budgeted level.

(b)   Capacity ratio: $\dfrac{190}{200}$ = 95%

Only 95% of budgeted hours were actually worked and used to produce units.

(c)   Efficiency ratio: $\dfrac{180}{190}$ = 94.74%

According to the budget, 50 units should have been produced in an hour and therefore in the 190 hours that were actually worked, 9,500 units should have been produced. Only 94.74% of that quantity (9,000) were actually produced.

Note that the three ratios are related to each other:

Efficiency ratio	×	Capacity ratio	=	Activity ratio
94.74%	×	95%	=	90%

5.4   Value added

Definition

Value added is the pool of wealth created, out of which a business provides for:

- payment of wages, salaries and other employee benefits
- reward for providers of capital, in the form of interest and dividends
- payment of government taxation
- maintenance and expansion of assets.

It is also defined as:

- the value of revenue less the cost of bought in materials and services.

Example 5

Value added statement

Horn Ltd

	£m
Revenue	1.35
Bought in materials and services	0.55
Value added	0.80
Applied as:	
To pay employee wages and other benefits	0.28
Providers of capital dividends	0.13
Government taxation	0.04
Maintenance and expansion of assets	
Depreciation	0.15
Retained profit	0.20

Number of employees = 20

- Value added per '£' of employee costs

$$\frac{0.80}{0.28} = 2.86$$

- Value added per employee

$$\frac{0.80}{20} = £0.04m \text{ or } £40,000$$

- Value added per '£' of employee costs and depreciation

$$\frac{0.80}{0.43m} = 1.86$$

or, in a highly mechanised process, related to use of machinery:

- production per machine hour

- production per machine.

5.5 Unit costs

Unit costs are the actual average cost of production of each unit of product in the period. Management will attempt to drive down unit costs over time.

5.6 Resource utilisation

This is a measure of the extent to which resources were used in relation to maximum capacity. Examples of utilisation and related measures for different resources include the following:

Machines	–	utilisation (hours used : potential hours)
	–	down time (machine down hours : total hours)
Materials	–	wastage (normal/abnormal loss percentage)
	–	inventory turnover (linked to levels of slow-moving inventories)
Labour	–	utilisation (productive : total hours)
	–	absenteeism, lateness
	–	mix variances (where different grades are used)
	–	idle time (non-productive hours : total hours)
	–	labour turnover (leavers replaced : total employed)

5.7 Quality of service

For a manufacturing business, this can be categorised into quality of service to customers and quality of service from service departments. The latter is covered in the section on the service departments.

Quality of service to customers is essentially a subjective, qualitative measure, although some quantitative measures can be used in connection with it – for example, ratios such as customer returns to total sales and customer complaints per units sold. Speed of service can be measured in retail outlets or numbers waiting per checkout in a supermarket.

The main source of measure of customer satisfaction will generally be through some sort of questionnaire. This is all considered in more detail later in this chapter.

5.8 Other non-monetary measures

Quality is a particular area in which such indicators are required; two others that have recently been identified as important attributes of world-class manufacturing are innovation and flexibility.

5.9 Innovation

Innovation is concerned with the business's ability to beat their competitors in developing new products, improvements to existing ones or additional customer services.

Measurement of innovation must concentrate on its effectiveness as well as its existence – counting the number of new products developed is of little help without knowing the extent to which they have been accepted by the market. Possible measures include the following:

(a) research and development expenditure related to new sales (in value and timing, i.e. payback)

(b) viable new products to existing products

(c) percentage of total profits relating to new products/improvements.

5.10 Flexibility

Flexibility is concerned with the business's ability to respond to customers' needs, in terms of speed of delivery of existing products, speed of reaction to changes in demand patterns and ability to respond to particular customer requests or specifications.

In a manufacturing context, it is often the case that flexibility is connected with the amounts of products using common parts. If demand for one type of product falls, it is easier to switch inventory and processing to another if there is a common base between them.

6 Service departments

6.1 Introduction

Many of the measures discussed above will be relevant in the assessment of the performance of service departments within a business. Unless an internal charge-out system operates (for example, the charging of user departments per hour of computer department time spent on their work),the emphasis will be on costs rather than profits.

6.2 Types of performance indicator

As well as the normal cost variances (with activity levels based on the departments' own cost unit, e.g. maintenance hours, meals served, data processing hours), other cost ratios will be appropriate, for example:

(a) meal cost per employee per period (canteen)

(b) running costs per van-mile (deliveries)

(c) cost per call-out (maintenance department).

Example 6

Consider a transport/distribution department. What type of cost performance indicators might be appropriate?

Solution

(a) **Standing costs** (ascertained as a rate per day), including:

    (i)   road tax

    (ii)   insurance

    (iii) garage and administration costs

    (iv) drivers' wages

    (v)   depreciation.

(b) **Running costs** (ascertained as a rate per ton/mile), including:

    (i)   fuel and lubricants

    (ii)   tyres

    (iii) repairs

    (iv) maintenance.

Standing costs will be incurred for vehicles owned whether or not they are in use and are in the nature of stepped fixed costs. Fixed because, for each vehicle, they do not vary in amount and 'stepped' because for each additional vehicle required, costs, on a graph, will rise by a further step and remain fixed for a further range of activity until another vehicle is required.

In addition to these, there will be depot administration and establishment costs to be absorbed. These should be ascertained in total and related to the activity of the depot. Statistical information such as mileage run, loaded and empty, and tonnages carried should also be collected so that a reasonable method of absorption may be derived.

The analysis of expenditure between fixed and variable costs (standing and running costs) gives potential for the use of marginal costing and the consequent improvements in management information.

With such information available, management will be better equipped to deal with:

(a) control over costs for each vehicle or group of similar vehicles

(b) pricing

(c) choice of most economic vehicle for specific tasks

(d) acceptability of contracts

(e) vehicle purchase and replacement decisions

(f) many other day-to-day decisions.

7 Service sectors

7.1 Introduction

Service organisations include the following:

(a) **Professional services**, such as firms of accountants, architects, surveyors, solicitors, whose main assets will be their employees and who provide individual, personalised services to their customers.

(b) **Mass services**, such as transport, which are highly capital asset based and provide a standard range of services to a wide range of customers.

(c) **Public sector services**, such as health, education and local authorities.

7.2 Types of performance indicators

Service sector measures can be considered under very similar headings as those for manufacturing organisations, although there will be a different emphasis on their relative importance.

The main difference between the two types of organisation is the nature of their output.

Output from manufacturing businesses comprises tangible, clearly identifiable products, usually of a standard design and quality which can be rejected by a customer if not required or unsuitable, and produced in advance of demand and stored until needed.

Think about a service provided to you – can it be said to have any of these characteristics? This leads to a different approach needed for performance measurement where costs per product or units per hour are of little relevance or meaning. However, in earlier chapters, we have seen that cost units do not have to be in terms of products and that measures may be activity rather than product based.

So, using similar headings as before, performance indicators for service organisations are productivity, unit costs, resource utilisation, profitability and quality of service.

In assessments the tasks will ask for performance indicators which are tailored to the scenario set. Make sure that you read the scenario information carefully and actually calculate the indicators that are asked for.

7.3 Productivity

Productivity can be difficult to measure, because services rarely have a standard unit of output. For example, it would be meaningless to measure a conveyancing solicitor's productivity on the basis of 'property purchase completions per month', as each will have a different degree of complexity and value to the business. Similarly, it would be inappropriate to assess a bus line on the basis of 'journeys per day', as the contribution to the company's profits would depend upon the number of people carried at each stage of the journey and how many buses were operating on the line.

Meaningful measures of productivity or efficiency for a service depend upon a clearly defined measure of activity and resources.

So, for example, the measure of activity for the bus line might be 'passenger miles' and of the resource might be 'driver hours'.

Professional firms, such as accountants and solicitors, will generally use 'chargeable hours' as a measure of activity and employees' productivity will be judged by 'chargeable hours per employee'.

7.4 Unit costs

Again, the difficulty here is in defining an appropriate unit for the activity being measured. Once this has been established, appropriate costs need to be attributed to it. So the cost of a professional chargeable hour would mainly consist of employee costs (salaries, NICs, benefits, etc.) but will also include a recovery of general overheads.

The cost of a 'passenger mile' for a transport company will include driver costs, vehicle running costs and overheads.

7.5 Resource utilisation

Resource utilisation is the extent to which available resources are used for productive service. Examples of suitable measures for various types of service businesses are illustrated by the following ratios:

Professional	Chargeable hours : Total hours available
Transport	Passenger miles : Total train miles available
Hotel	Rooms occupied : Rooms available
Car hire	Car-days hired : Car-days available

7.6 Profitability

Clearly, for the service business overall, the usual measures can apply – ROCE, profit margins, etc. Unit profitability measures will again depend upon the clear definition of the cost unit or unit of activity. The profit can then be determined by comparison of the cost per unit (as discussed above) with the income generated (e.g. the charge-out rate for a professional chargeable hour or the average fare per mile on a bus/train route).

 Example 7

Transport company (AAT J94)

A transport company is reviewing the way in which it reports vehicle operating costs to the company management. In particular, it is interested in the use of performance ratios which will help to assess the efficiency and effectiveness of the use of its vehicles.

Information on the following items is available for each vehicle for the period as follows:

Costs

Variable costs

Fuel	Tyres
Oil	Other parts
Hydraulic fluid	Repairs and maintenance

Fixed costs

Road fund licence	Cleaning
Insurance	Depreciation
Drivers' wages	

Activity measures

Miles driven

Number of days available for use

Tonnes carried

Number of days vehicle actually used

Journeys made

Required

You are asked to indicate six suitable performance ratios which could be used to monitor the effectiveness and efficiency of the usage of each vehicle.

Three of your ratios should relate to the efficient control of costs and three should relate to the effective usage of vehicles.

Solution

Cost control performance ratios

Cost per mile
Cost per tonne carried
Cost per journey
Cost per tonne/mile

> Each of these ratios could be calculated for fixed and variable costs separately

Fixed cost per available day
Fixed cost per working day

Usage performance ratios

Tonne/miles per period

Days available as a percentage of total working days

Days used as a percentage of available days

Tonnes carried per available day

Journeys made per available day

Tonnes/miles per journey

Test your understanding 1

Barwin

As a trainee accountant, you have recently been transferred to the marketing department of Barwin, a company making sports caps, which are sold to a wide variety of wholesalers, retailers and sports clubs. Customers are categorised by the size of the account, measured in terms of annual revenue. There are a few large customers, which have a revenue greater than $2,000,000, mainly high street fashion chains..

At the other end of the scale, small customers have an annual revenue of less than $5,000. These mainly comprise of individual sports clubs and societies that tend to place orders for caps with their own club motif sewn on to the cap – the minimum order is $300. Medium-sized customers lie in the range of $5,001 to $200,000. The significance of categorising customers by the size of their account is to allow the application of different gross profit margins for sales quotations – large 10%, medium 20%, small 30%.

The sales manager is presently on holiday. His assistant, Alex Smart, has been asked to brief the sales manager on his return on the performance of the sales representatives. The sales manager is particularly keen to see which of Barwin's two regions has the better performance. He wants to give a bonus to the better team, according to Alex's recommendation. Alex has compiled the following information from the last period's account but is unsure what to do next.

Table 1	North region	South region
Orders taken and delivered	$	$
Large	2,000,000	4,000,000
Medium	1,200,000	2,300,000
Small	1,700,000	1,000,000
Total revenue	$4,900,000	$7,300,000

Table 2	North region	South region
Orders as a percentage of the company revenue	40.2%	59.8%
New business as a percentage of total orders	32.0%	15.5%
Cancelled orders as a percentage of total orders	9.0%	3.0%
Order value taken per km travelled	$13.61	$34.76

Table 3	North region	South region
Sales representatives		
– number of sales people	12	9
– total salaries of sales people	$180,000	$171,000
– fixed expenses (car leasing, telephones, etc.)	$72,000	$54,000
– total km travelled*	360,000	210,000
Sales manager's salary	$32,000	$34,000

* variable cost per km = $0.10

Required:

(a) Calculate the financial performance of the sales team in both of the two areas based on the gross profit less sales expenses. Show your results to the near $000.

(b) On the basis of the information supplied and the expenses and profit calculated in part (a), calculate at least FOUR suitable performance ratios that will help Alex to compare the two areas. Show your results in a table.

Note: Such measures should be in addition to the performance measures already in Table 2.

(c) Write some brief notes to assist Alex in understanding the performance of the two areas.

7.7 Quality of service

This has arguably more significance in the service sector than in the manufacturing sector. Customers will make their buying decisions in the service sector on the basis of how well they expect the service to be provided.

The factors contributing to quality of service will vary according to the nature of the business. As an illustration, consider the service provided to trainee accountancy students by a private college. Possible factors that would influence a potential student in their choice of college and the ways in which these might be measured are as follows:

Factor	Possible measures
Technical expertise	Pass rates
Communication	Clarity of lectures, study material and administrative information
Access	Staff/student ratios Availability of tutorial help outside lecture hours Ease of finding department/member of staff required Location of college
Friendliness	Approachability of staff
Flexibility	Ability to tailor service to individual student's needs
Facilities	Availability and standard of canteen, library, phones, etc
Aesthetics	Appearance of college Staff presentation
Comfort	Roominess of classrooms Heating/air-conditioning Comfort of seats, size of desks

You can no doubt think of some more factors and different ways in which those given could be measured. For example, it is perhaps a little glib to use pass rates as a measure of the college's technical expertise, as these are also likely to be significantly influenced by the abilities and commitment of the students themselves.

7.8 Quantitative and qualitative performance indicators

Having identified what needs to be measured, how can this be achieved? Some are a matter of fact or record – like pass rates or the existence of facilities; most of the rest are qualitative judgement and would need to be measured by the use of assessment forms completed by students.

An overall measure of the quality of service provided by the college could be the trend in the number of students enrolling for courses, although again this can be affected by other factors, such as the location of the college and students, the policy of the students' employers and the size of the market for trainee accountants.

Test your understanding 2

Hotel departments

A company owns and manages hotels. Each hotel has a general manager with responsibility for investment decisions.

Sub-managers are responsible for departments within the hotel. The departments and responsibilities in each hotel are:

- Accommodation (responsible for bedrooms and for the letting of rooms for meetings).

- Catering (responsible for all food and beverages).

- Household (responsible for maintenance, cleaning and laundry).

- Administration (responsible for accounting, marketing and recruitment and training).

The following information is provided for the Catering Department of one hotel for a period:

- 2,140 meals were served in the restaurant at an average price of $12.60.

- Further revenue of $4,620 was generated from the provision of food for meetings and room service.

- Sales of beverages were $18,610.

- Direct costs incurred were:

  Food/beverages $16,188
  Staff $11,784
  Other $2,640

- Target profit margin (net of direct costs) is 40%.

In addition to the direct costs incurred, the department is apportioned:

- 10% of the general occupancy costs of the hotel (e.g. rent, rates, heating, lighting). The general occupancy costs of the hotel totalled $47,320 in the period.

- 20% of the costs of the Household and Administration Departments which totalled $64,970 in the period.

Required:

(a) Determine the net profit of the above Catering Department in the period and assess the department's profit performance.

(b) Identify the type of responsibility centre that may be appropriate for each of the following:

    (i)   Catering Department

    (ii) Administration Department

    (iii) Hotel.

(c) Suggest two measures (one financial and one non-financial) that may be used to assess performance in each of the following:

    (i)   Accommodation Department

    (ii) Household Department.

(d) Outline difficulties that may be encountered in applying performance measures effectively in the hotel group.

8   Total quality management (TQM)

Definition

Total quality management (TQM) can be defined as 'a continuous improvement in quality, efficiency and effectiveness'.

- It aims towards an environment of zero defects at a minimum cost – the principle of 'get it right first time'.

- It requires an awareness by all personnel of the quality requirements involved in supplying the customer with products of the agreed design specification.

- It aims towards the elimination of waste where waste is defined as anything other than the minimum essential amount of equipment, materials, space and workers' time.

- It must embrace all aspects of operations from pre-production to postproduction stages in the business cycle.

Total quality management will, therefore, seek method changes which will help in achieving such objectives. Examples include the use of Just-in-time (JIT) production procedures whereby each component or product is produced or purchased only when needed by production or by a customer, rather than for inventory.

8.1 Quality circles

An important element of TQM is that every employee is involved and anyone with an idea about how to improve quality should be heard. This is done by forming groups of employees known as quality circles. These groups normally consist of about 10 employees of differing levels of seniority and with different skills who meet regularly to discuss quality problems and put forward ideas.

8.2 The cost of quality

Traditionally failure rates, scrap and reworking were subsumed within the costs of production while other aspects of poor quality were accounted for in either production or marketing overheads. TQM does not accept the cost of poor quality as inevitable and requires that the cost of quality is highlighted in management reports. This enables alternative approaches (such as built-in quality at the design stage) to be developed.

Quality-related costs are the expenditure incurred in defect prevention and appraisal activities and the losses due to internal and external failure of a product or service through failure to meet agreed specifications.

8.3 Types of quality-related costs

Quality-related costs may be classified as follows:

(a) **Failure costs** are the costs required to evaluate, dispose of, and either correct or replace a defective or deficient product.

(i) Internal failure costs are costs discovered before the product is delivered to the customer. Examples include the following:

- rework costs

- net cost of scrap

- disposal of defective products

- downtime due to quality problems.

(ii) External failure costs are costs discovered after the product is delivered to customers.

Examples include the following:

- complaint investigation and processing
- warranty claims
- cost of lost sales
- product recalls.

(b) **Appraisal costs** are costs of monitoring and inspecting products in terms of specified standards before the products are released to the customer. Examples include the following:

- measurement equipment
- inspection and tests
- product quality audits
- process control monitoring
- test equipment expense.

(c) **Prevention costs** include investments in machinery, technology and education programs designed to reduce the number of defective products during production. Examples include the following:

- customer surveys
- research of customer needs
- field trials
- quality education and training programmes
- supplier reviews
- investment in improved production equipment
- quality engineering
- quality circles.

Example 8

Carlton Limited make and sell a single product.

The following information affects its costs and revenues.

1   5% of incoming material from suppliers is scrapped owing to poor receipt and storage organisation.

2   4% of material X input to the machine process is wasted owing to processing problems.

3   Inspection of storage of material X costs 10 pence per square metre purchased.

4   Inspection during the production cycle, calibration checks on inspection equipment and other checks cost £25,000 per period.

5   Production quantity is increased to allow for the downgrading of 12.5% of product units at the final inspection stage. Downgraded units are sold as 'second quality' units at a discount of 30% on the standard selling price.

6   Production quantity is increased to allow for returns from customers which are replaced free of charge. Returns are due to specification failure and account for 5% of units initially delivered to customers. Replacement units incur a delivery cost of £8 per unit. 80% of the returns from customers are rectified using 0.2 hours of machine running time per unit and are re-sold as 'third quality' products at a discount of 50% on the standard selling price. The remaining returned units are sold as scrap for £5 per unit.

7   Product liability and other claims by customers are estimated at 3% of sales revenue from standard product sales.

8   Machine idle time is 20% of gross machine hours used (i.e. running hours = 80% of gross hours).

9   Sundry costs of administration, selling and distribution total £60,000 per period.

10   Carlton Limited is aware of the problem of excess costs and currently spends £20,000 per period on training staff in efforts to prevent a number of such problems from occurring.

Give examples of internal and external failure costs, appraisal costs and prevention costs borne by Carlton Limited.

Solution

Internal failure costs. The machine processing losses, downgrading of products, and materials which are scrapped due to poor receipt and storage.

External failure costs. Product liability claims and the costs of making free replacements, including delivery costs.

Appraisal costs. Inspection during the production process, inspection of materials in storage and calibration checks.

Prevention costs. Training costs.

9 The balanced scorecard

9.1 Introduction

The balanced scorecard approach to performance indicators recognises that historically too much emphasis has been placed on financial ratios in assessing an entity's performance. A successful business will only succeed in the long-term if it keeps its customers happy as well as by making profits. The approach therefore combines financial measures with operational, organisational innovation and customer service measures. All of these perspectives must be managed by managers if the business is to prosper in the long-term.

The balanced scorecard becomes the manager's instrument panel for managing the complexity of the organisation within a dynamic external environment.

9.2 Four perspectives of the balanced scorecard

The table below is an example of a balanced scorecard performance management system which demonstrates the role of critical success factors (CSFs) and key performance indicators (KPIs) in this process.

The balanced scorecard

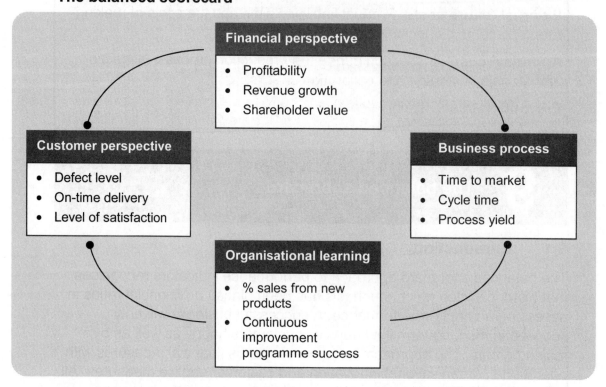

9.3 Key performance indicators

Typical key performance indicators for the balanced scorecard approach are illustrated below.

	Financial aspect	Customer aspect	Business process aspect	Organisational learning aspect
Strategic objective	Shareholder satisfaction	Customer satisfaction	Manufacturing excellence	New product innovation
Critical success factor	Grow shareholder wealth	Achieve preferred supplier status	State-of-the-art process plant	Successful new product development
Key performance indicators	ROCE	Number of new customers	Cycle times Unit cost % yield	% of sales represented by new products

Test your understanding 3

(a) Nicholson sells mobile telephones. It supplies its customers with telephone handsets and wireless telephone connections. Customers pay an annual fee plus a monthly charge based on calls made.

The company has recently employed a consultant to install a balanced scorecard system of performance measurement and to benchmark the results against those of Nicholson's competitors. Unfortunately the consultant was called away before the work was finished. You have been asked to complete the work. The following data is available:

Nicholson – Operating data for the year ended 30 November 20X7

Sales revenue	$480 million
Sales attributable to new products	$8 million
Average capital employed	$192 million
Profit before interest and tax	$48 million
Average number of customers	1,960,000
Number of telephones returned for repair	10,000
Number of bill queries	12,000
Number of customer complaints	21,600
Number of customers lost	117,600
Average number of bill queries unresolved at the end of each day	118
Average number of telephones unrepaired at the end of each day	804

Required:

Calculate the following ratios and other statistics for Nicholson for the year ended 30 November 20X7.

(i) Return on capital employed

(ii) Return on sales (net profit percentage)

(iii) Asset turnover

(iv) Annual number of complaints per thousand customers

(v) Percentage of customers lost per annum

(vi) Average time to resolve billing queries

(vii) Average wait for a telephone repair

(viii) Percentage of sales attributable to new products.

(b) The following information is for the mobile phone industry for the year ended 30 November 20X7.

Industry average statistics – Mobile telephones

Annual number of complaints per 1,000 customers	5
Percentage of customers lost per annum	3%
Average time to resolve billing queries	1.4 days
Average wait for a telephone repair	2 days
Percentage of sales attributable to new products	20%
Return on capital employed	15%
Return on sales (net profit percentage)	5%
Asset turnover	3 times

Required:

Using the industry average information and your answer to part (a), discuss the performance of Nicholson in the year ending 30 November 2007 under the four balanced scorecard headings of:

(i) financial success

(ii) customer satisfaction

(iii) process efficiency and

(iv) organisational learning and growth.

Note: State any assumptions that you make.

10 Cost reduction and value enhancement

10.1 Introduction

There are few organisations which would not benefit from real efforts to keep costs to a minimum. Businesses will make more money that way, assuming quality is not compromised.

Not-for-profit organisations will make their funds go further in providing necessary services, and will be better able to meet the requirements for 'good stewardship' normally imposed on them.

Definitions

Cost reduction is a process which leads to the achievement of real and permanent reductions in the unit costs of goods manufactured or services rendered without impairing their suitability for the use intended.

Cost control, on the other hand, aims simply to achieve the target costs originally accepted.

Note that cost reduction is aiming to reduce unit costs, i.e. the cost per item of output. It would be possible for a cost reduction programme to increase the total costs incurred, as long as the output volume rose even more, so that the unit cost was reduced.

10.2 Implementing a cost reduction programme

Once an organisation has adopted an objective of reducing costs, the following conditions need to apply if it is to be successful.

- A clear purpose – say, to reduce labour costs by 20%, or materials by 15%.

- A good reason – economic survival, say, or the ability in the future to compete with competitors with a lower cost base.

- Commitment and involvement by senior managers.

- Excellent and positive communication with workforce and, if possible, consultation.

- Gradual introduction.

10.3 Application of cost reduction techniques

Virtually all areas of businesses and not-for-profit organisations are open to the use of cost reduction techniques, including product design, production, purchasing, marketing, distribution, finance and personnel.

Two important cost reduction techniques are target costing and value engineering.

(a) **Target costing**

Target costing starts by subtracting a desired profit margin from the market price at which an item could be sold; this gives the target cost. It is then up to the designers to plan how the product can be manufactured for that cost. If the product is currently planned to cost more than the target cost, then the plan must be modified.

(b) **Value engineering**

Value engineering is a philosophy of designing products which meet customer needs at the lowest cost while assuring the required standard of quality and reliability. The idea is to understand what it is that customers want from your products, and save costs by eliminating items that add no value in customers' eyes. For example, a manufacturer of computer components may decide that its customers place no value on a paper instruction manual or on fancy packaging, and will decide to sell its products with no manual and in a plain cardboard box.

10.4 Value enhancement

The 'flip side' of cost reduction is value enhancement namely, getting the best value from the resources that are used in the organisation. Use of the performance indicators that we have seen in this chapter will provide useful comparative measures to assess value enhancement before and after an active 'value-for-money' programme.

It should be emphasised that cost reduction and value enhancement are not just the responsibility of the accounts department of a business. All the functional specialists (designers, marketing, engineering, quality control, etc) must pool their knowledge and work side-by-side to achieve the required objectives.

10.5 Benchmarking

One way of closely monitoring one's own business is to compare the results in your business with those of closely related businesses. **Benchmarking** is the establishment of targets and comparators, through whose use relative levels of performance (particularly areas of under-performance) can be identified. By the adoption of identified best practices it is hoped that performance can be improved.

One common example is internal benchmarking, where a company is split up into business divisions, all operating in more or less the same industry, and performance indicators are calculated and compared for each division. Perhaps it is then found that one division has receivables of four months sales, while all the other divisions have receivables of less than two months sales. The division with abnormally high receivables should be able to improve its liquidity by tightening up its credit control procedures.

KAPLAN PUBLISHING

11 Summary

As you have seen, there are numerous possible performance indicators and their relevance will depend upon the type of organisation and the aspect of performance being assessed.

The most important ratios for you to be able to compute (and interpret) are as follows:

Profitability: Return on capital employed (ROCE)
Gross and net profit margins

Liquidity: Current ratio
Quick (acid test) ratio
Inventory turnover
Receivables' collection period
Payables' payment (settlement) period

Remember that a ratio on its own is not particularly useful information; it needs to be compared, internally or externally. This gives rise to problems of comparability, which you should be able to discuss.

Many of the ideas covered in earlier chapters will have relevance here (e.g. variance analysis and the use of indices).

Make sure you are quite clear about the necessary attributes of a cost unit (or unit of activity) in order for it to provide a useful basis for measurement. This is particularly important for service activities. Try to think of services you have had experience of yourself and how the various aspects may be measured.

There will rarely be a unique right or wrong answer, so do not be afraid to use your imagination!

Test your understanding answers

 Test your understanding 1

Barwin

(a) **Financial performance per sales area**

Note that gross profit margins are given in the question. Gross profit can therefore be found by multiplying the sales revenue by the relevant margin.

		Northern region $000	Southern region $000
Gross profit per customer size			
Large	10%	200	400
Medium	20%	240	460
Large	30%	510	300
		———	———
Gross profit per region		950	1,160
		———	———
Less			
Sales representatives: Salaries		180	171
Overall expenses			
Fixed		72	54
Variable		36	21
Sales manager's salary		32	34
		———	———
		320	280
		———	———
Profit after charging sales expenses		630	880
		———	———

(b) Performance measures

		North	South
(1)	Sales expenses: Gross profit		
(i)	Sales expenses % of GP (N: 320/950 S: 280/1,160)	34%	24%
(ii)	Gross profit per $ of sales expenses (N:950/320 S:1,160/280)	$2.97	$4.14
(iii)	Sales per $ of sales expenses (N: 4,900/320 S: 7,300/280)	$15.31	$26.07
(2)	Average gross margin (N: 950/4,900 S: 1,160/7,300)	19%	16%
(3)	% gross profit per customer category to total gross profit		
	Large (N:200/950 S: 400/1,160)	21%	34%
	Medium (N: 240/950 S: 460/1,160)	25%	40%
	Small (N: 510/950 S: 300/1,160)	54%	26%
(4)	Gross profit per region as % of total company gross profit	45%	55%
(5)	Sales per company representative	$408,000	$811,000
(6)	Gross profit per representative	$79,000	$127,000
(7)	Profit after sales expenses as % of total for company	42%	58%

(c) Notes on performance of the two sales areas

The representatives in the Southern area out-perform their colleagues in the North as is highlighted by the performance measures sales and profit per employee. Also gross expenses as a % of GP is much lower.

The Southern team also performs better when focusing on cancelled orders, however in the North there is a higher % of new business, with the South concentrating on repeat business.

The North has lower total sales than the South, the North is concentrating on business in the small category customer band, giving a good margin but costly in terms of sales expenses.

The Northern region is undergoing a period of growth – new business. The South may well have to improve after sales service to attract new business.

Perhaps the future varies according to geography and concentration of business as indicated by total distance travelled in North compared to South.

The task of selling seems to be easier in the South than the North. It may be that the sales reps in the South are better trained and that the company should consider a staff development programme for the Northern region.

Test your understanding 2

Hotel Departments

(a) **Catering Department – net profit**

Income	
Restaurant meals (2,140 × $12.60)	26,964
Provision of food	4,620
Beverages	18,610
	50,194
Costs	
Direct	
Food/beverages	16,188
Staff	11,784
Other	2,640
	30,612

Contribution		19,582	(39.0%)
Apportioned costs			
General occupancy costs	4,732		
Household and admin	12,994		
		17,726	
Net profit		**1,856**	(3.7%)

The department has not achieved its target profit margin (net of direct costs) of 40%, being 1% below this at 39%. Its net profit after apportioned cost is $1,856, 3.7% of sales.

(b) (i) The Catering Department is likely to be run as a profit centre, being responsible for both income and costs, but not capital investment.

 (ii) The Administration Department is likely to be a cost centre as it has no revenue income.

 (iii) The Hotel will be treated as an investment centre, being accountable for costs, revenues and capital investment decisions.

(c) (i) (ii)

(*Tutorial note:* Only ONE measure for each category is required.)

Department	Financial	Non-financial
Accommodation	Sales revenue per bed-night	Occupancy rates (bed/meeting room)
	Letting income (per meeting-room hr)	
Household	Cost per bed-night	Hours worked: hours available
	Cost per customer stay	Customer complaint rate

(d) Difficulties that may be encountered in performance measurement in the hotel group include:

External (uncontrollable) factors – when comparing one hotel with another, it is difficult to take account of differences in location (e.g. rural/urban), size, local competition, changes in tourist attractiveness (e.g. building work nearby, threats of terrorism, local disease outbreak), etc.

Interdependence – when comparing departments within a hotel, it must be recognised that actions taken by one departmental manager can impact on the performance of other departments – for example, the number of bedrooms and meeting rooms let by the accommodation department will impact on the income of the catering department.

Test your understanding 3

Nicholson

(a) **Nicholson ratios and statistics**

Return on capital employed

$$\frac{\text{Profit before interest and tax}}{\text{Capital employed}} \times 100\% = \frac{\$48m}{\$192m} = 25\%$$

Return on sales

$$\frac{\text{Profit before interest and tax}}{\text{Sales revenue}} \times 100\% = \frac{\$48m}{\$480m} = 10\%$$

Asset turnover

$$\frac{\text{Sales revenue}}{\text{Capital employed}} = \frac{\$480m}{\$192m} = 2.5 \text{ times}$$

Annual number of complaints per 1,000 customers

$$\frac{\text{Number of customer complaints}}{\text{Average number of customers (in thousands)}} = \frac{21,600}{1,960} = 11$$

Percentage of customers lost per annum

$$\frac{\text{Number of customers lost}}{\text{Average number of customers}} \times 100\% = \frac{117,600}{1,960,000} = 6\%$$

Average time to resolve billing queries

$$\frac{\text{Average number of bill queries unresolved at the end of each day}}{\text{Total bill queries}} \times 365 = \frac{118}{12,000} = 3.6 \text{ days}$$

Average wait for a telephone repair

$$\frac{\text{Average number of telephones unrepaired at the end of each day}}{\text{Number of telephones returned for repair}} \times 365 = \frac{804}{10,000} \times 365 = 29.3 \text{ days}$$

Percentage of sales attributable to new products

$$\frac{\text{Sales revenue attributable to new products}}{\text{Total sales revenue}} = \frac{\$8m}{\$480m} = 1.7\%$$

(b) **Discussion of performance**

(i) **Financial success**

Nicholson's return on capital employed at 25% is much higher than the industry average and this indicates that it is generating a good return on the money invested in it. This is largely explained by a return on sales of 10%, exactly double that of the industry average company. This could be due to higher prices, lower costs, or both. The only financial weakness apparent is that Nicholson does not enjoy as high a sales per $ of capital employed as its competitors. Overall the company appears to have performed well financially.

(ii) **Customer satisfaction**

Nicholson does not perform as well as the industry average in this area. It is losing customers at twice the rate of the industry average company. It is often much easier to retain existing customers than to win new ones. The level of customer complaints is also much higher than average. These factors will result in lost sales. They should be seen as leading indicators of future financial problems.

(iii) **Process efficiency**

The two processes that appear in the statistics are telephone repair and bill enquiries. On both counts Nicholson performs badly. Telephone repair appears to take an average of nearly 30 days (as compared to a two day industry average). This will prove annoying to customers and will probably result in lost sales (customers cannot make calls without telephones). Similarly delays in processing bill enquiries will eventually result in dissatisfied customers and poor financial results.

(iv) **Organisational learning and growth**

Less than 2% of Nicholson's income comes from new products, as compared to 20% for the industry average company. In a sector characterised by changing technology and product innovation this is very poor. Failing to innovate is a failing to compete. Eventually this will result in lost sales and profits.

In conclusion the company's financial results have been good in the past year, but the prospects for the future appear poor unless improvements are made to customer service, process efficiency and innovation.

MOCK ASSESSMENT

1 Mock Assessment Questions

Task 1 (20 marks)

(a) **Match each item of budget data below with its appropriate source.** **(3 marks)**

Budget data	Appropriate source
Global Economic Trends	Customer Relationship Management (CRM) system
Likely future government policy	World Bank, International Monetary Fund
UK Inflation Trends	Market research
Details of orders placed by your company's customers	Office for National Statistics SWOT Analysis
	Political consultancies/ commentators

(b) **Match each task with the individual or group that you will need to contact for information.** **(4 marks)**

Task	Contact
You want to know plans to disrupt the firms' operations	Firms' customers
You want to identify the firm's production capacity	Suppliers
You want to check the availability of a raw material	Competitors' price lists
	Pressure groups
	Production planning manager

(c) **Select the most appropriate accounting treatment for each of the following items.** **(6 marks)**

- Ingredients wastage in the production process

- Administrative wages

- Holiday pay for production workers

- Direct marketing costs

- Depreciation of equipment located in the materials store.

- Office stationery

- Basic pay for production workers

Options available against each item are:

- Allocate to marketing overheads

- Allocate to administrative overheads

- Direct cost

- Charge to production in a machine hour overhead rate

- Charge to production in a labour hour overhead rate

(d) **Select the appropriate term to match each of these descriptions.** **(1 mark)**

A cost that fluctuates in direct proportion to changes in activity

- Variable cost

- Fixed cost

- Semi-variable cost

- Stepped cost

Detailed budgets prepared by functional managers are collated to form a master budget

- Top-down budgeting

- Bottom up budgeting

- Invariable budgeting

- Zero based budgeting

Collecting data about every item in the population

- Census
- Random sampling
- Stratified sampling

A financial measure of the difference between budget and actual performance

- Flexed budget
- Financial difference
- Inequality
- Variance

(e) **The budget committee has set the sales volume growth and pricing assumptions for years 2, 3, 4 and 5 in the form of indices. Complete the sales revenue forecast below.**

Do not show decimals. Round each figure to the nearest whole number. (6 marks)

	Year 1	Year 2	Year 3	Year 4	Year 5
Sales volume index	110	111	115	116	119
Sales price index	112	115	120	122	125

Sales revenue	Actual Year 1 £	Forecast Year 2 £	Forecast Year 3 £	Forecast Year 4 £	Forecast Year 5 £
At Year 1 prices	350,000				
At expected prices					

Task 2 (20 marks)

(a) **Complete the following production forecast for product 'Mauve'. Round any decimal figures up to the next whole number of units, if necessary.** **(10 marks)**

Units of product Mauve

	Week 1	Week 2	Week 3	Week 4	Week 5
Opening inventory	16,000				
Good production					
Sales volume	68,000	69,000	67,000	70,000	72,000
Closing inventory					

Rejected production			
Total manufactured units			

Closing inventory should be 25% of the following week's forecast sales. 5% of all production fails quality control checks and is rejected.

(b) The quarterly production requirements for product B are shown below.

3% of production fails the quality checks and must be scrapped.

How many items of product B must be manufactured to allow for waste? **(2 marks)**

	Month 1	Month 2	Month 3
Required units	50,600	49,500	49,800
Manufactured units			

(Round **up** to nearest whole unit)

(c) **Raw material purchases**

50,000 items of product G are to be manufactured in April.

Each requires 1.5 metres of raw material.

20% of raw material is wasted during manufacture.

The opening inventory will be 10,000 metres.

The closing inventory will be 11,000 metres.

How much material must be purchased? **(1 mark)**

Select from

94,750m   94,550m   94,900m   95,000m   96,750m

(d) **Labour hours**

114,000 units of product X are to be manufactured in May.

Each one takes 2 minutes to produce.

20 staff will each work 160 hours basic time.

How many overtime hours must be worked to complete the production? **(2 marks)**

Select from

600   200   360   300   3,800

(e) Department C manufactures three products, D, E and F.

Calculate the machine hours required to manufacture these in November.

Product	Units	Hours per unit	Hours required
D	50	1.5	
E	130	2.0	
F	250	2.5	
Total hours for department X			

There are seven machines in the department.

Each machine can be used for 120 hours in November. Additional machines can be hired if required.

How many additional machines should be hired?

(5 marks)

Task 3 (20 marks)

Operating budgets

Enter the missing figures in the working schedules and operating budgets using the data from the production budget and the notes below.

Production budget	Units
Opening inventory of finished goods	82,000
Production budget	115,000
Sub-total	185,000
Sales	115,000
Closing inventory of finished goods	70,000

(a)   Complete these three working schedules.   **(9 marks)**

Materials

Each unit produced requires 0.5 kgs of material. Closing inventory will be valued at the budgeted purchase price per kg.

Materials	Kg	£
Opening inventory	49,000	76,000
Purchases at £1.45 per kg		
Sub-total		
Used in production		
Closing inventory	51,000	

Labour

Each item takes 15 minutes to produce. 162 staff work 160 basic hours each in the period. Overtime is paid at 30% above the basic hourly rate.

Labour	Hours	£
Basic time at £15 per hour		
Overtime		
Total		

Overhead

Variable overhead is recovered on total labour hours.

Overhead	Hours	£
Variable at £2.60 per hour		
Fixed		94,440
Total		

KAPLAN PUBLISHING

(b) Now complete the operating budget. **(6 marks)**

Operating budget	Units	£ per unit	£
Sales revenue		8.00	
Cost of goods sold			£
Opening inventory of finished goods			70,740
Cost of production		£	
Materials			
Labour			
Overhead			
Closing inventory of finished goods			
Cost of goods sold			
Gross profit			
Overheads		£	
Administration		112,000	
Marketing		168,000	
Operating profit			

(c) **Prepare a cash flow forecast using the budget data that you have calculated in parts (a) and (b) of this task and the additional information below**. **(5 marks)**

Cash flow forecast		£
Opening cash balance/(overdraft)		92,000
Sales receipts		
Payments:	£	
Materials		
Labour		
Production overheads		
Other overheads		
Capital expenditure	70,000	
Closing cash balance/(overdraft)		

Enter receipts and payments as positive figures.

- The sales receivables balance is expected to decrease by £12,000 over the year.

- The materials payable balance is expected to increase by £4,000 over the year.

- All other payments are made in the year in which they are incurred.

- Production overheads include a depreciation charge of £35,000.

Task 4 (20 marks)

You have prepared a draft budget for direct labour costs. It is based on this year's costs plus an expected pay rise and increased staffing.

- The manager of human resources has forecast the pay rise.

- You have calculated the required staffing from the agreed production budget, which is itself based on the agreed sales budget.

- Major labour shortages have required salaries to increase significantly.

- Senior management require increased productivity.

Direct labour budget	Current year	Next year
Production units	1,400,000	1,700,000
Minutes per unit	15	14
Labour hours	350,000	396,667
Annual hrs per staff member	4,650	4,650
Number of staff	76	86
Average salary pa	£40,000	£45,000
Direct labour cost	£3,040,000	£3,870,000

Write an email to the budget committee, in three sections:

(a) Submit the draft budget for approval, and explain the key planning assumptions.

(b) Explain why planning assumptions in this draft budget are not totally within the control of management.

(c) Recommend appropriate performance measures that would assist managers to monitor direct labour performance against budget.

To: Production Director

Date: (Today)

From: Budget Accountant

Subject: Review of operation statement

(a) Budget submission

(b) Control

(c) Performance measures

Task 5 (20 marks)

(a) **Select the appropriate term to match each of these descriptions.**

(2 marks)

Description	Term
A budget kept continuously up to date by adding another accounting period (e.g. month or quarter) when the earliest accounting period has expired. It is suitable if accurate forecasts cannot be made.	Top-down budgeting
	Bottom up budgeting
	Zero-based budgeting
	Budget flexing
	Budget revision
	Rolling budgets
A cost that fluctuates in direct proportion to changes in activity.	Variable cost
	Fixed cost
	Semi-variable cost
	Stepped cost

(b) **Calculate these sales and cost budgets for July. Complete the table by using the information below.** **(8 marks)**

	Budget for the year	Budget for July
Units sold	60,000	6,000
Units produced	55,000	6,500

	£	£
Sales	924,000	
Materials used	825,000	
Labour	222,000	
Variable production overhead	68,750	
Fixed overhead	3,600	

- Each unit is made from 3 kg of material costing £5 per kg. It takes 15 minutes to make each item.

- 750 hours of basic time is available in the month. Any extra hours must be worked in overtime.

- The basic rate is £12 per hour. Overtime is paid at double time (100% more than basic rate.)

- Variable overhead relates to labour hours, including overtime.

- Fixed overhead costs are incurred evenly through the year.

(c) This task is about budget revision. You have submitted a draft operating budget to the budget committee. The committee has asked you to budget for an alternative scenario, and calculate the increase or decrease in expected profit.

Complete the alternative scenario column in the operating budget table, and calculate the increase or decrease in profit. Apart from the sales price per unit, do not enter decimals. Round to the nearest whole number, if necessary. **(10 marks)**

Assumptions in the first scenario

Material and labour costs are variable.

Depreciation is a stepped cost, increasing at every 12,000 units.

There is an allowance for an energy price rise of 8%.

Alternative scenario

Increase the selling price by 4%

Reduce the sales volume by 5%

Revise the energy price rise to 5%.

Operating budget	First draft	Alternative scenario
Sales price £ per unit	55	
Sales volume	65,000	
	£	
Sales revenue	3,575,000	
Costs		
Material	130,000	
Labour	65,000	
Energy	108,000	
Depreciation	19,000	
Total	322,000	
Gross profit	3,253,000	
Increase/(decrease) in gross profit		

Task 6 (20 marks)

(a)   **Select the appropriate term to match the following description.**
                                                                    (2 marks)

Description	Term
Variation in the total cost on account of the actual quantity being different from the standard quantity for the actual output achieved.	Performance indicator
	Labour rate variance
	Material usage variance
	Labour efficiency variance
	Variance analysis
	Variance

(b)   The operating statement for October showed that direct raw material costs were £145,660. That month, 9,500 kilograms of material were used and 4,500 items were made and sold.

The standard cost allows 2 kilograms of material for each item at a standard price of £16.00.

Complete the table of direct raw material costs, indicating whether each variance is favourable or adverse.   **(10 marks)**

Direct raw material costs	£	Fav/adverse
Flexed budget (standard cost)		
Actual material price per kg (correct to £0.01)		
Actual material used per item (correct to 2 dp)		
Price variance		
Usage variance		
Cost variance		
Cost variance % (correct to one decimal place)		

KAPLAN PUBLISHING

(c) **Prepare the direct labour cost statement from the activity data provided. Round to the nearest whole number if necessary.**

(8 marks)

Variance analysis

Prepare the raw material cost statement from the activity data provided.

Activity data	Items produced	Kgs used	Cost
Budget	3,000	4,500	18,000
Actual results	2,000	2,900	18,810

Raw material cost statement	£
Standard raw material cost of production	
Variance (adverse shown as negative)	
Material price	
Material usage	
Material cost	

Task 7 (20 marks)

A monthly operating statement is shown below with some explanatory notes. You are required to flex the budget, calculate variances and show whether each variance is favourable or adverse.

Monthly operating statement

	Budget	Actual
Volume	36,000	33,000
	£	£
Revenue	396,000	371,250
Costs		
Material	99,000	89,900
Labour	54,000	50,750
Distribution	1800	1,550
Energy	37,400	35,830
Equipment hire	480	455
Depreciation	21,000	21,000
Marketing	30,000	28,000
Administration	45,000	47,350
Total	288,680	274,835
Operating profit	107,320	96,415

Monthly operating statement

Volume 33,000

	Flexed budget £	Actual £	Variance Fav/(Adv) £
Revenue		371,250	
Costs			
Material		89,900	
Labour		50,750	
Distribution		1,550	
Energy		35,830	
Equipment hire		455	
Depreciation		21,000	
Marketing		28,000	
Administration		47,350	
Total		274,835	
Operating profit		96,415	

Enter adverse variances as minus

Notes

Material, labour and distribution costs are variable.

The budget for energy is semi-variable. The variable element is £0.90 per unit.

The budget for equipment hire is stepped, increasing at every 5,000 units of monthly production.

Depreciation, marketing and administration costs are fixed.

Task 8 (20 marks)

You are asked to review the operating statement shown below, and the background information provided, and to make recommendations.

Operating statement for May 2011

Revenue (units)   2,600,000

	Budget	Actual	Variance Fav/(Adverse)
	£000	£000	£000
Revenue	13,000	14,300	1,300
Variable costs			
Material	2,080	1,950	130
Labour	2,340	2,392	(52)
Transport	1,430	1,410	20
Power	1,300	1,352	(52)
Storage	416	416	–
	7,566	7,520	46
Contribution	5,434	6,780	1,346
Fixed costs			
Power	390	390	–
Storage	550	576	(26)
Depreciation	970	960	10
Maintenance	770	790	(20)
Administration	650	658	(8)
	3,330	3,374	(44)
Operating profit	2,104	3,406	1,302

The budget has been flexed to the actual number of units produced and sold. The original budget had been drawn up by the Chief Executive and communicated to senior managers by email.

Storage is a semi-variable cost and has been split between its fixed and variable elements.

Transport is a stepped cost. For every £130,000 spent on transport, the company can carry 250,000 units.

Write an email to the Chief Executive in which you:

(a) Suggest ONE possible reason for each of the following variances:

    (a) Revenue

    (b) Materials

    (c) Labour

    (d) Power

    (e) Storage

    (f) Transport.

(b) Explain TWO methods of assisting departmental managers to be more involved in preparing the budgets.

(c) Explain how the introduction of standard costing could assist effective budgetary control.

To:	Chief Executive
Date:	(Today)
From:	Budget Accountant
Subject:	Review of operating statement

(a)	Reasons for variances
(b)	Two steps to assist departmental managers to be more involved in preparing the budgets:
(c)	Standard costing

2 Mock Assessment Answers

Task 1

(a)

Data	Answer
Global Economic Trends	World Bank, International Monetary Fund
Likely future government policy	Political consultancies/ commentators
UK Inflation Trends	Office for National Statistics
Details of orders placed by your company's customers	Customer Relationship Management (CRM) system

(b)

Task	Answer
You want to know plans to disrupt the firms' operations	Pressure groups
You want to identify the firm's production capacity of the firm	Production planning manager
You want to check the availability of a raw material	Suppliers

(c)

- Ingredients wastage in the production process — Direct cost
- Administrative wages — Allocate to administrative overheads
- Holiday pay for production workers — Charge to production in a labour hour overhead rate
- Direct marketing costs — Allocate to marketing overheads
- Depreciation of equipment located in the material store — Charge to production in a machine hour overhead rate
- Office stationery — Allocate to administrative overheads
- Basic pay for production workers — Direct cost

(d)   A cost that fluctuates in direct proportion to changes in activity: variable cost

Detailed budgets prepared by functional managers are collated to form a master budget: Bottom up budgeting

Collecting data about every item in the population: Census

A financial measure of the difference between budget and actual performance: Variance

(e)   The budget committee has set the sales volume growth and pricing assumptions for years 2, 3, 4 and 5 in the form of indices. Complete the sales revenue forecast below.

Do not show decimals. Round each figure to the nearest whole number.

	Year 1	Year 2	Year 3	Year 4	Year 5
Sales volume index	110	111	115	116	119
Sales price index	112	115	120	122	125

Sales revenue	Actual Year 1 £	Forecast Year 2 £	Forecast Year 3 £	Forecast Year 4 £	Forecast Year 5 £
At Year 1 prices	350,000	353,182	365,909	369,091	378,636
At expected prices		362,642	392,045	402,045	422,585

Workings for the 'Forecast Year 2' column

In Year 2 we have a sales volume index of 111, compared to a sales volume index of 110 in Year 1. To calculate the numbers to enter in the 'Forecast Year 2' column, we can:

•   First, multiply our actual sales of £350,000 in Year 1 by 111 (= £38,850,000), then divide this number by 110.

$$\frac{£350,000}{110} \times 111 = £353,182.$$ These are the forecast sales for Year 2 before we adjust for the sales price index.

- Then, to adjust for the sales price index forecast in Year 2, we take our forecast sales of £353, 182 at Year 1 prices, then divide them by 112% to get a '1%' of that total:

$$\frac{£353,182}{112} = £3,153.411 \text{ (you should leave this number in your calculator)}$$

We can then multiply this by the index of 115 for Year 2:

£3,153.411 × 115 = £362,642.

Task 2

(a)

Units of product Mauve

	Week 1	Week 2	Week 3	Week 4	Week 5
Opening inventory	16,000	17,250	16,750	17,500	
Good production	69,250	68,500	67,750	70,500	
Sales	68,000	69,000	67,000	70,000	72,000
Closing inventory	17,250	16,750	17,500	18,000	

Rejected production	3,645	3,605	3,566	3,711
Total manufactured units	72,895	72,105	71,316	74,211

Workings

We start by calculating the values for the 'closing inventory' row.

- 'Closing inventory' in week 1
  - = 25% of week 2 sales
  - = 25% × 69,000
  - = 17,250

- 'Closing inventory' in week 2
  - = 25% of week 3 sales
  - = 25% × 67,000
  - = 16,750

- 'Closing inventory' in week 3
  - = 25% of week 4 sales
  - = 25% × 70,000
  - = 17,500

- 'Closing inventory' in week 4
  - = 25% of week 4 sales
  - = 25% × 72,000
  - = 18,000

We can then fill in the **'opening inventory'** row: the opening inventory in week 2 is the same as closing inventory in week 1, and so on and so forth.

Once this has been done, we may calculate, for each week, the **'Good production'** numbers as follows:

Good production units = sales units + closing inventory – opening inventory.

For example, in week 1:

Good production units = sales units 68000 + closing inventory 17250 – opening inventory 16000 = 69,250

Then, to calculate the **'total manufactured units'**, we take the 'good production' units that are only 95% of the total production, and we calculate what 100% of the total production would be. For example, in Week 1, we have 69,250 good units and they represent only 95% of the total production, so the total production is

$$\frac{69{,}250 \text{ good units}}{0.95} = 72{,}895 \text{ units}$$

Finally, to calculate the 'rejected production' units, we deduct the 'good production units' from the 'total manufactured units'. For example in Week 1:

Rejected production units = Total manufactured units – good production

Rejected production units = 72,895 – 69,250 = 3,645 units.

(b)

	Month 1	Month 2	Month 3
Required units	50,600	49,500	49,800
Manufactured units	52,165	51,031	51,341

(Round **up** to nearest whole unit)

(c) 94,750m

Working

50,000 items @ 1.5 metres = 75,000 metres.

75,000m × 100/80 (wastage) = 93,750m

Plus 11,000m closing inventory less 10,000m = 94,750m

(d) 600

Working

114,000 × 2/60 = 3,800 hrs required.

3,800 – (20 × 160) = 600 hrs overtime needed.

(e)

Product	Units	Hours per unit	Hours required
D	50	1.5	75
E	130	2.0	260
F	250	2.5	625
Total			960

How many additional machines should be hired? | 1 |

Task 3

(a) Materials

Materials	Kg	£
Opening inventory	49,000	76,000
Purchases at £1.45 per kg	59,500	86,275
Sub-total	108,500	162,275
Used in production	57,500	88,325
Closing inventory	51,000	73,950

Workings:

- Number of kilograms used in production : Production 115,000 units @ 0.5 kgs per unit = 57,500 kgs.

- Closing inventory (kgs) = Kgs purchased 59,500 + Opening inventory of kilograms 49,000 – Kgs used in production 57,500 kgs = 51,000 kgs

- These 51,000 kgs are valued at the **budgeted purchase price** of £1.45 per kg : £73,950 in total.

- The value (£) of kgs used in production is calculated by deducting the closing inventory value £73,950 from the sub-total £162,275 : £88,325.

Labour

Labour	Hours	£
Basic time at £15 per hour	25,920	388,800
Overtime	2,830	55,185
Total	28,750	443,985

Workings:

- The number of hours available can be calculated as 162 staff × 160 basic hours = 25,920 hours. These are paid £15 each for a total of £388,800.

- Each item takes 15 minutes to produce and there were 115,000 items produced. Therefore the **total** amount of hours amounted to

$$\frac{15 \text{ minutes per item} \times 115,000 \text{ items}}{60 \text{ minutes in an hour}} = 28,750 \text{ hours needed.}$$

- The difference between hours needed and hours available is the amount of overtime hours: 28,750 hours needed – 25,920 hours available = 2,830 hours of overtime are necessary to complete production.

- These are paid at £15 ×1.30 = £19.50 and the total amounts to 2,830 × £19.50 = £55,185.

Overhead

From the previous schedule, total labour hours amounted to 28,750.

Overhead	Hours	£
Variable at £2.60 per hour	28.750	74,750
Fixed		94,440
Total		169,190

(b)

Operating budget	Units	£ per unit	£
Sales revenue	115,000	8.00	920,000
Cost of goods sold			£
Opening inventory of finished goods			70,740
Cost of production		£	
Materials		88,325	
Labour		443,985	
Overhead		169,190	701,500
Closing inventory of finished goods			427,000
Cost of goods sold			345,240
Gross profit			574,760
Overheads		£	
Administration		112,000	
Marketing		168,000	280,000
Operating profit			294,760

(c)

Cash flow forecast		£
Opening cash balance/(overdraft)		92,000
Sales receipts		932,000
Payments:	£	
Materials	82,275	
Labour	443,985	
Production overheads	134,190	
Other overheads	280,000	
Capital expenditure	70,000	940,450
Closing cash balance/(overdraft)		13,550

Workings for the cash budget:

- Sales receipts will equal sales revenue, but we also need to take into account the movement in receivables. Here, our receivables have reduced by £12,000. This means that not only have we received the cash from our sales, but also reduced our receivables by £12,000 (i.e. they have paid £12,000 of their debt to us). Therefore, total cash received equals £920,000 + £12,000 = £932,000.

- Materials payments will equal materials expenditure, unless there is a movement in 'Materials payable', i.e. in the amount of money we owe to our creditors. Here, the 'materials payable' item increases by £4,000, which means we have a cash outflow for the expenditure of £86,275 less the £4,000 which increases our debt to creditors.

- There is no delay in paying labour costs so the expenditure will equal the cash outflow.

- Production overheads expenditure is equal to the production overhead cost of £169,190 less non-cash items (depreciation) of £35,000 = £134,190.

- Payments for other costs will equal expenditure unless there is a movement in 'Other payables', i.e. in the amount of money we owe to our 'other' creditors. Here, there is no 'Other payables' movement, which means we have a cash outflow for the expenditure of £112,000 (administration) + £168,000 (marketing) = £280,000.

Task 4

To: Budget committee

From: Accounting Technician

Date: xx/xx/xxxx

Subject: Direct labour budget

(a) **Budget submission**

I attach the proposed direct labour budget for next year for your consideration and approval. This is calculated from the agreed production volume budget and staffing increases.

The agreed production plan indicates an increase in volume to 1,700,000 units next year. An increase in productivity has been assumed from 15 minutes per unit to 14 minutes per unit. Overall the staffing level needs to increase by 10 to 86.

The manager of human resources estimates that average pay will increase by 12.5% next year to £45,000. This reflects labour shortages.

Please let me know if you need any further information.

(b) **Control**

Management cannot control all the variables in this budget:

- The sales and production budgets have already been approved but, of course, sales will be influenced by competitor activity and demand in the market.

- The salaries/direct labour cost will depend on the availability of labour and could vary significantly from the HR Director estimate.

- Labour productivity will be influenced by factors such as training and motivation.

(c) **Performance indicators**

There is a range of useful measures to monitor cost, efficiency, effectiveness and employee satisfaction. Staff hours and output data should be available on a daily basis. Labour rates are reviewed periodically. However employee satisfaction is probably best canvassed once or twice a year. I recommend that we conduct a weekly review of performance based on:

- Minutes per unit

- Hours of overtime

- Percentage of good output (or similar quality measure)

- Average hourly rate

We should also commission a confidential employee satisfaction and involvement questionnaire.

A Technician

Task 5

(a)

Description	Term
A budget kept continuously up to date by adding another accounting period (e.g. month or quarter) when the earliest accounting period has expired. It is suitable if accurate forecasts cannot be made.	**Rolling budgets**
A cost that fluctuates in direct proportion to changes in activity.	**Variable cost**

(b)

	Budget for July
Units sold	6,000
Units produced	6,500
	£
Sales	92,400
Materials used	97,500
Labour	30,000
Variable production overhead	8,125
Fixed overhead	300

(c)

Operating budget	First draft	Alternative scenario
Sales price £ per unit	55	57.20
Sales volume	65,000	61,750
	£	
Sales revenue	3,575,000	3,532,100
Costs		
Material	130,000	123,500
Labour	65,000	61,750
Energy	108,000	105,000
Depreciation	19,000	19,000
Total	322,000	309,250
Gross profit	3,253,000	3,222,850
Increase/(decrease) in gross profit		–30,150

Workings

- Alternative scenario – Price per unit

  £55 × (1+ 4% price increase) = £55 × 1.04 = £57.20 new price to use in the alternative scenario.

- Sales volume down 5%

  65,000 units × (1 – 5%) = 65,000 units × 95% = 61,750 units in the alternative scenario.

- Then, we multiply these 61,750 units by the new sales price of £57.20 for sales revenue of £3,532,100.

- Material costs are variable and calculated as (using 'first draft' column information):

  $$\frac{\text{Material costs } £130,000}{65,000 \text{ units}} = £2 \text{ per unit}$$

  We then use that cost and multiply the number of units in the alternative scenario column to obtain the total material cost of £2 × 61,750 = £123,500.

Labour costs are variable and calculated as (using 'first draft' column information):

$$\frac{\text{Labour costs } £65,000}{65,000 \text{ units}} = £1 \text{ per unit}$$

- We then use that cost and multiply the number of units in the alternative scenario column to obtain the total material cost of £1 × 61,750 = £61,750.

- Energy costs include a price rise of 8% (using 'first draft' column information) that needs to be taken away from the calculations:

$$\frac{\text{Energy costs } £108,000}{1.08} = £100,000$$

We then use that cost and apply the revised energy price increase of 5%: £105,000.

- Depreciation is a stepped cost and every 'step' is 12,000 units. In the 'first draft' we had 65,000 units, so this represents

$$\frac{65,000 \text{ units in total}}{12,000 \text{ units per step}} = 5.416667 \text{ so 6 steps.}$$

6 steps have incurred a cost of £19,000 in the first draft, and therefore the cost per step is $\frac{£19,000}{6 \text{ steps}} = £3,167$ per step.

In the 'alternative scenario column we have 61,750 units and each step contains 12,000 units. We therefore have

$$\frac{61,750 \text{ units}}{12,000 \text{ units per step}} = 5.1458 \text{ so 6 steps.}$$

Task 6

(a)

Description	Term
Variation in the total cost on account of the actual quantity being different from the standard quantity for the actual output achieved.	Material usage variance

(b)

Direct raw material costs	£	Fav /adverse
Flexed budget (standard cost)	£144,000	
Actual material price per kg (correct to £0.01)	£15.3	
Actual material used per item (correct to 2 dp)	2.11 kg	
Price variance	£6,340	FAV
Usage variance	£8,000	ADV
Cost variance	£1,660	ADV
Cost variance % (correct to one decimal place)	−1.2%	

Workings

- Flexed budget (standard cost)

  The standard material cost of 1 unit is £16.00 × 2 kgs per unit = £32.00 per unit. So, for an actual output of 45,000 items, we have a standard material cost of 4,500 × £32.00 = £144,000

- The actual material price per kilogram (correct to £0.01) is calculated as (actual total material cost £145,660/9,500 kgs) = £15.2631, i.e. £15.3

- Actual material used per item is £9,500 kgs/4,500 items = 2.11 kgs per item. We can already see that this is more than the standard usage of 2 kgs per item. Therefore, before any further calculation, we can already conclude that the material usage variance will be adverse.

- Price variance is based on actual purchases. Actual purchases of 9,500 kilograms should have cost 9,500 × £16 = £152,000, but did cost £145,660. This is a favourable variance of £6,340 F.

- Usage variance is based on actual output. 4,500 items should have used 4,500 × 2 kgs per item = 9,000 kgs. However, 9,500 kilograms were used. That is an adverse variance of 500 kilograms adverse, at £16.00 per kilogram = £8,000 A

- The cost variance is the sum of the price and usage variances: £6,340 F + £8,000 A = £1,660 A

- Cost variance %: the flexed budget tells us that actual activity should have cost us £144,000. A cost variance of £1,660 A represents (−£1,660/£144,000) × 100% = −1.152% or 1.2% rounded up.

(c)

Raw material cost statement	£
Standard raw material cost of production	12,000
Variance (adverse shown as negative)	£ fav/-adv
Material price	−7,210
Material usage	400
Material cost	−6,810

Task 7

Monthly operating statement

Volume   33,000

	Flexed budget £	Actual £	Variance Fav/(Adv) £
Revenue	363,000	371,250	8,250
Costs			
Material	90,750	89,900	850
Labour	49,500	50,750	(1,250)
Distribution	1,650	1,550	100
Energy	34,700	35,830	(1,130)
Equipment hire	420	455	(35)
Depreciation	21,000	21,000	–
Marketing	30,000	28,000	2,000
Administration	45,000	47,350	(2,350)
Total	273,020	274,835	(1,815)
Operating profit	89,980	96,415	6,435

Task 8

To: Chief Executive

Date: (Today)

From: Budget Accountant

Subject: Review of operation statement

(a) **Reasons for variances**

Revenue

The favourable revenue variance is due to an increased selling price which could have arisen due to increased demand for the product.

Materials

The favourable material variance is due to a lower price being paid for materials. This could be because of an overall reduction in prices due to fall in demand for the material or other economic factors or to better buying techniques.

Labour

The adverse labour variance could have arisen because of using less (or more) skilled staff or incurring higher overtime than expected.

Power

The adverse power variance is due to the increase in price per unit. This could reflect the increase in demand for this resource or it could be due to prices rises being higher than the expected level of inflation.

Storage

The adverse storage variance is due to an increased fixed cost which could have been caused by rises in underlying costs such as business rates or the rents charged by landlords.

Transport

The favourable transport variance arises because the budgeted stepped cost rises by fixed amounts whereas actual costs can vary because of differences in costs for such things as fuel , maintenance or improved usage.

(b)   **Two steps to assist departmental managers to be more involved in preparing the budgets**

The accounts staff can give advice and support to the department or cost centre managers and in the process can ensure consistency in approach whilst not reducing their responsibility for the preparation of the budgets.

Strategic plans and goals must be made clear by senior management and then communicated to the departmental managers both before the budgets are prepared and part of the feedback process after the budgets have been co-ordinated and reviewed.

(c)   **How standard costing can assist effective budgetary control**

Standard costing is an effective mechanism for bringing rigour to budgetary control. It makes sense to set standards for production resources at the level of a single unit of production. The standards can be multiplied by planned production levels to create cost budgets.

The system facilitates the calculation of detailed cost variances which helps managers to understand and manage the resources effectively. For instance, looking at the operating statement, we could analyse the material variance into the price and efficiency aspects and also see whether the labour variance was wholly due to saved overtime premium.

INDEX

KAPLAN PUBLISHING

KAPLAN PUBLISHING